Praise for The Great Speckled Bird

"By the year 2000, one-third of America's total population will consist of people of color. Education has become a primary site for struggles to redefine the cultural image of what America has and may become. *The Great Speckled Bird* illustrates the importance of redefining education to be relevant to America's great cultural transform~·' which is now occurring."

> *Manning Marable, Professor of H^i*
> *Director of The Institute for Resea.*
> *Columbia University*

"Catherine Cornbleth and Dexter W   ₋ ᴜᴏ̣ld step in exposing the politics of curriculum. The.   ₋₋ ᵢₛ a wonderful mix of ethnography and journalism providing both insider and outsider perspectives on the way that curriculum decisions get made. Especially important in this volume is the way that the authors demonstrate how voices of resistance get marginalized, muted, and distorted so that their participation in the process is minimized. . . . The book is exciting to read as the authors take us from one end of the country to the other. . . . It has a strong narrative voice that allows the reader to care about the people and the decisions that are made. . . . At the heart of their work is a plea for more democratic, equitable, and just education to create the kind of national character and community that sustains both our diversity and sense of unity."

> *Gloria Ladson-Billings, Assistant Professor, Department of Curriculum and Instruction, University of Wisconsin-Madison*

"*The Great Speckled Bird* opens a range of new perspectives on the meanings of multiculturalism in American schools today, and on the relation between what is understood to be multiculturalism and the conception of a national identity. Catherine Cornbleth and Dexter Waugh examine the debates surrounding curriculum policymaking in California and New York with uncommon lucidity and candor. Shibboleths and stereotypes both stand exposed . . . and a way is opened for new modes of communication and the kind of affirmation of our differences that may infuse the making of a new, dynamic, wondrously diverse community. This book may disturb some readers, inspire others, provoke still others to enter into the conversation. What is important is the conversation; these authors have done a great deal to enrich and expand what is being said. There is an excitement in their book and I recommend it enthusiastically."

> *Maxine Greene, Professor Emerita of Philosophy and Education, Teachers' College, Columbia University*

"For me, this book provided a lot of insight into dynamics that I had seen glimpses of. . . . The overall issues of race in America and the use of power in defining knowledge are important ones that Cornbleth and Waugh argue very well. . . . As this book compellingly shows, the stands taken in California and New York, and the debates surrounding the construction of social studies curricula, go to the heart of the very different lived experiences, subsequent viewpoints, and political power of Americans on either side of the color line. . . . Thanks for the opportunity to read this book!"

> Christine Sleeter, Professor of Teacher Education, University of Wisconsin-Parkside

"In *The Great Speckled Bird*, Catherine Cornbleth and Dexter Waugh provide critical accounts of the campaigns and deliberations which have gone into the recent initiatives of the states of California and New York to reform their social studies curricula along multicultural lines. Writing respectively as an academic who has participated directly in those battles and as a journalist who has been covering them, Cornbleth and Waugh report and analyze both the processes and events which have transpired and the media representations of those developments, offering from their unique vantage points many valuable insights and observations about the politics of American culture, education, and curriculum. . . . Cornbleth and Waugh have written an original and important book . . . you must read *The Great Speckled Bird*."

> Harvey J. Kaye, Rosenberg Professor of Social Change and Development, University of Wisconsin-Green Bay

The
Great
Speckled
Bird

MULTICULTURAL POLITICS and EDUCATION POLICYMAKING

Catherine Cornbleth

University at Buffalo

Dexter Waugh

The San Francisco Examiner

ST. MARTIN'S PRESS • New York

To Masaye and Midori Waugh,
and tomorrow's students

EDITOR: Naomi Silverman
MANAGER, PUBLISHING SERVICES: Emily Berleth
PUBLISHING SERVICES ASSOCIATE: Kalea Chapman
PROJECT MANAGEMENT: Richard Steins
COVER DESIGN AND PHOTO MANIPULATION: Rod Hernandez
COVER PHOTO: ©93 Pete Saloutos, The Stock Market

Library of Congress Catalog Card Number: 94–65155

Manufactured in the United States of America.
98765
fedcba

For information, write:
St. Martin's Press, Inc.
175 Fifth Avenue
New York, NY 10010

ISBN: 0–312–10824–9

Preface: Finding a Way

He was a Buffalo Soldier
in the heart of America
stolen from Africa
brought to America
fighting on arrival
fighting for survival
If you know your history
then you would know where you're coming from
then you wouldn't have to ask me
who the hell do I think I am
          Bob Marley, "Buffalo Soldier," 1973*

Bob Marley's reggae rhythms and bold words coming from the tape deck seemed suddenly jarring while driving on a cold autumn day along Interstate 80 across the great pastel plateaus of Nevada and down onto the Great Salt Lake. Marley seemed initially too incongruous, too stark a contrast to imagined images of covered wagons rumbling slowly in the opposite direction, westward, a hundred or two hundred years before, and to those quite-different folk songs that the pioneers from the East sang on their journey. But after only a few minutes Marley, the late Jamaican artist, seemed as logically and comfortably an American choice of music as any other. This was 1991, not 1841. This desolate landscape had not changed much in that time, but the country had.

Today's culture, if there is some such thing as one American culture—and there can't be, despite those who imagine us still swirling in a melting pot—has expanded to include many different kinds of singing, many different songs. Listening to Marley, his music, and especially his lyric in this dry, barren landscape seemed particularly symbolic of how swiftly the country had be-

---

v

come a place echoing the dramatic, stratified mountains, with their layers upon geological layers thrown one upon another, intermingling, symbiotic.

It is commonplace to say that education is political. It is less common to show how the politics of education policymaking operate, how power is wielded to shape public and professional perception, policy, and perhaps classroom practice as well. In *The Great Speckled Bird* we highlight the political, the configurations of power and how they play out with respect to history–social studies curriculum policy. Our focus is on California and New York, two contrasting cases of state-level policy process and outcome, set against the national education policy scene that they shaped as well as reflected.

It also is commonplace to say that schooling reflects society and that education change or reform is a function of change in the host society. At the same time it is clear that the schools are key arenas in which battles are fought over our values and priorities as a nation and what vision of ourselves should be transmitted to the next generation—for example, sacred or secular, monocultural or multicultural. And the schools are called on to resolve societal problems ranging from racial segregation to family breakdown to lagging competitiveness in the global economy. But rarely have the intersections of national issues and education policy questions been examined systematically.

In *The Great Speckled Bird* we examine the politics of multicultural curriculum policymaking in California and New York within the context of the national "America debate." We purposely use *America* rather than the more specific *United States of America* when referring to debates about U.S. national identity and (re-)definition because, unfortunately, the terms of the debate already have been set by the critics and opponents of a transformative conceptualization of U.S. national identity, who have cast the issues in the language of "American" and "un-American." This language dates to the colonial and early national periods of U.S. history and the emergence of the myth of American exceptionalism.

The Great Speckled Bird, then, is about ongoing efforts to redefine America and about the politics of education policymaking as different individuals and groups endeavor to legitimate their definition of America by having the schools endorse and transmit it via curriculum. Means of exercising influence include state policymaking processes and emerging state policies and, perhaps as important, discourses that (re-)define what is considered legitimate and appropriate knowledge to include in school curricula.

Race remains this nation's central unresolved dilemma. In this work we focus primarily on racial and ethnic concerns about multicultural history–social studies curricula and instructional materials; how these concerns were made known to a wider audience; and how they were received, absorbed, and rejected—in short, how education policy comes about in a rapidly changing society. Corollary concerns were raised by others in California, including religious groups—Muslims, Jews, Christians—as well as gays and lesbians. As has been said in many ways over the centuries, "A fight for the rights of one is a fight for all." The Great Speckled Bird is our counter symbol to the Bald Eagle; to us it represents the racial-ethnic-cultural diversity that has characterized the United States since its beginnings. It is our metaphor both for the multicultural reality of American society today and for its as-yct-unrealized expression in school social studies curricula.

STARTING POINTS

In California in 1990 a public debate over new social studies text-books gained national media attention. Before that, in 1987, the state drafted a new history–social science curriculum framework that pushed history into the center of the table. It was a framework widely applauded by education professionals—so it was reported, as California's brand of multi-culturalism later became the media darling of the day.

We have serious doubts if California's version of America will survive, or should survive, into the next century. For all its virtues it is based on an immigrant ethos that largely ignores centuries of oppression of enslaved Africans, the slaughter of indigenous peoples, and the conquest of Mexicans. While the state's framework encouraged discussion and study of multiple perspectives—the Taino as well as Columbus, for instance—primarily it called for an immigrant analysis that mentioned but did not give serious attention to the conflicts brought about by cultural hybridization or the creolizing that actually took place through countless individual and group interchanges.

We focus on the public debate over this immigrant ethos and on the paeans to a "common culture" that embroiled educators, historians, and others dur-ing the late 1980s and early 1990s in California and New York, states with the largest immigrant populations. In California the curriculum debate was low key and attracted little public attention during the mid-1980s as committees and state officials, under the leadership of state Superintendent of Public Instruction Bill Honig, created a new History–Social Science Framework, a 120-page document that encompassed the ideas of various history advocates. Soon, however, public interest in history in the schools took a significant turn, fueled by the residual concerns of people of color, particularly African-American men and women in academic life who were deeply worried about conditions in society that were affecting, directly or indirectly, the future lives and livelihoods of their children. The schools and the history curriculum from which they had been excluded became a focus of their concerns—which should not be surprising, since most people savor aspects of their heritages and having their stories told. Appreciation and respect for these community ties have always had the potential to sustain us, in some way or another, much more than to divide us.

In California the public debate in 1990 over textbooks—summarized through the media as it nearly always was in terms of ethnocentrists versus cultural pluralists, or variations on that theme—obscured some crucial questions. First of all there was (and is) the assumption that there is "a history" to teach and that somehow consensus can be reached about what that history is; then there was the assumption that history is paramount to a child's education and should—must—be taught. In the context of the economic recession that hit the nation and devastated California in 1990 it is interesting to ponder why the assumption that history is important gained so much primacy so as to not even be questioned. As for the former assumption, that there is "a history" to be taught, it is one that the critics of the textbooks in California essentially were challenging, although it was not publicly discussed in quite that way. The argument was whether the history that was contained in the textbooks satisfactorily embraced and included different— that is, nonwhite, non-Western—experiences and points of view. The more basic question—Is there a single, even if multifaceted, history that can be taught?—was not addressed directly. These considerations frame much of what is to come in the following pages.

PATHS AHEAD

The Great Speckled Bird comprises three parts. Part I, "Vistas," consists of two chapters. Chapter 1, "Vantage Points," provides historical perspective and the contemporary social and political landscape for the case studies in Part II. Chapter 2, "Lights and Shadows," offers the theoretical framework for our analysis—a critical pragmatism—and examines such key issues as conceptions of nationalism and multiculturalism, literary canon and historical master narrative, and the "America debate."

Part II, "Cases," consists of four chapters. Chapter 3, "California: Containing America," deals with the History–Social Science Framework adopted in 1987 and with the controversy surrounding adoption of K–8 social studies textbooks in 1990. Chapter 4, "New York: Extending America," begins with the public uproar over a 1989 task force report, *A Curriculum of Inclusion,* and continues with the saga of a second social studies review committee and report, *One Nation, Many Peoples,* and with the related "Understanding Diversity" state policy. Chapter 5, "New York: Muting Multiculturalism?" examines the renewed public clamor generated by the second report, the formation of a new committee charged with incorporating diversity concerns into a broader education reform program (the second state committee to which co-author Cornbleth was appointed and the one from which she eventually resigned), and the apparent outcomes in terms of more multicultural social studies curricula. Chapter 6, "California: Making the Grade," returns to the West Coast three years after the controversial textbook adoption to glimpse what is happening in some San Francisco Bay Area school districts and classrooms, to see policy in practice at the ground level.

These case studies of the politics of state education policymaking in California and New York—of the battles for control over the history and social studies knowledge that is selected for inclusion in school curricula, clearly illustrate how social issues and education policy are intertwined and how influence is exercised in the making of education policy.

In the context of the larger media and academic debate over multiculturalism and national identity during the late 1980s and early 1990s we approached these case studies of policy-in-the-making from two different perspectives: in California, a San Francisco journalist who followed the 1990 state history–social studies textbook adoption process; in New York, a professor of education in Buffalo who served on two state committees charged with reviewing and revising the state's social studies curriculum. From the two coasts we came to write this book together by a serendipitous route. A colleague of Catherine Cornbleth's passed along a paper she had presented at the 1991 meeting of the National Council for the Social Studies to someone who knew Dexter Waugh and who shared it with him because of its relevance to the work he had been doing. Waugh contacted Cornbleth, and that led us to compare notes from our independent work on similar subject matter—what we came to call a "neo-nativist network." We met and talked further at the 1992 meeting of the American Educational Research Association in San Francisco, and we agreed to work out our ideas, first in an essay that appeared in *Educational Researcher* (October 1993) and now in this book. To our colleagues we owe a great deal. But we, of course, are responsible for deciding to juxtapose the California and New York cases and for attempting to blend journalistic and academic traditions.

We have not tried to mask or blend our different voices in the case-study chapters primarily because it would be ironic at best to try to speak in a single anonymous voice or to allow one voice to dominate the other in telling these stories of multicultural policy-in-the-making. Our perspectives meshed, however, in interpreting what we have observed.

The case studies are based on extensive data from direct observation (for example, of meetings and hearings) and from field notes, interview notes, tape transcriptions, and a range of documents from 1987 through September 1994. Analysis is in the tradition of critical interpretive field studies. Direct quotes, unless otherwise indicated, are from our field notes or transcriptions. We have chosen not to interrupt the flow of the case studies with more than essential citations.

We have found it critical to attend to the political, cultural, and racial-ethnic differences that influence state education policymaking. We have tried scrupulously to keep in mind our particular places in this dialogue, to be aware that we are building largely on the work of others—an array of voices too often dismissed or overlooked in mainstream scholarship. There is a significant and diverse stream of academics, educators, journalists, and reformers whose work on the issues that we examine spans at least a century.

Finally, in Part III, "Possibilities," our conclusions are presented in Chapter 7, "America Not Yet." Here we reflect on events in California and New York and on their implications, both educational and political. We further explore the possibilities of listening to historically marginalized or suppressed voices and of considering alternative visions of America as they are being practiced in the schools as well as being advocated by public figures and academics. We conclude by describing the kind of constructive dialogue among differences that might well supersede the divisive battles in what Bob Marley called "the war for America."

ACKNOWLEDGMENTS

From California, co-author Waugh acknowledges the invaluable role of K. Connie Kang, who, as his editor and frequent co-writer at the *San Francisco Examiner*, initiated and then brought focus to a subject they spent much of 1990 writing newspaper stories about: the deplorable lack of racial and ethnic representation in history textbooks, which they called "An American Tragedy." From New York, co-author Cornbleth thanks Lois Weis for her intellectual support and encouragement of risk taking, and Tom Popkewitz for his continuing challenge, even when our ideas diverged.

We thank the teachers and others in California who were interviewed for Chapter 6; and Joyce E. King for the many hours of conversation over the course of three years; and Sylvia Wynter for explaining her perspective and theories on several occasions during those years. We appreciate the thoughtful comments and questions of those who helped to shape and reshape aspects of this work by reading and responding to drafts of various segments: S. G. Grant, K. Connie Kang, Joyce E. King, Gloria Ladson-Billings, Elizabeth Leu, Susan E. Noffke, Hugh G. Petrie, Peter Seixas, Maxine Seller, Tim Stanley, Lois Weis, and Sylvia Wynter; and, for their assistance, University at Buffalo graduate students Chinyere Anunobi, Gretchen Duling, John Szabo, and Lucille Teichert; and, for critical conversations, members of Curriculum Politics and Policy seminars at the University at Buffalo and at the University of British Columbia.

And, finally, we thank our editor at St. Martin's Press, Naomi Silverman, and the reviewers who provided valuable feedback, including encouragement to St. Martin's to publish this book: Ursula Casanova, Arizona State University; Pearl Oliner, Humboldt State University; Alan Singer, Hofstra University; Dianne Smith, University of Missouri, Kansas City; and several anonymous reviewers.

In the end, of course, the interpretations and conclusions we offer are our own. We are very much aware of the charged nature of the issues examined here—and, certainly, that not all readers will agree with our selections, emphases, and interpretations.

Contents

PART I • Vistas

CHAPTER 1   Vantage Points   3

Historical Perspective   3
Resurgence of Nativism   5
Discrimination against Newcomers   7
Restricting and Assimilating Immigrants   9
The America Debate and the Schools as Battleground   11
Neo-Nativist Network   14
The Role of the Media   19
The Examiner's *Experience   20*
Other Battlefronts   22
REFERENCES   23
NOTES   26

CHAPTER 2   Lights and Shadows   27

A Critical Pragmatism   28
Contingency   29
Critical Analysis   29
Fallibility   30
Anti-fundamentalism and Community   31
Pluralism   32
In Sum   33
Issues and Implications   34
Multiculturalisms and Nationalisms   35
Literary Canon, Historical Master Narrative   41
Visions of America   43
Controlling Curriculum Knowledge   49
REFERENCES   52
NOTES   55

PART II • Cases

CHAPTER 3   California: Containing America   59

Reform and Response   60
    Textbook Challenges   61
    Public Culture, Prescriptive Rules   64
Building a National Identity   68
    Revising the Framework   68
Putting Everyone in the Covered Wagon   74
    The 1990 Evaluation and Adoption of History Textbooks   74
    The Great Divide   79
A Gathering of Neo-Nativists   85
REFERENCES   88
NOTES   90

CHAPTER 4   New York: Extending America   93

Prologue: Creating *A Curriculum of Inclusion*   95
Transition: 1989–1990   98
Creating *One Nation, Many Peoples*   101
E Pluribus Unum   106
    Political Sensitivity   110
    Constructing Consensus and Individual "Reflections"   115
Racism and Common Culture   118
Unveiling *One Nation, Many Peoples*   122
REFERENCES   122
NOTES   124

CHAPTER 5   New York: Muting Multiculturalism?   127

Policy and Debate   128
    "Understanding Diversity"   128
    Derisive Discourse: Misunderstanding Diversity?   130
    State Policymaking as Mediation   132
Framing America   133
    Business More or Less as Usual   135
    Bridging Pluralism and Unity   138
    Chains of Command   142
Mediating Multiple Demands   149
    Obstacles in the Way of the Diversity Initiative   149
    A Continuing Story   151
Postscript   152
REFERENCES   153
NOTES   154

CHAPTER 6   California: Making the Grade   157

San Francisco   158
    The Columbus Quincentennial: Multiple Perspectives   162
    Changes   164
South of the City   167
Oakland: There Is Plenty of There There   169
East Palo Alto and Hayward   172
Los Angeles and Houghton Mifflin   174
Teachers, Textbooks, and Curriculum Policy   177
REFERENCES   181
NOTES   182

PART III • Possibilities

CHAPTER 7   America Not Yet   185

Lessons   186
Standardizing America   189
Possibilities for Transformative Multiculturalism   193
    Black Studies Perspective   193
    Reciprocal History   197
Dialogue among Differences   198
REFERENCES   201
NOTES   203

Index   205

PART I

Vistas

1
Vantage Points

You are already a hybrid culture, which to me is a positive thing. I believe all cultures are richer when they assimilate others, and change. I don't believe in a pure culture. Here we are sitting and talking in New York, a city populated by the minorities that are the world's majority. It is marvellous, no?
Octavio Paz, 1990 Nobelist in literature (1993, p. 58)

I've never been a guy who thinks about history. I don't think it matters a damn in football.
Bill Parcells, coach of the New England Patriots football team (1993, p. 57)

HISTORICAL PERSPECTIVE

D oes history matter? Many professionals—educators, academics—who think so have devoted their professional and personal lives to making history, particularly U.S. history, the centerpiece of a social studies curriculum in the public elementary and secondary schools.

They always encounter infidels like Parcells, who suggest there are occasions when the past is best forgotten in order to get on with the task of rebuilding—in his case a team, when he took it over in 1993—and winning.

In other real-life pursuits, however, the past simply cannot be forgotten, not so much because we may be condemned to repeat it, as the saying goes, but because it gives us a greater, deeper appreciation for our humanity, our links with others throughout time. Marguerite Yourcenar, discussing the writing of her *Memoirs of Hadrian* ([1954] 1984), an account of the life of that early Roman emperor, provides a vivid metaphor when she writes about the "problem of time foreshortened in terms of human generations: some five and twenty aged men, their withered hands interlinked to form a chain, would be enough to establish an unbroken contact between Hadrian and ourselves" (p. 321).

Yourcenar's metaphor reminds us in stark terms that our links to the past are closer than we think, that our links with other human beings through our genetic code and aborning flesh are closer and more intimate than we in a Western, individualist society may like to realize or remember.

We don't, it is continually shown, learn from history's mistakes; we learn, if at all, from our own. Thus even Parcells will review game films, exhorting his players to look for the crucial mistakes made on the field and to learn from that different—historical—viewpoint to make corrections and improve performance.

In the field of written history there have been many recent attempts to do the same thing—to reexamine U.S. history from the viewpoint of those who were here when Columbus arrived, from the viewpoint of the indigenous peoples who were decimated by European-introduced diseases, from the viewpoint of later Irish, Chinese, and Jewish immigrants who came and experienced oppression at the hands of those who had come earlier. Throughout U.S. history newcomers have experienced suspicion, intolerance, and purposefully sanctioned discrimination from those native born, and such treatment—although transformed during the late twentieth century into sometimes more subtle expression—doubtless will not soon disappear.

There are many bountiful aspects to our "hybrid culture," as Paz and others well note. But there continues to be a racial divide in the United States—one that has become more complex, shifting from the classic division between whites and blacks to, depending on the region, whites and blacks and Koreans, Vietnamese, Mexicans, and Puerto Ricans. And there are many permutations of how racism is perceived. Bob Blauner (1992) has reported on how white students often see race in color-blind terms—as in, "We've made much progress, and now everyone has an equal chance"—while black students perceive themselves as still at the bottom of the social ladder; equality is still problematic as far as they are concerned.

In this context we offer in Part II case studies of what happened in New York and California during the 1980s and 1990s, of clashes over what it means to be an American, U.S. variety, going into the twenty-first century, and of the struggle over which version of history will be conveyed to the next generations via elementary and secondary curricula and textbooks. Of course, as Vincent Harding notes (1990), "The term *American* must either be expanded to include this American hemisphere in its totality, or condensed to the size of the setting we really intend, these United States of America" (p. 40). In New York, as contrasted with California, the clashes were more extended and more ambiguous in their outcomes. In both states a well-placed (either through outside influence, as in New York, or inside control, as in California) coterie of conservatives and neo-liberals were embraced by a generally sympathetic, if not discerning, media, enabling them to dominate the discussion.

Two interrelated movements frame our account of the struggle to control education policymaking processes and outcomes. One is the renewed "America debate" about how the United States of America should be or can be redefined to encompass our increasingly diverse population. It is a debate about what it means to be an American and which vision of a redefined

America should be passed on to the next generation, both formally by means of school curricula and informally via popular culture. One important aspect of this debate concerns how and to what extent different racial and ethnic experiences, cultures, perspectives, and histories—the Great Speckled Bird that is our metaphor for America—can be and should be represented in a revised national history. The question becomes important especially as a revised history enters the school classroom, sanctioned by state and national education policy, course guides, and examinations. Not unexpectedly, two places where the America debate has been most boisterous are New York and California, the states with the largest numbers of immigrants and the widest diversity of peoples, languages, and cultures.

The second movement is the continuing struggle for knowledge control within academic communities of historians (see e.g., Appleby 1992) and with respect to school curricula (e.g., Kliebard 1986; Cornbleth 1990, 1992). To control school or curriculum knowledge is a means of exercising power beyond school walls by shaping how we understand ourselves, others, the nation, and the world. Curriculum knowledge affects individual and collective identity, capacity, attitude, and action. As an illustration of how control is sought and power is exercised, we are particularly interested in the activity of a small but well-funded and media-savvy group of people who sought to preserve, or promote, a rather narrow conception of America and what it means to be American.

RESURGENCE OF NATIVISM

The making of an American begins at that point where he himself rejects all other ties, any other history, and himself adopts the vesture of his adopted land. This problem has been faced by all Americans throughout our history—in a sense it is our history—and it baffles the immigrant and sets on edge the second generation until today. In the case of the Negro the past was taken from him whether he would or no.
  James Baldwin (1955, p. 29)

The 1980s had given rise to a neo-conservatism which, says Henry Giroux (1992), focused on turning higher education (and we would include elementary and secondary education) into "an academic beachhead for defending and limiting the curriculum to a narrowly defined patriarchal, Eurocentric version of the Western tradition" (pp. 92–93; see also Kaye, 1991). The neo-conservative agenda, unfortunately, did not and does not now include a desire to engage in debate within the usual boundaries of critical exchange, says Giroux, who adds:

It is increasingly taking on the shades of McCarthyism rampant in the 1950s in the United States, with those in power using their influence in the press, in well-funded public symposiums, and through highly financed private think tanks to conjure up charges that academics who are questioning the relationship between the liberal arts and the discourse of power and citizenship are to be judged by their motives rather than their arguments. (p.93)

American University law professor Jamin B. Raskin writes that the day he saw a wizard of the Ku Klux Klan denouncing political correctness on a television show was the day he stopped making PC jokes. What once was used as a put-down for preachy leftist posturing, he says, "had not only been swiped by conservatives and emptied of irony; it had been dipped in poison and turned against the idea of inter-racial progress" (1994, p. 68). Observing that race is "at the heart of the anti-PC campaign," Raskin says that the

> PC-bashers . . . may make it impossible for our new multicultural real-
> ity to blossom, bringing back the old American baseline majority of
> racial animosity and exclusion [recalling] . . . Reconstruction, when a
> majority of white Americans—not simply unrepentant Confederates,
> but Northern liberals as well—tired of the exhausting business of racial
> progress and moved to undo "special privileges" for the recently freed
> slaves. (p. 71)

The neo-conservatism described by Giroux transmuted into what we have called "neo-nativism" (Cornbleth and Waugh 1993), an ethos that involves attempting to portray America's increasingly diverse society in school curricula by simply adding more historically excluded people to the old immigrant diorama of America and minimizing serious examination of racial and ethnic conflict.

Another term, such as *assimilationism,* could be used, since we are intend-ing to portray a latter-day version of that turn-of-the-century approach to dealing with immigrants: Dissolve their cultural differences and absorb them. We believe, however, that *neo-nativism* more directly captures the phenomenon that has arisen in recent years and that we encountered in our case studies. It is one that turns practically on its head the definition of nativism (Higham [1955, 1963] 1977) as a defensive nationalism that has led to lashing out against perceived perils—usually religious, revolutionary, or racial-ethnic outsiders. Recognizing that immigrants already have forever changed life, society, and the "culture" in places like California and New York, policymakers as well as a broad swath of others now say that "we are all immigrants" and that immigrants are who made America in the first place.

While superficially seeming to be inclusionary, in fact the neo-nativist position has the same exclusionary effects (intended or not) as the earlier nativism, despite—or because of—its having been (in the case of California's history–social science curriculum) "multiculturalized." The issue of race remains far, far away from the central role it has played in America, as Raskin and others have shown. Instead, inclusions are made within the existing framework, without changing the story of European immigrant

America (cf. Higham [1955] 1977). Whether or not one agrees that, of the several forms of organized bigotry in the United States, "the three most virulent are racism, anti-Semitism and nativism," it cannot be denied that nativism is about as old as the republic and "as American as violence, capitalism and democracy" (Remini 1992, p. 15).

Discrimination against Newcomers

As they made steady inroads into lands occupied by indigenous peoples, the early European settlers also fought rear-guard actions against newcomers: Early colonial fervor was anti-Papist and anti-Germanic. During the eighteenth century, before and after Independence, says Stephen Steinberg (1981), America—needing labor to build the country—imposed no restrictions on immigration, yet "foreigners were generally regarded with suspicion, if not outright hostility" (p. 11). He continues:

> Long before the onset of mass immigration, there was a deeply rooted consciousness of the nation's Anglo-Saxon and Protestant origins. From the beginning, the nation's political institutions, culture, and people all had an unmistakably English cast, and despite denominational differences, Protestantism was the near-universal creed. The early stirrings of nativism clearly signaled the fact that however much the nation might tolerate foreigners in its midst, it was determined to protect its Anglo-Saxon and Protestant legacy. (p. 13)

During the nineteenth century anti-immigrant activity focused variously on the Irish, Jews, Chinese, and southern and eastern Europeans. But while earlier non-Anglo immigrants suffered prejudice, the Chinese, who began arriving shortly before 1850, became the first victims of overtly racist discrimination directed against immigrants. As Lawrence H. Fuchs (1990) reports, "The Chinese were, as the Democratic party platform of 1884 later said, 'unfitted by habits, training, religion or kindred . . . for the citizenship which our laws confer' " (p. 112).

Chinese immigrants, who came here to make their fortune and move on—just as many other immigrants to California during the mid-1800s hoped to do—were at the bottom of the social ladder. Although initially viewed ambiguously, they soon became social pariahs much like African Americans and Native Americans. As Fuchs notes (1990) it was "something else beyond 'habits, training, religion or kindred' [that] kept the Chinese outsiders. . . . That something else was race" (p. 112).

The first Chinese to arrive in California were regarded as curiosities; according to Roger Daniels and Harry H. L. Kitano (1970), "The state's racism was not yet catholic enough to include all men of color" (p. 35). But by 1852, after Chinese joined other forty-niners in the search for gold in the Sierra foothills, antagonism based on class and race distinctions—later fueled by fears that the Chinese were a threat to organized labor—became manifest.

A poignant account of bigotry against Chinese immigrants is told by Frank Leach (1917), in his memoir of early days in Sacramento. Leach was a youth in 1855 when the event transpired. His account:

> A Chinaman was killed by a blow on the head from a club wielded by a boy fifteen or sixteen years old. A half-dozen boys about that age had undertaken to tease the Oriental. They succeeded beyond their expectations, for he started after them, following them with bulldog persistence. After a chase of some distance the boys took refuge behind some cordwood piled up along the sidewalk. One of the boys seized a four-foot stick and when the Chinaman came up struck him on the head, with fatal result. I came in view of the affair just at the time the Chinese was felled. The affair happened near Chinatown and caused great excitement among the residents of that locality, but I never heard of any arrest being made on account of it. (p. 35)

By 1870 anti-Chinese feelings reached their height in San Francisco, where, according to the 1870 Census, a quarter of the state's 50,000 Chinese resided (Daniels and Kitano 1970, p. 38). There was an economic depression nationwide, and in San Francisco the Chinese in particular were singled out. The city imposed special taxes on Chinese laundries and even a tax on Chinese who wore their hair in the traditional queue. Pressure grew from the Workingmen's Party, the Anti-Coolie Union, and other groups to cut off further immigration of Chinese. Only two groups spoke in favor of continued immigration: employers who valued the Chinese as a source of cheap labor and some Protestant denominations that viewed China as a vast opportunity for missionary work (Daniels and Kitano 1970). The electoral success of the Workingmen's Party—which endorsed a number of other populist issues but which used as its rallying cry, "The Chinese must GO!"—ultimately led to congressional passage in 1882 of the Chinese Exclusion Act. It prohibited immigration from China for 10 years and was renewed for another 10 years in 1892 and extended indefinitely in 1902.

Although organized labor has been often cited as the driving force for exclusionary immigration laws against Chinese and, later, Japanese, in his study of newspaper coverage in San Francisco of the Japanese and Chinese between 1882 and 1924, Jules Becker (1991) found that anti-Asian campaigns "were scarcely altered by economic conditions. In good times and bad, Asians became targets" (p. 202). Crime stories in particular constituted the majority of the coverage of the Chinese. In these crime articles the Chinese were depicted as

> criminals, drug addicts, different and unassimilable, and provided the reasons why they should be, and were, excluded. . . . Chinese crime provided the major justification for the campaign against Chinese immigration. . . . Over the long haul . . . economic conditions were never key issues in campaigns against the Asians. The key issue was that they were Asians. (pp. 202–203)

The anti-Chinese reaction was significant. Early non-English-speaking newcomers, such as the Germans, had faced assimilationist efforts since the eighteenth century. But the Chinese immigrant experience in the middle to late nineteenth century—characterized by California's and then Congress's blatantly racist discrimination—was a watershed in U.S. immigration history and "helped to shape a restrictive pattern to which our immigration laws adhered for almost a century" (Daniels and Kitano 1970, p. 44).

Restricting and Assimilating Immigrants

During the 1890s, when eastern and southern Europeans began pouring into New York's harbor, the same restrictive patterns that had been developed against the Chinese were brought to bear against them. At the same time cultural pluralists and educators began to remake these diverse newcomers by using the schools as vehicles to assimilate them into the American community. The Pledge of Allegiance, first published in 1892 to celebrate the 400th anniversary of Columbus's arrival, caught on quickly, and by the end of 1892, according to one account, 12 million children were reciting it in classrooms every day (Fletcher 1992).

There were at least two aspects of the movement to assimilate and Americanize immigrant children. According to David B. Tyack (1993), some wanted the public schools to drive a sharp wedge between the children and their native culture, to Americanize them as fast as possible. Others preferred a slower, social-worker approach, helping to keep alive the children's native cultures while acculturating them into American life, society, and good citizenship. The outbreak of World War I brought a heightened frenzy to "eradicate 'hyphenism' among foreign born adults and to ensure that their children were superpatriots" (p. 15). Tyack (1976) writes:

> Clearly, Americans had enormous faith in the power of schooling to transform all kinds of people—even "enemies"—into citizens. . . . Characteristically, Americans intensified their attempts at political socialization in schools whenever they perceived a weakening of loyalties (as in World War I), or an infusion of strangers (as in peak times of immigration), or a spreading of subversive ideas (whether by Jesuits or Wobblies or Communists). (p. 367)

The economic depression of 1920–1921, an influx of immigrants from southern and eastern Europe (Catholics, Jews, and Greek Orthodox), the revival of the Ku Klux Klan, and popular writings stressing the superiority of the "Nordic race" all contributed to passage by Congress in 1924 of a new immigration law that discriminated against not only Asians but also these white ethnic groups from Europe. The new law, the National Origins Quota System, severely restricted immigration based on nationality (Daniels and Kitano 1970, p. 54; Feldstein and Costello 1974, p. 146). The restrictions remained in effect for more than 20 years until, after the end of World War II, a series of immigration reform laws canceled the 1924 national quota system.

The year 1965 brought further immigration reforms, and these, coupled

with the end of the war in Vietnam in 1975 and the beginning of an unprecedented flow of refugees from Southeast Asia, resulted in the second-greatest
influx of newcomers to these shores in a century. Throughout the years of
the 1980s and 1990s California absorbed an estimated half of all new legal
and illegal immigrants; New York, Texas, and Florida took fewer but, still,
large numbers.

During the late 1980s California entered a severe recession brought on
by (in addition to national economic conditions) a decline in property tax
revenues resulting from passage of Proposition 13, in 1978, and the col-
lapse of the defense industry. By the early 1990s the impact of immigration
to California led to growing resentment among native borns and earlier
immigrants toward the newcomers, who, they feared, were taking away
jobs, adding to the public costs of welfare and education, and generally
creating an unbearable burden on society. In an October 1990 *New York
Times* article noting America's growing uneasiness about immigration, reporter Felicity Barringer (1990, p. E4) wrote that:

> Despite some disturbing incidents, there are few signs that the kind of
> organized anti-immigration movements of decades past are rising again.
> The strident voice of the nativist has faded. . . . But political scientists say
> that the immigration debate has created new political fault lines and
> disrupted old alliances. As often as not, the voices expressing concerns of
> increased immigration come from people who once would have been
> called liberals.

Very shortly the storm clouds gathered. A 1993 Gallup poll found that 65
percent of Americans felt the number of immigrants admitted to the country
should be decreased—twice the number of those who felt that way in 1965
(Gallup Organization 1993). In that same year, buffeted by sinking revenues
and soaring expenses, California Governor Pete Wilson wrote an open letter
to President Clinton, placed as a full-page advertisement in the *New York
Times*, that called for drastic steps to halt illegal immigration, including denying citizenship to children of illegal immigrants born in the United States and
cutting off education and health services for undocumented residents. "We
can no longer allow compassion to overrule reason," he said (Rohter, 1993, p.
E4). California and other states with large immigrant populations—legal and
illegal—sued the federal government, accusing it of failing to stem the tide of
illegal border crossings and demanding that it repay the states for the costs of
providing health and education services to undocumented residents. Latino
activists called Wilson's demand an "election gimmick" and vowed to "beat
the anti-immigrant backlash" (McCormick and Martinez, 1993, p. A4).

In 1993, a year after jury verdicts acquitting police officers of nearly all
assault charges stemming from the videotaped capture and beating of an
African American, Rodney King, the Los Angeles Times took a poll of racial
attitudes in Southern California around Los Angeles. It discovered a complex
mixture of feelings: Although Angelenos in general held favorable impressions toward Asians, they did not feel that way toward new Asian immi-

grants. Prompted by then-current news events surrounding the smuggling of Chinese boat people into this country, 64 percent supported sending the Chinese back without a hearing; 55 percent favored a three-year ban on all immigration. Even Asians backed the return of Chinese boat people without hearings, by a margin of 53 percent to 35 percent (Los Angeles Times 1993). Moreover, a Los Angeles Times poll published in September 1994 (Sontag, 1994) found that 62 percent of those likely to vote in the November election that year supported a ballot initiative that encompassed Wilson's proposals denying benefits to illegal immigrants. In contrast to Barringer (1990), Lawrence Cremin (1989) had noted:

> Every indicator in the early 1980s pointed toward the beginning of a new nationwide Americanization movement not unlike the one that flourished during the second and third decades of the century, and toward a return to definitions of what it meant to be an American that closely resembled those of the earlier era. (p. 117)

But the Los Angeles Times polls made it clear that if there were to be a new round of skirmishes between nativists and newcomers, the combatants now were quite different. Whereas in the past white natives carried the banner of anti-newcomer attitudes, during the 1990s their implicit claims to ownership of America were being challenged by Native Americans, Latinos, Asians, and African Americans, who claimed equally deep generational title to the country. In addition to being roiled by similar misgivings about newcomers, these groups had far more potent and lingering concerns about the failure of America to live up to its ideals of institutional equality than did whites. As Steinberg (1981) notes, "A pluralism based on systematic inequalities is inherently unstable" (p. 256).

THE AMERICA DEBATE AND THE SCHOOLS AS BATTLEGROUND

The things that we have used to bind us over the years aren't going to be the things that are going to bind us into the next century. It's not going to be the story of Plymouth Rock, it's not going to be the traditional story of Thanksgiving as we know it. . . . We're going to have to be a little more sophisticated, a little deeper and find out what does it mean to be an American. . . . The binding elements are not going to be the color of skin or same last names or same accent . . . or same heritage, but it's going to be some deeper things that make us function as a country, even after we acknowledge that we're different, and made up of different people.
    Henry Cisneros, former mayor of San Antonio and later secretary of
    the Department of Housing and Urban Development in the Clinton
    administration (Public Broadcasting System 1990)

During the early 1990s there developed growing national concern, in the face of intense global economic competition, over a perceived loss of

United States' prestige and place in the international economy. Many policymakers and opinion makers focused their ire downward, on the schools, for failing to produce graduates capable of carrying the American "empire" into the twenty-first century. The Union of Soviet Socialist Republics collapsed, the European Community came closer to unity, and, constantly, the American people were told that the test scores of their children were lagging far behind the scores of their counterparts in France, Germany, Japan, and elsewhere.

During the 1980s conservative administrations reigned in Britain and the United States. Paralleling these administrations was a growth in the number and influence of think tanks funded by conservatively oriented foundations. These think tanks generated thousands of position papers, many of which were reprinted on opinion pages of newspapers throughout the United States. In this climate, free market and privatization were pushed into the forefront of options for addressing social and economic problems facing the United States. Although not always acknowledged, at the heart of these approaches was a belief that America had to rediscover or return to the kind of rugged "can-do" individualism that reputedly had made it great. Some politicians and educators decided that this could be accomplished by having the schools convey a revised patriotism. It was to be embodied in the teaching of history, an expansive kind of history that acknowledged the contributions of a wider variety of peoples than previously but one that at the same time emphasized a unifying set of "common values."

Many of these educators and politicians often referred to a vaguely defined common American culture as "glue." In 1984 William Bennett, chair of the National Endowment for the Humanities (NEH) who became secretary of the Department of Education in the Reagan administration, referred to democratic principles that he claimed "descended directly from great epochs of Western civilization" as "the glue that binds together our pluralistic nation" (1985, pp. 14–15). Lynne Cheney, later head of the NEH, said that knowledge of democratic values "functions as a kind of civic glue" (1988, p.7).

"Glue" was ubiquitous during discussions and debates over Americanism during the late 1980s and early 1990s, even among those purporting to take a neutral stance. For example, in their description of California's *History–Social Science Framework,* (History–Social Science Curriculum Framework and Criteria Committee, 1988), education professors James Guthrie, Michael Kirst, and Allan Odden of PACE (Policy Analysis for California Education) said that history is "the glue that makes the past meaningful and provides the lens [sic] through which children and adults can come to understand the world they live in and how it is shaped" (PACE 1991, p. 76).

California's version of American history was based on an immigrant perspective that in effect subjugated Native Americans, African Americans, and former Mexican citizens in the Southwest to the status of ride-alongs, rather than primary participants and shapers of America's dynamic, hybrid culture. "They put everyone in the covered wagon," said Joyce E.

King, a Santa Clara University education professor who fought a losing battle against California's brand of modest multiculturalism while a member of California's state Curriculum Commission (Waugh and Hatfield 1992, p. A18).

According to Stanford University's Sylvia Wynter, who held a joint appointment in the departments of African and Afro-American Studies as well as Spanish and Portuguese, California's multiculturalist curriculum promoted a culturally pluralistic version of American society downplaying, if not ignoring, its racial and cultural hierarchy. California's version of history functioned to represent Euro-immigrant America as the "universally valid perspective of all America" (1990, p. 6). In this master narrative, hierarchy was flattened, race faded away, and everyone became immigrants.

Although this kind of modest multiculturalism purported to include hitherto excluded voices, only certain voices were selected. As Henry Giroux says in *Border Crossings* (1992), this brand of multiculturalism

> glosses over any attempt to designate how dominant configurations of power privilege some cultures over others, how power works to secure forms of domination that marginalize and silence subordinated groups. . . . Absent is any account of how various social movements have struggled historically to transform a Eurocentric curriculum that, in part, has functioned to exclude or marginalize the voices of women, blacks, and other subordinated groups. (p. 234)

As an example, Diane Ravitch, in her 1990 *American Reader,* offers a celebratory selection of primary source documents including speeches, poems, songs like "Home on the Range" and "Clementine," cartoons, and essays from America's past and present. Where Ravitch's *Reader* includes instances of conflict, they mostly are patriotic dissents such as Patrick Henry's "Give me liberty, or give me death!" and pleas from slaves and Native Americans for equal treatment, although occasionally anger was allowed inside, as in Frederick Douglass's "Independence Day Speech at Rochester." In her introduction Ravitch acknowledges that she did not include "every major voice; I did not include, for example, those who preached disunion or hatred toward others" (1990, p. xiii; cf. Singer 1991).

The neo-nativist's version of multiculturalism as demonstrated in the Houghton Mifflin textbooks adopted in California in 1990 promotes a highly selective kind of inclusion, along the lines suggested by Ravitch in her *American Reader*. Martin Luther King Jr. is there; Malcolm X is not. This selectivity threw into doubt the credibility of the neo-nativists' "glue." Much more is included than before, but there is still much left out, and the central driving focus or narrative remains that of European immigrants. The consequence of this is a self-serving "politics of erasure." According to Giroux (1992):

> Through her insistence on a common culture, Ravitch erases the institutional, economic, and social parameters that actively construct deep structural inequalities and forms of domination that characterize relations

between privileged and subordinated groups, as well as the challenges that have been waged against such practices. (p. 234)

This "politics of erasure" was at the base of conflicts in California and New York over the design of elementary and secondary school programs, textbooks, and exams. Questions of multicultural education—specifically, more inclusive history and social studies education—took on increased significance after the violence in Los Angeles following the Rodney King beating verdicts in 1992, as President Bush and his appointees moved toward national education standards and assessments. According to Bush's secretary of education, Lamar Alexander, consensus had been created "about what children should know and be able to do in order to live, work and compete in today's world" (1992, p. 1). Alexander further claimed that there was a "new consensus about the need for and the shape of a voluntary national examination system. . . . In just one year the question has become not whether to do it, but how best to do it." Actually, there was considerable disagreement over whether it was best to do it at all. But with or without consensus, it remains highly questionable whether national goals, standards, and testing by themselves can solve the problems that have led to urban uprisings or bolster the nation's competitiveness in the global economy. Insofar as standards engender standardization, however, they could thicken the neo-nativists' glue.

The debates over multicultural education in California, New York, and elsewhere were contests over drawing up the version of the United States that would gain widespread if not universal allegiance, one that would be passed on to future generations in the nation's schools. The public schools, after all, have long been one of the principal arenas in which battles are fought over public values and priorities (Cremin 1989, Kliebard 1992) and over what vision of itself the nation would transmit to future generations. Witness, for instance, the campaign of Christian fundamentalists to gain strongholds on community school boards in order to influence how, or whether, creationism and evolution and traditional family values are taught in the schoolroom. The school curriculum is seen as a major vehicle of cultural definition and transmission; hence the battle for control of curriculum knowledge.

NEO-NATIVIST NETWORK

Father Latour reflected. "And the silver of the Spaniards was really Moorish, was it not? If not actually of Moorish make, copied from their design. The Spaniards knew nothing about working silver except as they learned it from the Moors."

"I am glad to think there is Moorish silver in your bell. When we first came here, the one good workman we found in Santa Fe was a silversmith. The Spaniards handed on their skill to the Mexicans, and the

Mexicans have taught the Navajos to work silver; but it all came from the Moors."
"I am no scholar, as you know," said Father Vaillant rising.
Willa Cather, *Death Comes for the Archbishop* (1971, p. 45)

Neo-nativism blurs the usual political distinctions, appealing to liberals as well as to conservatives. The 1990s neo-nativists proposed to contain diversity and difference through a standardized education—with national standards in core subjects, national assessments, and a de facto national curriculum. They wished to establish a peculiarly standardized version of multicultural history, one that would both create and maintain their notion of a common culture.

The neo-nativist opposition to multiculturalism has been reactive and is characterized by an unfortunate penchant to conflate multiculturalism with Afrocentrism, to pose an either–or choice between assimiliation and Americanization on the one hand, and racial separatism and centrism on the other (Erickson 1992, p. 99). It may seem absurd to place an old-line liberal like Arthur Schlesinger Jr. with the neo-nativists, but there are different kinds of liberalism. As Erickson notes in discussing Schlesinger's *Disuniting of America,* conventional liberalism as represented in Schlesinger's discourse fails to move beyond an "additive" version of multiculturalism (that is, simply including more material), as contrasted with progressive liberals like Henry Louis Gates Jr., who advocate a transformative multiculturalism that "implies disrupting and restructuring the whole field" (Erickson 1992, p. 99). (Additive and transformative multiculturalism are considered at greater length in Chapter 2.) Distinguishing these different liberal stances helps explain why the neo-nativist attack on multiculturalism (and "political correctness" and a host of other issues often tied up with multiculturalism) dovetailed with conventional "individual rights" liberalism.

Debate during the 1980s and early 1990s over national identity and education policy was influenced by a relatively small group of neo-conservative academics, educators, and federal appointees in the Reagan and Bush administrations who managed to establish a tone and set the terms of the America debate. Following the 1989 governor's conference that led to the national goals and standards package that became known as America 2000, many of them became involved in the work of developing standards in various core subject areas, including history.

Their growth in influence—as illustrated in the California and New York case studies in Part II—paralleled the rise during the Reagan years of a network of conservative and libertarian think tanks and advocacy groups concerned with a variety of political and social reforms. These think tanks, such as the Heritage Foundation, derived their support from essentially the same places as the key players in the neo-nativist curriculum effort: from the conservative John M. Olin Foundation, for instance (Waugh and Hatfield 1992, p. A18).

Former chair of the National Endowment for the Humanities, Lynne

Cheney, former assistant education secretaries Diane Ravitch and Chester Finn, and historian Schlesinger were prominent standard-bearers of the neo-nativist movement in history-social studies education. One of their main allies was UCLA education professor Charlotte Crabtree, whose National Center for History in the Schools—established at UCLA in 1988 with a $1.5-million grant from Cheney's NEH—later garnered $1.6 million from both NEH and the federal Department of Education for a project to draw up national standards for history education. Supporters of these principal players have included people like Albert Shanker, head of the American Federation of Teachers, whose weekly paid-advertisement column in the *New York Times* often extolled the virtues of a far-reaching "common American culture" and who joined Ravitch and Schlesinger in heaping abuse on New York State schools' chief Thomas Sobol while castigating multiculturalists in general and Afrocentrists in particular. Shanker's presence here demonstrates the breadth of appeal of the neo-nativists' message; while they may have differed about many other issues, they joined in the late 1980s and early 1990s to become the de facto defenders of common culture, "legitimate" history, and the curriculum knowledge deemed appropriate for elementary and secondary schoolchildren.

The neo-nativist network's genealogy can be traced to 1982, when Chester Finn and Diane Ravitch co-founded the Educational Excellence Network (EEN), which described itself as a confederation of about 800 educators, scholars, and journalists devoted to improving America's schools and the quality of education. Finn was an education professor at Vanderbilt University, and Ravitch was an adjunct professor of history and education at Teachers College, Columbia University.

Five years later the EEN spawned the Bradley Commission on History in the Schools, with historian Kenneth Jackson of Columbia University as chair and historian Paul Gagnon—then at the University of Massachusetts-Amherst—serving as executive secretary. Among the 17 commission members were Ravitch and UCLA's Crabtree. Supported by a grant from the Bradley Foundation, the commission published its report, *Building a History Curriculum*, in 1988 and then transformed into the Westlake, Ohio–based National Council for History Education, with the avowed goal of promoting the importance of history in school and society. Ravitch, Jackson, Finn, and Gagnon all have been involved with the Westlake group.

In California, Crabtree and Ravitch collaborated to write the final draft of the state's framework for history–social science education, approved by state officials in 1987. Crabtree, whose background was in elementary social studies education, had been involved in the committee discussions leading up to the framework and later was appointed to the Curriculum Development and Supplemental Materials Commission, an advisory body to the state board of education commonly referred to as the Curriculum Commission. In 1988 her proposal to Cheney's NEH to establish a National Center for History in the Schools at UCLA won out over proposals from UC-Berkeley and elsewhere. The center's purpose was to "provide a broad program of research and dissemination activities to improve history teaching and learning in the nation's elementary and secondary schools" (National Center for History in the Schools, undated pamphlet). UCLA historian Gary Nash was Crabtree's associate director at the center, and Paul Gagnon was among those listed as a staff scholar.

At the same time, in New York, the American Textbook Council opened its offices in Manhattan to "advance the quality of social studies textbooks and all instructional materials" (*Social Studies Review* [Spring 1991], p. 16). The council was established with a $300,000 grant in 1988 from the Donner Foundation of New York to Gilbert Sewall, who that year also became a co-director (with Finn) of the Educational Excellence Network. Sewall and Gagnon went to California in 1990, at Crabtree's invitation, to give presentations to the panel of teachers and professors assembled by the state to review history textbooks then up for adoption. The advisory board of Sewall's American Textbook Council has included Gagnon, Crabtree, Kenneth Jackson, and Bill Honig, former California Superintendent of Public Instruction.

Virtually a one-person operation during its early years, Sewall's council and especially its quarterly newsletter *The Social Studies Review*, helped shape the America debate in the public arena; with a print run of about 4,000, it was distributed widely to the media and educators, and Sewall emerged as an "expert," frequently called by reporters to comment on issues related to textbooks. In occasionally turgid prose he castigated the textbook critics who attended a California State Board of Education hearing in the fall of 1990: "Their interest was in image and self-promotion, in panegyric and hagiography, in past grievances and scores to settle. Truth did not matter. What counted was prominent and favorable treatment for themselves and excoriation of their enemies" (*Social Studies Review* [Fall 1990], p. 12). In the same issue, Sewall also noted with pleasure the receipt of additional funding from three foundations, including the Olin Foundation, to "help us publish and distribute forthcoming issues, so we can continue to provide crucial information to educators around the country who must decide what textbooks their schools will use and who more than ever need access to *impartial*, independent reviews" (Fall 1990, p. 2; emphasis added). Sewall's dramatic flair sometimes sacrificed credibility in the interest of highlighting what he presumably assumed his readers would find bizarre: His description in the same issue of a Muslim wearing a jellaba and unfurling a prayer rug outside a textbook hearing in Sacramento was repeated almost verbatim by one magazine writer (Kirp 1991).

Sewall's account was disputed by Shabbir Mansuri, the leader of the Muslim contingent to the public hearing, who also took responsibility for leading the traditional noon prayer on the lawn outside. Neither he nor anyone else unfurled a prayer rug, he said; nor did any of the Muslims in attendance that day wear a jellaba, as Sewall had claimed. "My daughter wore a scarf," said Mansuri, "but that is not a jellaba." (interviews, December 13, 1990, May 15, 1994.)

In 1991 Ravitch went to the U.S. Department of Education as assistant secretary in the Office of Educational Research and Improvement (OERI). Gagnon soon followed, to serve under Ravitch. Later that year UCLA reaped two more important grants. One of four Academies for History Teachers was established in association with Crabtree's center with a $495,000 grant from Ravitch's OERI. The Bradley Commission's Westlake successor was another recipient. The other two grantees had no previous connection with the neo-nativist network: Brigham Young University and the State University of New York at Buffalo.[1] The second UCLA grant was a joint $1.6-million award from the Department of Education and Cheney's NEH to Crabtree's history center for a history standards project. This project was to develop "world-class" national standards for history education (U.S. Department of Education 1991). Its advisory council included Kenneth Jackson, Gary Nash, and Gilbert Sewall, as well as other members of the Westlake group.

These players continued their work in the national history standards movement during the early 1990s. Cheney and Finn served on the 1991–1992 National Council on Education Standards and Testing, with Cheney heading the council's history task force. Finn and Crabtree both served on the National Assessment of Educational Progress governing board, where Finn was the liaison to the committees planning the 1994 U.S. history national assessment.

Among the noteworthy aspects of this neo-nativist network, in addition to its complex interconnections, was the mix of public and private funding that the various individuals and groups received. Funders of two or more of the organizations just mentioned include the U.S. Department of Education and the National Endowment for the Humanities, which in addition to the grants already mentioned gave $27,000 in "general support" money to the Westlake group; and from the private sector, monies came from the John M. Olin Foundation of New York, the Lynde and Harry Bradley Foundation of Milwaukee, and the Donner Foundation of New York. The Educational Excellence Network received numerous grants over the years from foundations, including $250,000 in 1989 and 1990 from Bradley and a $300,000 three-year grant from Olin in 1989. Olin gave Chester Finn another $92,000 for a Vanderbilt University–based education reform project in 1991. Diane Ravitch received research grants of $85,000 in both 1989 and 1990 from Olin.

Also noteworthy is the organizational location of individual members, which lent status and authority to their pronouncements. One speaks not for oneself but for a committee, commission, council, or center or for a university or federal government agency. Network members supported one another and their reform cause by praising each other's work in public statements and journal articles, appointing one another to advisory boards, hiring one another as consultants for their various projects, and helping fund those projects. Their position gained seeming legitimacy largely through repetition and overlap, and the appearance of consensus that they were able to generate.

While they were successful in getting their opinions and viewpoints expressed in the media, members of the neo-nativist network were less successful in seeing their vision of America adopted officially in New York than they were in California. California endorsed the neo-nativists' America, while New York continued to move, albeit slowly, counter to a national trend of adopting that version of America and its modest brand of multiculturalism.

THE ROLE OF THE MEDIA

In New York only a few people, including historian Arthur Schlesinger Jr., were able to have their voices magnified by the media and to stall a 1989 minority task force effort to steer New York's social studies curriculum away from its traditional Eurocentric perspective. Schlesinger and education historian Diane Ravitch railed against people who were disturbed by the move toward a sanctioned national history that downplayed the more challenging aspects of diversity, calling them "ethnic cheerleaders" and "tribalists" out to "balkanize" the country. Their catchphrases were catnip to the mainstream media. There was hardly a liberal, moderate, mainstream, or conservative publication that did not pick up and endorse their views.

Beyond the easily grasped "identity crisis" suggested by the America debate, the issues raised by the *Curriculum of Inclusion* report in New York in 1989 and the history textbook adoption process in California in 1990 were complex and difficult for the media to cover. In New York attention was focused on a few instances of so-called "inflammatory" language and "controversial" metaphors such as King Arthur's Round Table that were used in the task force report (see Chapter 4). In California questions about historical perspective and whether California would move beyond a modest, inclusionary form of multiculturalism did not receive serious attention; the media dealt mainly with some of the more gripping citations that critics said demonstrated "distortions, stereotypes and inaccuracies" in the K–8 textbook series (see Chapter 3).

Newspapers, needing concrete examples, seized on these to attempt to convey to readers what the dispute was all about. Very few reporters or editors had the chance, time, or inclination to give careful readings to the textbooks, relying instead on the "thumb test," a quick flip through the books which usually proved impressive because of the books' heavy reliance on photos and graphics. The underlying problem with the immigrant narrative perspective raised by textbook opponents was difficult to convey and usually got lost as supporters and opponents quarreled over various passages.[2]

A second factor is that the textbooks did represent an improvement over past textbooks in their increased inclusion of literature and stories of ethnic and racial minorities. As the debate got increasingly hot over the summer and early fall of 1990, it seemed that many in the media simply became impatient with the critics, agreeing with Superintendent of Public Instruction Bill Honig's caustic assessment of them as mere "special interest groups." One of the most admiring news articles written about the new textbooks appeared in the *Los Angeles Times* the morning the state board of education was to take its final vote on adoption (Banks and Trombley 1990):

> *Sacramento*—They are not like any history books you've ever seen.
>
> American history doesn't begin with the country's "discovery" by Christopher Columbus. The Italian explorer isn't even introduced until the fifth chapter of one of the controversial history texts that received approval Thursday from a key committee. . . .
>
> The "melting pot" concept of American diversity taught to generations of students is tossed out in favor of the "salad bowl" approach. U.S. history is presented not just through the eyes of European immigrants, but through the stories of American Indians who were pushed off their land and blacks brought from Africa and enslaved. . . .
>
> [They] are a far cry from the dull collection of dates and places common to many history texts. . . .
>
> The new books are chockablock with colorful maps and graphs and rely on first-person narratives and excerpts from literature by a diverse group of authors. . . . (p. A1)

It is only after ten paragraphs of such breathless praise that the reporters note that the books "have brought a firestorm of protests from ethnic and religious groups."

Textbook adoption in California usually is a mundane proceeding, unless there is a controversy. There had been one, for instance, a few years earlier over the treatment of creationism versus evolutionism in new science textbooks. And the focus for the media usually is an "event," in this case the public hearing in July before the state's Curriculum Commission, which recommended the textbooks, and another before the state board in September. Newspaper coverage before September was minimal; it only started building as the September hearing neared. One newspaper, however, the *San Francisco Examiner*, followed the entire adoption process from beginning to end. It is our belief—based on word from numerous teachers, parents, and education activists who asked for reprints—that this coverage probably stimulated coverage by other media and brought more attention to the ongoing process than otherwise might have occurred, given its generally esoteric nature.

The *Examiner's* Experience

Here we briefly summarize how the *San Francisco Examiner* got involved, to give insights into both how media coverage can exert some influence on education policymaking and how reporters who have the opportunity to follow a process can develop deeper understanding of the process and the issues—and can draw conclusions that journalists who cover an issue only occasionally might not.

The *Examiner's* coverage originated in 1989 with K. Connie Kang, then an assistant metro editor who for many years had wanted to write about the apparent lack of inclusion of Asians in U.S. history textbooks—a particular concern in San Francisco, where about 45 percent of the K–12 students are of Asian descent. Kang gathered a team of reporters which developed a survey to be taken of graduating high school seniors, and then she convinced the *Examiner's* management to pay for it. Its purpose was to determine how widely educated about their own and other racial and ethnic groups the graduating seniors had become during their sojourn in San Francisco's schools. The results showed generally that the various ethnic groups had not learned much about each other; and some immigrant groups—Chinese, Vietnamese, and Koreans—were more likely to feel that others viewed them as foreigners.

The *Examiner's* three-part series (May 6–8, 1990) also reported on California's *History–Social Science Framework* and the opportunities it held out for publishers to develop new and exciting and authentically multicultural textbooks. In subsequent months a total of 24 articles reporting on various steps in the process appeared, usually in the Sunday editions, which reached a large audience in Northern California. One reported that review books available for public perusal were going largely unnoticed by parents (May 20, p. B1). Another reported the results of the Instructional Materials Evaluation Panel, which rejected seven of the nine publishers that had submitted materials (July 1, 1990, p. A1); another reported that public written response to the textbooks was overwhelmingly negative (July 8, 1990, p. B1); another was the first report of state Curriculum Commissioner Joyce E. King's public protest of the anointed textbooks for what she called "egregious racial stereotyping" (July 18, 1990, p. A1). Another article examined the propriety of Commissioner Charlotte Crabtree's participation in the voting, since one of the textbooks' co-authors, historian Gary Nash, was an associate of hers at UCLA (July 29, 1990, p. B3).[3] Another said the state legislature's black caucus would ask for a delay on the textbook vote (September 12, 1990, p. A4). And another reported Houghton Mifflin's unusual step of hiring a high-powered public relations firm to help win public approval (a far cry from the old days, when textbook publishers routinely wined and dined state education officials) (October 2, 1990, p. A10).[4] The *Examiner* also editorialized against adoption, one of the few (if any) major dailies to do so: "Ignorance is the real root cause of ethnic tensions. These proposed textbooks would do little to help today's students—tomorrow's citizens—to learn to live and work together" (October 11, 1990, p. A25).

Although co-author Waugh had begun observing the textbook adoption process not knowing what to expect, he became increasingly concerned as the textbooks seemed to gather steamroller momentum, while people who raised serious doubts about them seemed either to receive little serious attention or had their concerns trivialized by state education officials. In the view of the *Examiner* series' principal authors, Waugh and Kang, the adopted textbooks fell short of what was needed by the state's diverse student population. In a final commentary they argued that the state should have held out for better textbooks (October 14, 1990, p. B1).

The articles did bring public attention to these concerns, and in one reported case (Der 1992) they helped unite opposition to the textbooks in a local school district (Oakland).

With nearly all the large newspapers in California that had anything to say about the events approving of, and thus legitimating, the state board's adoption of the texts, the media played its own role in the education policy-making process.

Other Battlefronts

The national media continue to play a significant role as they switch attention from one flashpoint in the debate over America's schools to another, and during the early 1990s there were numerous controversies that involved both the public schools and higher education: expanding the canon, the English-only movement, bilingual education, political correctness, speech codes, dress codes, all-male schools for black youths, school choice, national standards and assessments, so-called outcomes based education (OBE), distribution of condoms in the schools, and sex education.

Two of the most contentious issues were interrelated: the controversy in New York over the "Rainbow Curriculum" and the growing phenomenon of the conservative Christian movement to capture seats on local school boards.

Adopted in 1991 by the New York City school chancellor's office, the 440-page multicultural guide "Children of the Rainbow" raised hackles in some quarters because of one small section that called on first grade teachers to include references to gays and lesbians in classroom activities. One community school district board rejected the curriculum outright; the board's president launched a campaign of mailings attacking the guide for containing "dangerous misinformation about sodomy" (Karp 1993, p. 49). The issue tapped a wellspring of populist resentment as busloads of angry parents and residents flocked to community school meetings. The campaign against teaching about same-sex families, wrote Stan Karp, "masks a deeper resistance to other forms of multiculturalism" (1993, p. 55). Maxine Greene (1993) commented:

> There are paradigms throughout our culture that function deliberately to repress, to belittle other ways of being, and sometimes to make those alternative ways appear threatening, requiring censorship or prohibition or even a violent demise. The response to the "Children of the Rainbow" curriculum is a sad example, especially in the way its linking of gay and lesbian families (presented on one page as "real people") to a range of atypical or minority families aroused fear and loathing, and a conscious distortion. (p. 216)

A much broader campaign to halt the tide of multiculturalism in school curricula began in 1988, when Richard Simonds formed Citizens for Excellence in Education (CEE) with the avowed purpose of helping conservative Christians gain control of local school boards. By 1993 CEE and other religious organizations on the right had made stunning inroads in many communities· Simonds claimed that his organization had helped elect almost 5,000 school board members between 1991 and 1993 and that it controlled 2,200 school boards nationwide—a claim that was disputed by his opponents (Shogren and Frantz 1993, p. A38). Although the media often are guilty of "overspeak" in dealing with such matters, Shogren and Frantz may not have been exaggerating when they wrote:

> From San Diego County to New York City, the religious right has turned the public schools into the primary battleground in a divisive conflict over the most fundamental issues of national identity. At issue is nothing less than what values should be taught to the next generation of Americans. (p. A1)

"Schools have been an ideological battleground for decades, but there is no precedent for the breadth of the religious right's current campaign," they added (p. A38). School board disputes involving the religious right and their opponents most often centered on books, sex education, and homosexuality—anything in the curriculum that went beyond the basics or seemed overconcerned with raising students' self-esteem or seemed to represent behavior modification.

Although gays and lesbians were involved in California's history textbook protests in 1990—in fact, they were first on the signup sheets to speak at public hearings—their concerns were not taken seriously by state education officials (see Chapter 3). If the religious right becomes more of a factor in curriculum policymaking, sexual orientation and how to address it in the public schools is likely to remain near the top of the issues agenda.

But the long-unresolved issues of racial hierarchy and the tantalizing promise of developing a transformative multicultural history—and the debate over what it means to be American—were raised most cogently in the 1990 California history textbook controversy, which set the stage and preceded magazine cover stories about the America debate in the national media by almost a year. We turn our attention to the California controversy in Chapter 3.

REFERENCES

Alexander, Lamar. 1992. America 2000: One year later. *America 2000*, no. 23 (March 30): 1–3.

Appleby, Joyce. 1992. Recovering America's historic diversity: Beyond exceptionalism. *Journal of American History* 79 (2): 419–431.

Baldwin, James. 1955. *Notes of a native son*. Boston: Beacon Press.

Banks, Sandy, and William Trombley. 1990, New textbooks: Out with dull, in with diverse. *Los Angeles Times* (October 12): pp. A1, 38.

Barringer, Felicity B. 1990. A land of immigrants gets uneasy about immigration. *New York Times* (October 14): p. E4.

Becker, Jules. 1991. *The course of exclusion, 1882–1924: San Francisco newspaper cover-*

age of the Chinese and Japanese in the United States. San Francisco: Mellen Research University Press.

Bennett, William. 1985. To reclaim a legacy. *American Education* 21 (1): 4–15.

Blauner, Bob. 1992. Talking past each other: Black and white languages of race. *American Prospect* 10:55–64.

Cather, Willa. 1921. *Death comes for the archbishop.* New York: Vintage.

Cheney, Lynne V. 1988. *American memory: A report on the humanities in the nation's public schools.* Washington, D.C.: GPO, 216–283.

Cornbleth, Catherine. 1990. *Curriculum in context.* London: Falmer.

———. 1992. Controlling curriculum knowledge. Paper presented at the annual meeting of the American Educational Research Association, San Francisco.

Cornbleth, Catherine, and Dexter Waugh. 1993. The great speckled bird: Education policy-in-the-making. *Educational Researcher* 22 (7): 31–37.

Cremin, Lawrence A. 1989. *Popular education and its discontents.* New York: Harper and Row.

Daniels, Roger, and Harry H. L. Kitano. 1970. *American racism: Exploration of the nature of prejudice.* Englewood Cliffs, N. J.: Prentice-Hall.

Der, Henry. 1992. Cultural context of Oakland protests against Houghton Mifflin history textbooks. Unpublished paper.

Erickson, Peter. 1992. Multiculturalism and the problem of liberalism. *Reconstruction* 2 (1): 97–101.

San Francisco Examiner (listed chronologically):

Kang, K. Connie, and Dexter Waugh. 1990. Minority students feel like outsiders who were robbed of their past (May 6): pp. A1, 14.

Ramirez, Raul. 1990. Students feel unprepared for life in multicultural society (May 7): pp. A1, 8.

Waugh, Dexter. 1990. Framework puts color in state history books to show ethnic diversity (May 8): pp. A1, 14.

Kang, K. Connie, and Dexter Waugh. 1990. New school textbooks getting little attention (May 20): pp. B1, 4.

Waugh, Dexter, and K. Connie Kang. 1990. Textbooks fail to make grade for state panel (July 1): p. A1, back page.

Waugh, Dexter. 1990. Public flunks most publishers' efforts (July 8): pp. B1, 5.

———. 1990. Official rips textbooks under review (July 18): pp. A1, back page.

———. 1990. Questions raised in textbook vote (July 29): p. B3.

———. 1990. Black lawmakers ask delay in adopting new textbooks (September 12): p. A4.

———. 1990. PR firm enters schoolbook fray (October 2): p. A10.

Accurate textbooks. 1990. Editorial (October 11): p. A25.

Waugh, Dexter, and K. Connie Kang. 1990. Textbook controversy shifts over to schools (October 14): pp. B1, 5.

Feldstein, Stanley, and Lawrence Costello, eds. 1974. *The ordeal of assimilation: A documentary history of the white working class.* New York: Anchor Books.

Feynman, Richard. 1985. *Surely you're joking, Mr. Feynman! Adventures of a curious character.* As told to Ralph Leighton; edited by Edward Hutching; pp. 288–302. New York: Norton.

Fletcher, George P. 1992. Update the pledge. Week in Review. *New York Times* (December 6): p. xx.

Fuchs, Lawrence H. 1990. *The American kaleidoscope.* Hanover, Conn.: Wesleyan University Press.

Gallup Organization. 1993. Public wants fewer immigrants. *San Francisco Chronicle* (July 23) : p. A26.

Giroux, Henry. 1992. *Border crossings: Cultural workers and the politics of education.* New York: Routledge.

Gordon, Beverly M. 1993. African-American cultural knowledge and liberatory education: Dilemmas, problems, and potentials in a postmodern American society. *Urban Education* 27 (4): 448–470.

Greene, Maxine. 1993. Diversity and inclusion: Toward a curriculum for human beings. *Teachers College Record* 95 (2). 211–221.

Harding, Vincent. 1990. Gifts of the black movement toward "A new birth of freedom." *Journal of Education* 172 (2): 28–44.

Higham, John. [1955] 1977. *Strangers in the land: Patterns of American nativism, 1860–1925.* New York: Atheneum.

History-Social Science Curriculum Framework and Criteria Committee. 1988. *History-Social Science Framework.*

Karp, Stan. 1993. Trouble over the rainbow. *Z Magazine* (March): pp. 48–54.

Kaye, Harvey J. 1991. *The Powers of the Past.* Minneapolis: University of Minnesota Press.

Kirp, David. 1991. The battle of the books. *San Francisco Examiner IMAGE* magazine (February 24): pp. 17–25.

Kliebard, Herbert M. 1986. *The struggle for the American curriculum, 1893–1958.* London: Routledge and Kegan Paul.

———. 1992. Constructing a history of the American curriculum. In Philip W. Jackson, ed., *Handbook of research on curriculum.* New York: Macmillan. pp. 157–184.

Leach, Frank. 1917. *Recollections of a newspaperman.* San Francisco: Samuel Levinson.

Los Angeles Times. 1993. Southern California Survey (August).

McCormick, Erin, and Don Martinez. 1993. Protesters hit Wilson's plan on immigrants. *San Francisco Examiner* (September 17): p. A4.

National Center for History in the Schools. Undated pamphlet.

PACE (Policy Analysis for California Education). 1991. Conditions of education in California 1990. Berkeley: School of Education, University of California.

Parcells, Bill. 1993. The control freak meets the geeks. By Charles P. Pierce. *New York Times* magazine (September 12): pp. 56–57, 69–71, 91.

Paz, Octavio. 1993. Talk of the Town. *New Yorker* (December 27): pp. 57–58.

Public Broadcasting System. 1990. America's schools: Who gives a damn? Panel discussion.

Ravitch, Diane, ed. 1990. *The American reader: Words that moved a nation.* New York: HarperCollins.

Remini, Robert V. 1992. No foreigners, Catholics, slaves, or whiskey, please. *New York Times* (October 18): pp. 15–16.

Rohter, Larry. 1993. Revisiting immigration and the open door policy. *New York Times* (September 19): p. E4.

Sewall, Gilbert T. 1990. *Social Studies Review* (Fall): 2, 12.

Singer, Alan. 1991. Review: *The American reader* by Diane Ravitch. *OAH Magazine of History* (Summer): 55–57.

Shogren, Elizabeth, and Douglas Frantz. 1993. School boards become the religious right's new pulpit. *Los Angeles Times* (December 10): pp. A1, 38.

Sontag, Deborah. 1994. Illegal aliens put uneven load on states, study says. *New York Times* (September 15): p. A8.

Steinberg, Stephen. 1981. *The ethnic myth: Race, ethnicity, and class in America*. Boston: Beacon Press.

Tyack, David B. 1976. Ways of seeing: An essay on the history of compulsory schooling. *Harvard Educational Review* 46 (1): 355–389.

———. 1993. Constructing difference: Historical reflections on schooling and social diversity. *Teachers College Record* 95 (1): 8–34.

U.S. Department of Education and National Endowment for the Humanities. 1991. News release (December 16).

Waugh, Dexter, and Larry D. Hatfield. 1992. Rightist groups pushing school reforms. *San Francisco Examiner* (May 28): p. A18.

Yourcenar, Marguerite. [1954] 1984. *The memoirs of Hadrian*. New York: Modern Library.

NOTES

1. Co-author Catherine Cornbleth was one of three co-directors of the History Academy at the University at Buffalo.
2. Sewall's assessment of the textbooks: "While the Houghton Mifflin series is elegant in format and lively in content, it makes no effort to restore running narrative to a primary position and simplify design. Quite the opposite. With a look not entirely foreign from *USA Today*, the books are kaleidoscopic in appearance" (*Social Studies Review* [Fall 1990], p. 10).
3. Crabtree was quoted in the story as saying she was unaware of Nash's work on the Houghton Mifflin history textbooks until December 1989, about seven months before she voted with others on the Curriculum Commission to recommend state adoption of her colleague's textbooks.
4. An entertaining account of this former activity was described by the physicist Richard Feynman, who served on a textbook review panel during the early 1960s (Feyman 1985).

2
Lights and
Shadows

Never have you been able to think in terms of blacks and whites, goods and evils, God and the devil. . . . You know that every extreme includes its contrary: cruelty, tenderness; courage, cowardice; life, death. In some manner, almost unconsciously, by being who you are and where you are and what you have lived, you know this, and therefore you can never be like them, who do not know it. Does that disturb you? Yes, it's troubling. How much more comfortable to be able to say: this is the good, and this is the evil.
Carlos Fuentes, *The Death of Artemio Cruz* ([1964] 1987, p. 28)

To highlight some part of the world as a focus of study is also to turn the light of attention away from something else and thereby cast it into shadows. Similarly, the concepts and theoretical framework one employs influence what one pays attention to and how one interprets what is "seen," inevitably highlighting some aspects and obscuring others. This chapter presents our theoretical framework, which we term a *critical pragmatism*, and we note where it casts both lights and shadows by considering implications for key issues in the America debate and multicultural education policymaking.

The metaphor of lights and shadows also suggests the limits of human knowledge and understanding. Our views of the world and aspects of it—even minute fragments of it, such as the place where one lives—are necessarily partial. There simply is no such thing (in the human sciences) as a total picture or complete story. Even if there were, the picture or story would be outdated immediately because the world does not stand still. So it is too with our interpretations and explanations, our theories and conceptual frameworks. However much we might like them to be comprehensive and to stay put is the measure of our inevitable disappointment.

Grand theories, all-embracing systems, or master narratives all are seductive as well as dogmatic and totalizing. As Berger and Kellner (1981) say:

27

On the cruder level, this is because they make the intellectual enterprise easier. . . . One of the basic drives of the human intellect is the drive for meaningful order—and ideological systems provide just such an order. Having readily applicable schemas of interpretation at hand makes the task of trying to grasp the endlessly fluid, often chaotic-seeming reality of the human world less burdensome. But there is a deeper level of seductiveness. Ideological systems provide . . . knowledge that not only provides intellectual understanding but also provides existential hope and moral guidance. (p. 144)

This is to say that we make no seductive claim to offer a singular or whole story of recent multicultural education politics and policymaking in California and New York. But we hope that the stories we do tell will make some difference in the course of future education politics and policymaking in these states and elsewhere, thus rendering our account "historical."

A CRITICAL PRAGMATISM

Our theoretical stance can be described as a critical pragmatism. A philosophical stance emerging in the post–Civil War United States, pragmatism has particular relevance to the political and ethical issues in the late twentieth century United States, including the vision or visions of America to be transmitted to future generations.

More than a century ago William James (1876; cited in Gunn, 1992, p. 36) suggested that pragmatism be considered a habitual way of thinking that continually sees alternatives, imagines other states of mind, refuses to take the usual for granted, and makes "conventionalities fluid again." Pragmatism, as disciplined skepticism and imagination, is made possible by difference, by the inevitable cracks in dominant social systems, and by democratic political institutions that provide space for alternatives to take hold.

Approximately a half-century later W. E. B. Du Bois, described by Cornel West (1989, p. 138) as a "Jamesian Organic Intellectual," took both Emerson and James seriously and showed how American democracy was falling far short of its promise. Du Bois's 1935 *Black Reconstruction*, in West's analysis, "illustrates the blindnesses and silences in American pragmatist reflections on individuality and democracy" (p. 146). West continues:

Although none of the pragmatists were fervent racists themselves—and most of them took public stands against racist practices—not one viewed racism as contributing greatly to the impediments for both individuality and democracy. (pp. 146–147)

Du Bois saw pragmatism as relevant to the predicament of African Americans, and he provided pragmatism with what at the time was a radical perspective on racist and capitalist obstacles to the fulfillment of individuality and democracy. James's pragmatism allowed for but did not elaborate structuralist issues such as institutionalized racism (West 1989). And subsequent portrayals of pragmatism varied in their recognition of both Du Bois's work and his arguments.

Periodically over the last century, philosophers and others have retrieved or reconstructed a version of pragmatism as an alternative to the prevailing modes of thought and theorizing. This is one of those times. David Harvey, for example, tells us that in a postmodern world, where comprehensive representations and global projects are either oppressive or impossible, pragmatism "becomes the only possible philosophy of action " (1990, p. 52). Changing the world begins with reinterpreting it.[1]

How we "see" the world or some part of it—our assumptions, conceptions, explanations—influences how we think about and act within or on it. Theory can be seen as an instrument, an intellectual tool, for gaining understanding and for considering possible courses of action. So our theories, however fuzzy, are not merely of academic interest. A major question of contemporary pragmatic theory asks what it would mean to adopt one rather than another way of looking at things (Gunn 1992). What would it mean to adopt, for example, one rather than another vision of America? Several overlapping facets of our conception of critical pragmatism are introduced in the following sections: (1) contingency, (2) critical analysis, (3) fallibility, (4) anti-fundamentalism and community, and (5) pluralism.

Contingency

Pragmatism, like postmodernism, rejects so-called meta- or master narratives or grand theories that purport to offer interpretations or explanations of universal scope and application. It also is impatient with the boundaries and dichotomies of intellectual bureaucracy. Pragmatism is a mode of thought, inquiry, or analysis that recognizes its location in time and place and considers how its particular locality influences investigation, interpretation, and action. The localism of pragmatism is not provincialism but the specificity or practicality of a concrete situation. Pragmatic inquiry is situated and contingent. The present inquiry, for example, juxtaposes specific and necessarily partial cases of multicultural education politics and policymaking in California and New York against our view of the national U.S. scene with a focus on the six-year period from 1987 through 1993. While multiculturalism may be a transnational phenomenon (Kalantzis and Cope 1992), it manifests itself in particular places and ways.

Critical Analysis

We specify a *critical* pragmatism to make clear the perspective we bring to this project. Although some pragmatists might see this specification of a critical dimension as redundant, we are reminded by W. E. B. Du Bois (1935) and others that wide-ranging skepticism ought not to be taken for granted.

A critical theory perspective entails questioning appearances and everyday practices, probing assumptions and implications, in order to foster individual and collective enlightenment, empowerment, and freedom from various forms of oppression. It recognizes and values human intention and action in relation to both the limiting and the enabling aspects of people's historical, material, and cultural circumstances. The questioning and probing associated with a critical perspective extend beyond the immediate situation in time and space to historical antecedents and social structures. Oppressive regimes—political, military, and ideological—cannot tolerate critical perspectives in their midst. Instead they impose their truths and suppress alternative points of view—including questions that raise doubts about their authority or beneficence.

A critical perspective emphasizes questioning or skepticism in the interests of freedom from oppression in order to further human dignity, equity, and social justice. Its concerns are political and ethical as well as epistemological. In other words, not only are theory and practice intertwined, but interpretations are judged in part by their consequences in action. Who benefits directly or indirectly from the consequences in each case? From, say, the consequences of one or another vision of America or version of multiculturalism?[2]

Fallibility

Critical pragmatism aims to be self-questioning, subjecting its own values and presuppositions to scrutiny. What, for example, does it mean to value human dignity? What might or could it mean? What are the consequences of one or another interpretation? These questions illustrate two key aspects of a critical pragmatism in addition to its skepticism.

One is that values such as human dignity, equity, and social justice are not absolute, fixed, or transcendent. Instead their specific meanings change—are reinterpreted—as time, place, and circumstance change. Whereas the fundamentalist takes values to be invariant standards, directives, or mandates, the critical pragmatist sees values as indeterminate concepts that orient inquiry, decision, and action. Critical pragmatists have not, for example, clung to an eighteenth-century interpretation of "All men are created equal" that excluded women and all people of color.

Second, critical pragmatists reject an eccentric form of relativism that claims the inherent worth of some value or practice (for example, representative government, female infanticide) simply because it is part of a larger cultural package. Critical pragmatism is not without guiding values or principles. It "merely" subjects its own as well as others' values to scrutiny and possible reinterpretation. A prime example in the U.S. context is the continuing reinterpretation and expansion of the meaning of "We hold these truths to be self-evident, that all men are created equal."[3]

A critical pragmatism minimizes the possibility of privileging or reifying a particular form or source of critique that serves to liberate only some of us (see, e.g., Ellsworth 1989). Pragmatism recognizes its fallibility, realizing according to Bernstein (1991), that although we must begin any inquiry with prejudgments and can never call everything into question at once, nevertheless there is no belief or thesis—no matter how fundamental—that is not open to further interpretation and criticism. (p. 327)

Critical pragmatism's openness to, even insistence on, cultural critique makes it particularly appropriate as a framework for analysis of the continuing America debate and its intersections with multicultural education policymaking.

Anti-fundamentalism and Community

In addition to contingency or context sensitivity, critical analysis, and fallibility, the "pragmatic *ethos*" has been characterized by anti-foundationalism, community, and pluralism (Bernstein 1991). Anti-foundationalism, or *anti-fundamentalism*, means rejection of the possibility of absolute or certain knowledge, of first premises or final conclusions. Instead knowledge (or truth) is seen as provisional—as far as we can tell, for the time being. A pragmatist would wonder whether the search for or claim to foundations or fundamentals masks an attempt to justify and eternalize a particular account or practice and its attendant benefits.[4]

Community refers to the ideal social setting in which knowledge is constructed and individuality is formed. Ideally this conversational community is a "critical community of inquirers" of which we all are or might become active participants. We test our claims and understandings not only by our own review but by submitting them to the critical scrutiny of public discussion, to the "serious encounter with what is other, different, and alien" (Bernstein 1991, p. 328).

Rorty (1991) joins pragmatism's anti-fundamentalism and community in a manner that both anticipates pluralism and undermines the simplistic "anything goes" version of the relativist epithet. He notes that

to say that what is rational for us now to believe may not be *true* is simply to say that somebody may come up with a better idea. It is to say that there is always room for improved belief, since new evidence, or new hypotheses, or a whole new vocabulary, may come along. For pragmatists, the desire for objectivity is not the desire to escape the limitations of one's community, but simply the desire for as much intersubjective agreement as possible, the desire to extend the reference of "us" as far as we can. (p. 23)

Although Rorty may not have had in mind the current America debate and the professed concerns of many, especially neo-nativists, for national unity, critical pragmatism offers another route to unity as well as to rationality and objectivity and provisional truth—not standardization but widespread negotiated agreement that extends and redefines the reference of "us."

Rorty goes further, showing that putative questions about objectivity, truth, relativism, rationality, and knowledge are moral and political as well as epistemological. They are questions

about what self-image our society should have of itself. The ritual invoca-
tion of the "need to avoid relativism" is most comprehensible as an
expression of the need to preserve certain habits of contemporary European [or American, or other] life. (p. 28)

The critical pragmatist would go further, asking, "Whose need?" and "Who
would benefit from these habits' being preserved?"

While critical pragmatism casts light on an expanding conversational
community, it risks leaving in shadow the everyday world in which most
people live. In this world, individuals and groups jockey for survival and,
beyond survival, for position and power to practice their beliefs and pursue
their interests.

Pluralism

Pluralism, the fifth aspect of the "pragmatic *ethos*" identified by Bernstein, "pervades" the themes of contingency, critical analysis, fallibility, anti-
fundamentalism, and community. "There can be no escape from plurality—
a plurality of traditions, perspectives, philosophic orientations" (Bernstein
1991, p. 329). After dismissing versions of pluralism that he characterizes as
fragmenting, flabby, polemical, and defensive, Bernstein argues for pluralism
that means

> resolving that however much we are committed to our own styles of
> thinking, we are willing to listen to others without denying or suppress-
> ing the otherness of the other. It means being vigilant against the dual
> temptations of simply dismissing what others are saying by falling back
> on one of those standard defensive ploys where we condemn it as ob-
> scure, woolly, or trivial, or thinking we can always easily translate what
> is alien into our own entrenched vocabularies. . . . What makes this task
> so difficult and unstable is the growing realization that there are no
> uncontested rules or procedures [for reaching rational agreement on
> every point]. (p. 336)

From this perspective, disagreement is unavoidable, and consensus is not
necessarily desirable. Instead of confrontation or adversarial debate, dialogue or conversation is sought where

> one begins with the assumption that the other has something to say to us
> and to contribute to our understanding. The initial task is to grasp the
> other's position in the *strongest* possible light. . . . There is a play, a to-
> and-fro movement in dialogical encounters, a seeking for a common
> ground in which we can understand our differences. The other is not an
> adversary or an opponent, but a conversational partner. (p. 337)

As our exploration of possibilities for dialogue in Chaper 7 further
shows, pragmatic dialogue is what Catharine Stimpson (1994, p. B1) aptly
calls "hard work." Beyond some minimal degree of civility, participants

must be willing to subject their views to scrutiny. But too often the dia-logue is adversarial.

Describing pragmatism similarly, Gunn (1992) also acknowledges the politics of pragmatism. Without advocating a particular politics, pragmatism possesses a politics

> distinguished by the democratic preference for rendering differences conversable so that the conflicts they produce, instead of being destruc-tive of human community, can become potentially creative of it; can broaden and thicken public culture rather than depleting it. (p. 37)[5]

From a pragmatic perspective,

> It is healthier to keep looking for, and listening to, and making up new stories than it is to insist that all of our experience—and perhaps every-one else's to boot—must be encompassed within . . . one single story. (p. 16)

The intent is less to maintain and select from existing traditions or stories than to envision and enact new possibilities.

Efforts to make cultural discourse univocal can be seen as leading to totalitarianism. At the same time Gunn acknowledges that encouraging plu-ralism may yield so much difference that it will be ignored. In other words, pluralism can be a means of managing or in effect "suppressing difference rather than for acknowledging and interacting with it" (p. 216). A related danger is that widening and deepening the conversation may not change anything; it may only dissipate the energies of difference. Yet, in a democ-racy, he tells us, we do not have a better choice. "The fate of everyone human these days is becoming more and more interdependent on people and groups whose contrary tastes and temperaments they can neither alter nor avoid" (p. 38).

In Sum

Bringing together critical and pragmatic traditions in this way links the contextual emphasis and equity goal of critical theory with the self-questioning and pluralism of pragmatic philosophy. The critical perspective gives depth and direction to pragmatic inquiry and dialogue. Pragmatism, in return, reminds us that cultural critique encompasses us all; none of us or our cherished beliefs, individually or collectively as a member of one or another group, is above or beyond question.[6] Emergent and oriented toward action, this critical pragmatism eschews materialist and theological determin-isms on one side and postmodernist quicksands on the other. Critical pragma-tism employs standards or principles of judgment, and it subjects them to ongoing scrutiny and possible modification. Without such provision for change Western science, for example, might not have survived the Spanish Inquisition. Thus critical pragmatism is neither authoritarian nor anarchist.

In the absence of 360-degree vision, all views are partial and necessarily distorting. To approach truth and justice requires the interaction (not merely the availability or presence or pasting together) of multiple perspectives. For critical pragmatists, this interaction is governed by criteria or principles agreed upon by participants—principles of access and participation as well as of justification—principles which are subject to scrutiny and renegotiation as are the substantive points in question.

This middle ground between authoritarianism and anarchy is not a comfortable one for those who would claim that their views should be accepted, without reference to any substantive guiding principles, simply because they exist and perhaps have been excluded or marginalized in the past. While critical pragmatists would insist on the procedural justice of equitable access and participation of multiple voices, they also would recognize that "procedural justice is neither a necessary nor a sufficient condition for substantive rationality (or epistemic worthiness more generally)" (Siegel 1993, p. 18). This middle ground also would be uncomfortable for those who would insist that their preferred principles be followed and their conclusions be accepted without question. Whereas the former emphasize principles of access and participation (theirs), the latter emphasize principles of justification (theirs). Critical pragmatism encompasses both and works toward "ours." In contrast, absolutists of all stripes favor dialogue about as much as corporations favor regulation.

We now turn to an overview of some implications of our critical pragmatic stance for key issues in the America debate and multicultural education policymaking—issues to which we return in the concluding chapter. Perhaps the clearest implication is critical pragmatism's opposition to efforts to limit or close off debate, either by putting topics or issues out of bounds or by *a priori* rejecting particular viewpoints or the participation of particular individuals or groups.

ISSUES AND IMPLICATIONS

Next we examine three interrelated issues relevant to multicultural education policymaking. The issue of pluralism and unity (versions of multiculturalism and forms of nationalism) and the issue of canon–historical master narrative can be seen as two sides—political and cultural—of the same coin. The third issue, which we characterize as visions of America, or the America debate, can be seen as encompassing and future-oriented.

There are, of course, more than two sides to each issue, and in the spirit of critical pragmatism we present multiple positions—examining a wider range of options than was considered publicly in either the California or the New York cases of curriculum policymaking. This broader background is intended to provide perspective or context for understanding the case studies in Part II—and to suggest what might have been or may yet be (see Chapter 7). Individual and group self-interests are embedded in these issues, each one more than it appears to be on the surface. Among the questions that

might be raised in each case is "Who benefits?" from one or another position
or resolution of the issue.

Multiculturalisms and Nationalisms

Ethnic Versus Civic Nationalism. Based on examination of the emergence of nation-states in England, France, Russia, Germany, and the United
States, Greenfeld (1992) distinguishes between the civic nationalism of England, France, and the United States and the ethnic nationalism of Germany
and Russia. Nationhood and national identity are ideas or concepts; they are
not necessarily linked to common ethnic cultures or geopolitical divisions.
Whereas *civic nationalism* is individualistic and emphasizes a sovereign people united by an agreed-upon social contract, *ethnic nationalism* is collective
and emphasizes a unique people or ethnic culture. Whether or not one finds
Greenfeld's categories apt, the key point is that nations are "imagined communities," humanly created and modified over time, not primordial or natural communities fixed for all time (see Anderson 1991).

Both civic and ethnic nationalism emphasize "the people" (as in "the
American people"), and they locate individual identity within that peo-
plehood ("I am an American"). But "the people" may be defined in presumably universalistic terms of human rights and citizenship or in terms of a
particular shared history, heritage, religion, or race. Similar to Greenfeld's
civic nationalism, Jaenen (1981, p. 81) refers to the British tradition of
defining national unity in political rather than cultural terms. Unity in Britain and Canada has been a function of widespread recognition and acceptance of a parliamentary and legal system and symbols such as the Crown.
The U.S. counterparts are the constitutional system and symbols such as the
Flag and the Bald Eagle. In this view, unity is a matter of reaching agreement
on how to live together peaceably, not of how to look or sound or act alike.[7]

In looking to a vaguely defined common culture for national unity, neo-
nativists conflate ethnicity and nationality. They do not always make it clear
whether their common culture is the U.S. civic culture, especially its encompassing democratic political ideals and institutions (see, e.g., Fuchs 1990) or
a mythical culture of harmonious everyday life. One wonders, then, who
would benefit from the neo-nativists' version of common culture—or from
any "centric" concept of the nation-state.

Additive, Revisionist, and Transformative Multiculturalism. Several forms of
multiculturalism also are possible, and meanings given to the term vary
widely. Here we focus on the selection and organization of knowledge in
multicultural history and social studies curricula rather than on multicultural
education in general or multiculturalism writ large.[8] The several varieties of
multicultural history–social studies can be grouped into three clusters: additive, revisionist, and transformative (cf. Banks 1987, 1988; Erickson 1992).
While all three forms of multiculturalism support inclusion, they do so from
different conceptual and political-ideological positions and with potentially
different social consequences.

Within additive multiculturalism one finds at least two forms: (1) separate studies and (2) heroes and contributions. Separate studies are an add-on to the conventional curriculum, usually in the form of elective courses that enable senior high school students, in the schools that offer such electives, to sample the histories and cultures of specific groups such as African Americans or Asian Americans. Separate studies are parallel tracks. Any interaction between or among the various studies or courses would come from the initiative of individual teachers or students. Potential conflict among the various tracks, studies, or stories is minimized by maintaining their separation. Since the separate, "other" studies usually are electives—meaning that no one is *required* to take them—they remain marginal. In contrast, U.S. history is required by 47 of the 50 states; 35 require at least two years of study in grades 5–12 (New York and California require at least three years of U.S. history).

The heroes-and-contributions form of additive multiculturalism adds "other" heroes and contributions to the conventional stories of U.S. history, usually indigenous peoples and people of color. Photographs, boxed inserts, special features, and suggested activities in history and social studies textbooks, for example, are much more diverse than they were even 20 years ago. Despite its limitations, or perhaps because of them, heroes-and-contributions tokenism has wide appeal (see Olneck 1990).

One limitation is that heroes-and-contributions multiculturalism maintains the conventional European-dominant historical narrative by "mentioning" only those "other" individuals and events that are deemed a proper fit. By definition the heroes and contributions that are included are not ordinary people or everyday activities; they certainly are not "troublemakers" or "problems." In this way, "others" are portrayed one-dimensionally, and historical understanding remains stunted.

A second, related limitation is that the inclusions in this additive form of multiculturalism are safe (Seller 1992). Heroes and contributions of whatever color, class, culture, or gender are selected because—by dominant or mainstream cultural standards—they are role models. They sustain rather than challenge the status quo. Compare, for example, how most elementary and secondary school textbooks have treated Martin Luther King Jr. and Malcolm X.

A third limitation is the individualist bias of the heroes-and-contributions approach. It does not reach or reveal the institutional or structural arrangements in U.S. and other societies that perpetuate inequity and relationships of domination-subordination. Highlighting female heroes and contributions, for example, masks the lesser rights and opportunities accorded females in the United States and elsewhere by suggesting that since these examples have "made it," you can too. This approach also perpetuates largely bourgeois standards of what makes one a hero and what counts as a contribution.

Revisionist multiculturalism offers a change in viewpoint (for example, from the bottom up), a different focus, or different themes for the story of America, its history, and its peoples. A widely known example is Howard

Zinn's *People's History of the United States* (1981); a recent attempt is Ronald Takaki's *Different Mirror: A History of Multicultural America* (1993). Changes in academic history such as these usually take decades to find their way into school curricula and textbooks, and their degree of acceptance depends in particular on how radical they are considered.

Another example of a revised story, which is elaborated in Chapter 3 about the California experience, is provided by the 1990 Houghton Mifflin textbook series for elementary social studies. The fifth grade U.S. history text, *America Will Be*, offers a European immigrant framework. The text is more multiculturally inclusive than most of its predecessors, but the terms of such inclusion are high. Various groups—including indigenous and conquered peoples, and those enslaved and brought here involuntarily—are treated as immigrants and as if their experiences were essentially no different from or worse than those of European immigrants.

Revised stories, with a different focus or theme than conventional histories, vary in the extent to which and how they are multiculturally revisionist. While more inclusive than the older syntheses, they usually operate from a single interpretive framework or story line. The single story line provides coherence at the expense of the diversity of the peoples and cultures whose stories are being told. In contrast, a second variety of revisionist multiculturalism, characterized by multiple perspectives, would accommodate and highlight diversity at the expense of a single story line. It would make the interests of various individuals and groups explicit rather than giving the appearance of being interest free.

A multiple-perspectives approach would include the experiences and points of view of various participants throughout the events being studied, not merely in separate sections as some textbooks do. Participants' voices would be heard as directly as possible. Swartz and Goodwin (1992) urge that the multiple perspectives presented in school texts be authentic. Rather than text authors speaking for one or another person, group, or point of view, people ought to be speaking for themselves. Authorial interpretation of others increases the possibility of misrepresentation while implying that they are incapable of speaking for themselves. The extent to which the multiple perspectives are organized so that they become interrelated or interacting could vary. Also variable is the extent to which the events selected for inclusion and their organization reflect traditional versions of U.S. history or the multiculturality of that history. Thus multiple-perspectives approaches span a wide range from additive to transformative.

While increasingly advocated, a comprehensive multiple-perspectives approach remains to be realized. School texts do include special features such as "opposing viewpoints." One of the most common offers a "British view" of the American Revolution or asks, "What happened at Lexington Green?" Some also include features such as Native American perspectives on the "westward movement." In most cases, the multiple perspectives are "featured" outside the main text. It is as if excerpts from separate studies were brought under the same roof, or between the same covers, as the main story of U.S. history. Alternatively, multiple perspectives appear in collections of supplementary readings or other supplementary instructional materials. As with the heroes-and-contributions approach, the "other" perspectives selected for inclusion depend on who is doing the selecting, and the perspectives usually have been relatively "safe"—that is, far enough in the past or moderate enough or so widely accepted that they are unlikely either to offend traditionalists or to disrupt the status quo.

An example of multiple-perspectives advocacy that goes beyond the safe and the supplementary, which is elaborated in Chapter 4 regarding the New York experience, is provided by the 1991 report *One Nation, Many Peoples* (New York State Education Department, Social Studies Review and Development Committee 1991). In this case, multiple perspectives are advocated as a principle of teaching and learning to infuse the entire curriculum (p. 13), and the need for multiple perspectives is cited as a key finding of the review of New York State social studies syllabi (pp. 18–19). Instead of a single narrative *One Nation* calls for giving priority to depth over breadth of subject matter content in a social studies curriculum that involves students in systematically examining questions like "What is an American?" and "What holds us together as a nation?" (p. 9) Multiple perspectives, including those of the students, would be primary and pervasive.

Whereas additive forms of multiculturalism selectively enlarge the history to be conveyed within an existing framework, and revisionist versions alter as well as extend the narrative historical framework, transformative versions of multiculturalism would remake the framework altogether.[9] It is this transformative restructuring or redefining of America and its history and culture(s) that upsets neo-nativists, including cultural traditionalists, political conservatives, and many liberals.[10]

An example of transformative multiculturalism is an emergent approach that can be termed *reciprocal history*. Even less in evidence, and perhaps more radical, than multiple-perspectives approaches, it has considerable potential for accommodating both racial-ethnic-cultural diversity and interconnections among diverse individuals and groups. Our sketch of reciprocal history draws primarily on the recent work of Sylvia Wynter (1992) and Toni Morrison (1992) and is elaborated in Chapter 7.

In *Do Not Call Us Negros*, prompted by the 1990 textbook adoption controversy in California, Wynter (1992) argues that the dominant "EuroAmerican cultural model" ignores its own genesis *in interaction with* indigenous native Americans and enslaved Africans. Rather than merely making contributions to an already formed western-European cultural heritage, Wynter suggests that so-called marginalized groups have been and continue to be an *integral* part of a dynamic American culture. One way to begin to see this reciprocity is to view the past, and the present as well, through the alternative lens of what Wynter calls a "black studies cultural model," which would question the bases of the prevailing system of knowledge. Her intent is not simply to round out the standard, two-dimensional U.S. history but also to level its race- and class-biased hierarchy and reconceive it as a "community of communities based on reciprocal recognition (p. 35). Wynter, too, would begin to change the world by reinterpreting it.

Toni Morrison (1992) makes a complementary case for understanding American literature and Americanness by taking into account what she calls the "Africanist presence and personae" (p. 90). Her main point in this regard is that attention be given to how an Africanist presence has shaped both white America and American identity more generally, as well as how white America has constructed and portrayed Africanism and African Americans. For example, studies of racism typically examine its consequences for victims, ignoring racism's impact on its perpetrators. What Morrison proposes instead

> is to examine the impact of notions of racial hierarchy, racial exclusion, and racial vulnerability and availability on nonblacks who held, resisted, explored, or altered those notions. The scholarship that looks into the mind, imagination, and behavior of slaves is valuable. But equally valuable is a serious intellectual effort to see what racial ideology does to the mind, imagination, and behavior of masters. (pp. 11–12)

Fiction in the United States, Morrison observes, "has taken as its concern the architecture of a *new white man*" (p. 15). To the extent that U.S. history also has done so, it not only has left out most Americans but also has left out the intergroup relations that have shaped us.[11]

Earlier, James Baldwin (1985) admonished that white Americans could not fully understand their history without understanding black history, because the histories of blacks and whites in the United States were inextricably intertwined. Similarly, Cornel West (1933a) observes that

> from the very beginning we must call into question any notions of pure traditions or pristine heritages, or any civilization or culture having a monopoly on virtue or insight. Ambiguous legacies, hybrid cultures. By hybrid, of course, we mean cross-cultural fertilization. Every culture that we know is a result of the weaving of antecedent cultures. Elements of antecedent cultures create something new based on that which came before. (p. 3)

It is from "against the grain" observations such as these that a reciprocal multiculturalism might be created. This transformative approach would portray multiple acculturation—the numerous ways in which various groups have influenced and learned from as well as about one another. It also would be open-ended or ongoing as interaction continues and circumstances change. Taking up this challenge would be a daunting task, in part because there are as yet no comprehensive models to follow. Further, as Maxine Greene (1993) suggests,

> the tension with regard to multiculturalism may be partially due to the suspicion that we [that is, whites, European Americans] have often de-

fined ourselves against some unknown, some darkness, some "otherness" we chose to thrust away, to master, not to understand. (p. 15)

The selection, organization, and use of knowledge intended to convey a reciprocal multiculturalism would be much different from that found in curricula that did not portray interconnections and mutual influences among diverse individuals and groups and their social settings. A key difference is the manner of presentation, organization, and intended use of knowledge, not merely its presence or inclusion in the curriculum.

In an insightful construction of four categories of knowledge and analysis of their potential for curriculum transformation from a black studies perspective (see Chapter 7), Joyce E. King (1995, in press) addresses relevant aspects of the selection, organization, and uses of cultural and culture-centered knowledge. By culture-centered knowledge she refers to the information and beliefs that underlie and make coherent, and legitimate, a social framework such as "white middle class" or "black intellectuals." Drawing on a legacy of black history and black studies scholarship, King distinguishes between what she calls "invisibilizing knowledge" and "marginalizing knowledge," which serve to maintain existing hegemonies on one side, and "expanding knowledge" and "deciphering knowledge," which offer possibilities for social transformation on the other.

Whereas invisibilizing knowledge is monocultural, simply ignoring diversity as if "we" were all alike (usually like some Anglo-European Protestant model), marginalizing knowledge is selectively inclusive. The historical experiences of European immigrants are set as the norm, for example, and the experiences of others—as well as the prior experiences of Native Americans and African Americans and Latinos—are marginalized (see Chapter 3). Both invisibilizing and marginalizing knowledge, directly or indirectly, emphasize similar individual characteristics and interests across groups, as if group identities, experiences, and differences did not matter much. The curricular organization of invisibilizing and marginalizing knowledge is more likely to be chronological than thematic or conceptual, minimizing connections across time periods. Even immigration, for example is unlikely to be studied as a continuing theme or aspect of U.S. history. Native Americans disappear between "the westward movement" and "the civil rights movement." Invisibilizing and marginalizing knowledge are to be acquired, not actively used to effect change; they serve to sustain the social, political, and economic status quo.

Expanding knowledge, such as that provided by multiple perspectives, recognizes and incorporates diverse experiences, perspectives, social interests, and standpoints, but it does not necessarily challenge existing relationships of power and privilege. Both expanding and deciphering knowledge acknowledge group differences and interests, but in King's scheme only deciphering knowledge is sufficiently transformative to liberate consciousness and inform needed social action.

Building on the work of Sylvia Wynter (1992) and Michel Foucault

(1970, 1972), King calls for a curriculum that will help students decipher and reinvent cultural rules such as those regarding blackness and whiteness and their interrelations. Deciphering knowledge, then, is a heuristic selection and organization of cultural and culture-centered knowledge that enables students to critique and act to change prevailing social patterns and the assumptions that undergird and legitimate them. It is the most promising kind of knowledge use for a transformative, reciprocal multiculturalism (see Chapter 7). Whereas invisibilizing and marginalizing knowledge are passive, expanding and especially deciphering knowledge are potentially activist.

The range of alternative meanings of nationalism and multiculturalism that have entered the America debate and debates about curriculum policy is narrower than that just presented. What has been cast by neo-nativists as a dichotomy and choice between pluralism and unity is more complex. Critical pragmatists call for opportunities to shape the terms of public debates as well as to participate in them on terms previously set by others.

Literary Canon, Historical Master Narrative

Having looked at the political side of the coin of national identity, we flip now to the cultural side of the coin—to the issue of canon and master narrative. The question is whether there are or should be a canon and master narrative and, if so, what they are or should be. At least three positions are discernible in the continuing clamor:

1. An established canon and narrative exist, and they should continue as they have been,
2. There should continue to be a canon and master narrative, but they should be broadened (much like an additive multiculturalism),
3. The notions of canon and master narrative have outlived whatever usefulness they may have had and should be abandoned in favor of literary choice and multiple historical perspectives or reciprocal history.

The idea and assumption of a canon appear to date to medieval Europe, to a body of church law and/or the authentic books of the Bible as determined by a church or religious body. *Canon* has come to mean a body of established or otherwise authoritative rules, principles, standards, or texts. In medieval European education, knowledge of subjects came to mean mastery of selected texts, that is, a sacred-secular canon that would strengthen the mind and discipline one's character. These texts were assumed to carry wisdom, truth, and (high) culture.

The tradition of important, venerable, and venerated (if not sacred) texts referred to as *paedeia*, "Great Books," masterpieces, classics—or canon— serves the purposes of unifying people at least symbolically and, also symbolically, of offering the reassurance of seeming permanence and certainty. A secular, usually literary, canon and its historical-master-narrative counterpart also communicate what and who are considered important and worthy, at least within the canon's domain. What knowledge is included and whose work is admitted to the canon set the cultural-historical standard. Not surprisingly, canons and master narratives tend to sustain the status quo, including traditional conceptions of knowledge and distributions of power and privilege.

The traditional version of U.S. history, at least the school history offered to elementary and secondary students, has been a chronological political history (military and diplomatic as well as domestic) of leaders and laws, with a smattering of economics. The key actors have been presidents, statesmen, generals, and successful businessmen and bankers—almost always white men. The master narrative has been one of progress, of onward and upward movement, of expansionism.

In the past two or three decades this elite version of U.S. history has been challenged with some success by new and increasing scholarship, especially in the area of social history, and by the demands of historically misrepresented and marginalized groups for legitimate inclusion. In some high school textbooks and curriculum guides, progress, or forward movement toward national ideals, is now seen as being uneven and the result of struggle. Examples of new scholarship challenging established interpretations and cherished myths are recent works on the West in U.S. history (e.g., Brinkley 1992; Limerick, Milner, and Rankin 1991; Slotkin 1992) and on slavery (e.g., Kolchin 1993).

While it might appear neutral, a master narrative tends to represent the viewpoints and interests of the dominant groups in a society, who usually are its main actors. Master narratives, however, give the appearance of universality, usually by abstracting from individual and collective experiences and difference. Progress, for example, becomes an overriding ethos— everyone who works hard and lives within prevailing norms may succeed. Cultural and ethnic-racial diversity are muted by this ethos, and group-based discrimination is ignored. In this way, institutionalized racial or gender biases can be downplayed or avoided altogether.

Meanwhile, historians continue to dispute the nature of history—for example, whether history is any kind of narrative at all or an imposition of narrative form on non-narrative materials (see, e.g., White 1973; Carr 1986). The widespread public perception of history as a story or narrative, master or otherwise, may be a convenient fiction. History as a single, chronological, and linear story—even "a story well told," as called for by California's *History–Social Science Framework*—may be a primitive epistemology. The difficulties encountered in efforts to synthesize the recent work in social history (e.g., Appleby, Hunt, and Jacob 1994) lend credence to this view. Yet the possibility of a new synthesis or master narrative continues to have considerable appeal.

Similarly, the assumption of a literary canon imposes order and buttresses "high" (elite) culture. Mortimer Adler's *Paedeia Proposal* (1982) was in this vein. "The" literary canon in the United States which neo-nativists like Lynne Cheney and William Bennett among others sought to protect against multiculturalist onslaught during their tenures in public office, is less than a century old. It was constructed during the World War I period in ι<action to German militarism, Russian Bolshevism, and millions of eastern European immigrants' coming to America. The canon did not emerge naturally, like cream rising to the top. It was created purposefully in a particular time and circumstances "as a cultural bulwark" whose formation "was steeped in politics from the start" (O'Sullivan 1992, p. 17). As Henry Louis Gates Jr. has noted, "The grand canon" as a "fixed repository of valuable texts—never existed as such" (1992, p. 179).

Tracing the "intellectual lineage of the current opposition to 'multiculturalism,'" Gerry O'Sullivan (1992, p. 19) highlights prior assaults on and battles over a literary and cultural canon, "an imagined cultural unity" (p. 20). The recent and continuing debate is not new. Nor is it likely to turn back the clock:

> Against what is always seen as the rising tide of cultural anarchy, proponents of negative classicism turn to the Greeks and the Greats in a futile search for an illusory permanence and truth, located in an unrecoverable past. (p. 18)

The canon controversy also is an epistemological dispute over the nature of knowledge (e.g., Banks 1993a). Is knowledge to be taken as discovered, certain, and universal, as the supporters of an established canon would have it? Or is knowledge to be taken as constructed, provisional, and contingent, as opponents of an established canon would argue? Despite the temptation to simplify the question in a true-false, good-bad fashion, the canon—master narrative issue simultaneously raises questions about the nature of knowledge, valued literature-culture-history, and power relationships. The question is not simply whether or not students should study Shakespeare—or anyone else.[12] The often-used Shakespeare example highlights that the canon issue has been concerned at least as much with authors as with texts (see Gates 1992). In other words, who is to be represented? Which individuals and groups (or constituencies) are to be recognized as worthy and belonging?

Visions of America

The America debate, introduced in Chapter 1, is about what it means to be an American and the vision of America to be transmitted to future generations. It is a debate about national identity that encompasses the issues of nationalism and multiculturalism and of canon and master narrative. Here we focus on the contours of the America debate and the nature of the prevailing discourse. We also consider the openness of the continuing debate, including the individuals and groups who have access to participate and be heard, to shape the debate, and perhaps to dominate it.

The discourse—the language and manner of argument—is important because it shapes public and professional opinion, education policy, and classroom practice. Approximately 50 years ago, Walter Lippmann observed that "he [or she] who captures the symbols by which the public feeling is for the moment contained, controls by that much the approaches of public policy" (cited in Alterman 1992, p. 19).

Lippmann's observation about the power of symbols, and the power to shape policy by capturing or controlling public symbols, presaged Foucault's analysis of power, knowledge, and discourse. Power, Foucault concluded, resides not only in individuals and groups but also and perhaps more importantly in social organizations, institutions, and systems—both in their formal or authoritative roles and relationships (such as academic historian, high school teacher) and in their historically shaped and socially shared conceptions and symbols (such as history, America). In modern societies, power increasingly operates through the definition of these conceptions and symbols as well as through the definition of appropriate patterns of communication, including rules of reason and rationality, that is, "regimes of truth" (Foucault 1970). A residue of past practice and conventional ways of thinking exert a powerful hold on everyday life and discourse, as is evident in opposition to reform efforts to make history–social studies curricula more inclusive.

The roles that people fill, the relationships that they enter into, and the prevailing discourse in which they participate all precede their current participants. A focus only on the present or on the particular individual(s) is misleading at best. In other words, the America debate and related battles to control the knowledge that is included in curriculum are best understood not as current events but in their broader social and historical contexts—of historically recurrent nativism, for example.

Knowledge about prevailing conceptions, symbols, patterns, and roles—and with it, the opportunity to instigate change—is enhanced by further understanding of the nature of prevailing discourse or discursive practices. The discourse of history as cultural literacy, for example, seems to have become a code for Eurocentric or Western-dominated (not multicultural or inclusive) history. As code or symbol, cultural literacy can be seen as an attempt to control curricula not only by means of official education policy but also by dominating the discourse.

Following Foucault (1977), the discursive practices of a field are characterized and make a difference by

> delimitation of a field of objects, the definition of a legitmate perspective . . . and the fixing of norms for the elaboration of concepts and theories. Thus each discursive practice implies a play of prescriptions that designate its exclusions and choices. (p. 199)

Discursive practices delimit a field by specifying what is to be included and what is not. What is to count as historical knowledge or history? What historical knowledge is to be selected for inclusion in social studies curriculum? The definition of a legitimate perspective or perspectives and the fixing of norms for conceptual elaboration also can be seen to support some forms of historical and curriculum knowledge and not others. Should, for example, a traditional version of U.S. history be upheld for school curricula and textbooks? Or should a transformative version be instituted? Or should multiple perspectives prevail?[13]

Discursive practices are not merely of academic or theoretical interest. They derive from and enter into everyday practice. Further, their pervasiveness often renders them unseen and unacknowledged. Discursive practices are "embedded in technical processes, in institutions, in patterns for general behavior, in forms for transmission and diffusion, and in pedagogical forms which, at once, impose and maintain them" (Foucault 1977, p. 200). Particular discursive practices are not in any sense inevitable; they are constructed in specific times and places to serve particular interests and therefore are amenable, though usually not with ease, to reconstruction. In the current debates, not only social studies curriculum but history itself seems to be at issue. The discourse is in flux.

The America debate has a history of more than 200 years. Rather than reprise the course of that history, including the ritual references to Crevecoeur in the eighteenth century and Tocqueville in the nineteenth, we illustrate the mythic aspect of the America debate about the nation's identity with the discourse of American exceptionalism (Appleby 1992). Exceptionalism, the possession of enviable qualities that set one far apart from and above others, provided the collective national identity for the newly independent colonies-states which, during the 1780s and 1790s, had relatively little in common. Joyce Appleby (1992) notes that

> desire for a closer union, moreover, had not been widely felt, but rather reflected the aspirations of men who were already nationalist in their thinking and cosmopolitan in their outlook. From these leaders came the noisy complaints in the 1780s about state factions and the Cassandra-like predictions of political fragmentation. . . . The case for "a more perfect union" was made in a lawyerly fashion by nationalist leaders, most of them lawyers. Outside of their circles, there were abroad in the land few common sentiments, fewer shared assumptions operating at the intimate level of human experience, and a paucity of national symbols recognizable from Georgia to Maine. (p. 422)

Exceptionalism—nurtured by the European Enlightenment belief in the uniformity or universality of human nature and the autonomous individual, democratic institutions, and opportunities for ordinary people—provided the "compelling ideas to create the imagined community that forms a nation" (Appleby 1992, p. 424; cf. Anderson 1991). In the process, "[M]ost of what really happened in the colonial past was ignored because it fit so ill with the narrative of exceptionalism" (p. 425). For example, the

> cultures of Africans and native Americans could not be incorporated into American history, for those peoples' very claims to have culture would have subverted the story of progress. The self-conscious crafters of American identity took great pride in freedom of religion, but the major religious figures of the colonial era, the Puritans of New England, openly embraced orthodoxy—banishing dissidents, whipping Baptists, even executing four Quakers. And so it went with free speech. Congress com-

posed a Bill of Rights guaranteeing free speech, but colonial legislators had been much more likely to jail their critics than to protect their speech. And then there was the elaboration of slave codes by colonial legislatures. How were those laws to be integrated into the teleology of a peculiarly free people? (p. 425)

The vision of America based on the discourse of exceptionalism, created and maintained by means of "deep forgetting" (Appleby 1992, p. 425) and "induced amnesia" (p. 429), survived for 200 years, creating "formidable obstacles to appreciating America's original and authentic diversity" (p. 420).

Toni Morrison (1992) suggests how "a constituted Africanism . . . deployed as rawness and savagery . . . provided the staging ground and arena for the elaboration of the quintessential American identity" (p. 44) during the late eighteenth century. Key features of this identity are dramatically illustrated by Bernard Bailyn's account of Dunbar, the educated Scotsman turned frontier Mississippi planter during the 1770s (cited in Morrison 1992). They are autonomy (freedom, individualism), newness (innocence), distinctiveness (difference—from both Europe and Europeans and from Africa and Africans), and authority and absolute power (heroism, virility)—all of which, Morrison shows, play out against an Africanist presence as well as geographic "frontiers."

Recent social history scholarship has challenged the myth of American exceptionalism and the supposed cultural coherence and national unity of earlier periods. Along with substantial increases in the number and diversity of immigrants to the United States over the past three decades, and the revival of nativism, the new knowledge generated by social history scholarship during this time has contributed to the reopening of the America debate since the late 1980s.

In the mass media and among academics, the neo-nativists have sought to cast the America debate in terms of a choice between polar opposites, racial-ethnic-cultural group identity versus shared national values and unity (e.g., Ravitch 1990). This not only is an oversimplification but also masks issues of identity and power. First, it is not at all indisputable that a nation can be either deeply pluralistic or strongly united but not both. What is now the United States always has been culturally plural; it has been united nationally for more than 200 years.

The second aspect of oversimplification is the assumption of singular or agreed-upon meanings of pluralism and unity, especially the latter. Typically, national unity has been cast in terms of what Americans "share" or "have in common." The "one" of E pluribus unum is interpreted as one people sharing the same values, but the unspoken, underlying assumption is that this unity necessarily relies on an Anglo middle-class standard. This assumption belies that *unum*, or unity in the American context, can be interpreted as encompassing significant pluralism or difference; pluralism need not mean separatism. Consider, for example, the unity of an American League baseball team whose members—catchers, pitchers, outfielders—may hail from throughout the Western Hemisphere and around the world.

James Banks (1993b) has aptly observed that "multiculturalists view *e pluribus unum* as an appropriate national goal" (p. 24). But, he says,

> they believe that the *unum* must be negotiated, discussed, and restructured to reflect the nation's ethnic and cultural diversity. . . . [R]eformulation [of national unity] must also involve power sharing and participation by people from many different cultures who must reach beyond their cultural and ethnic borders in order to create a common civic culture that reflects and contributes to the well-being of all. This common civic culture will extend beyond the cultural borders of any single group and constitute a civic "borderland" culture. (p. 24)[14]

Interrelated issues of identity and power are bound up with the nature and extent of pluralism deemed acceptable by dominant groups and their preferred basis for national unity. At issue with respect to identity is who will name us—individually, collectively, and as a nation. How will our experiences, our histories and cultures and biographies, be defined? In whose image and to whose benefit? Naming and defining involve positioning, or attempting to position, oneself in relation to others—for example, at the center or toward the margins of society, at the pinnacle of the extant social hierarchy or some distance from it.

In explicating the meanings of pragmatism, William James (1876, repr. 1975) commented as follows on the power of naming:

> You know how men have always hankered after unlawful magic, and you know what a great part, in magic, *words* have always played. If you have his name, or the formula of incantation that binds him, you can control the spirit, genie, afrite, or whatever the power may be. Solomon knew the names of all the spirits, and having their names, he held them subject to his will. . . . That [power-bringing] word names the universe's *principle*, and to possess it is, after a fashion, to possess the universe itself. (p. 31)

To what extent do various individuals and groups have the power to name and position themselves rather than being defined by others?

Enslaved Africans in the United States, for example, were defined by Spanish- and European-American defenders of slavery as not fully rational beings and therefore, along with women of all colors, as less than human and not among all the men "created equal." African American and women's studies programs and scholarship can be seen as an effort toward self-definition and consciousness apart from that previously imposed by others (see, e.g., Hill Collins 1991). Not all those who have benefitted from this activism and scholarship, however, can be counted among its supporters. A contentious example of the power to define, or to negotiate the definition of, oneself and others—to distinguish what is public from what is private, to determine what matters and what does not—was provided by the 1991 Anita Hill–Clarence Thomas hearings regarding Thomas's fitness for a seat on the U.S. Supreme Court (see, e.g., West 1993a; Fraser 1992). In this case, Thomas's definitions of what the Senate Judiciary Committee and the public had a right to know (that is, what was public as opposed to private), and what mattered as opposed to what did not, held sway. Most important, Thomas was successful in redirecting attention from Hill's charges of sexual harassment to his own charge of being the victim of a lynching.

In a manner compatible with Banks's (1993b) call for renegotiating the *unum*, Alice Kessler-Harris (1992) argues that national identity is not abandoned by "expanding the definition of what it means to be an American." Instead, "it encourages us to rethink the meaning of identity as something that is fluid and susceptible to change" and "to redefine democratic culture as a culture in process—a culture in a continual state of construction" (p. B3). This rethinking and redefining is necessary, she points out, because of the knowledge generated by social history scholarship's examinations of the experiences of previously neglected groups and the raising of questions generated by that knowledge. For example:

> Black history, which had not proved especially troublesome when it evoked the moral possibilities represented by Frederick Douglass, Harriet Tubman, or Martin Luther King, Jr., became contentious when historians started to ask how racism had shaped the white mind and the dominant economy. . . . Writing women and people of color into our understanding of culture required redefining the concept of an American to incorporate multiple definitions of identity; it made a mockery of a single synthesis or interpretation of the American past. (p. B3)

It may be that the pluralism-unity dichotomy and debate have less to do with whether the United States will go the way of Yugoslavia as the neo-nativists have claimed (e.g., Schlesinger 1991) than with the balance of power between groups that have dominated the U.S. polity, economy, society—and curriculum—thus far and groups that currently are challenging this domination. The neo-nativists' emphasis on unity and their apparent concern for harmony can be seen as a means of smoothing over differences and inequities and thereby maintaining the political, economic, and cultural status quo—America as they know it. In effect, the neo-nativists have redefined "minority" objections to marginalization, exclusion, and misrepresentation as a problem of national unity.

Posing problems within a particular framework restricts the bounds of acceptable solutions and the means of reaching them. The typical emphasis on problem solving deflects attention from how the problem to be solved has been framed. So, in the America debate, the tables were turned to the extent that inclusion was cast as divisive pluralism, and attention was redirected to fostering unity. Once again, minority concerns were marginalized.[15] Tyack and James (1985), in their historical review of the efforts of various "moral majorities" to "legalize virtue" (p. 513) by passing laws that prescribed inclusion of their preferred knowledge and values in school curricula, conclude:

> Not until the recent generation would excluded groups develop the power legally to challenge the precedents set by this earlier legalization of values in order to broaden the scope of schooling and legitimize their values as well as those of dominant WASPs. Then, ironically, the results of their efforts to secure equality of dignity in public education would be labeled legislative meddling and litigiousness, partly because the pressure came from people who had traditionally lacked power. And, once more, conservative groups in the 1980s are again seeking to assert by law in public schools the religious and political values long prescribed as the prerogative of traditional moral majorities. (p. 533)

A last discursive note here is that the America debate is adversarial, a conflict among opposing camps. *Debate* implies arguing one's position and attacking opponents' weak points. It promises a winner, at least for the time being, and also losers. Instead of an open dialogue that extends, transforms, and enriches community—where the intent is to learn from, not defeat, one another—we see individuals and groups jockeying for position and to enshrine their version of America in school curricula. So far the battle has been lopsided, tilting heavily in favor of those subscribing to a less conflictual version of American history.

In the case studies that follow in Chapters 3 through 6, we further illustrate the nature of multicultural education policy discourse and particular discursive practices. The absence of a unified multicultural "voice" equivalent to that of the neo-nativists was significant. While explanations for the imbalance are beyond the scope of this project, it is worth noting that "multiculturalists" have been a diverse lot, with differing versions of multiculturalism and different visions of America; that, for the most part, the multiculturalists have not been in positions of political prominence with easy access to media nor "connected" to those who are; and that the multiculturalists have not been the recipients of substantial foundation support for their activities. Consequently, compared with the neo-nativists, they have lacked the power to shape the America debate and to create and distribute opportunities to speak.

CONTROLLING CURRICULUM KNOWLEDGE

The issues just examined directly influence history–social studies curriculum knowledge and its control. Curriculum knowledge—the information, issues, and ways of thinking selected for inclusion in school programs and made available to students in classroom practice—is important because different values and interests are sustained or modified depending on which curriculum knowledge (for instance, nativist or multiculturalist) is selected and how it is distributed among students. Curriculum knowledge is continually contested and renegotiated. The management of public schooling in the United States may be nonpartisan, but it is hardly apolitical.

What is taught in school, in social studies and other subjects, is necessarily only a small portion of available knowledge. Apart from the differences between the knowledge and practice of academic disciplines and their translation into school subjects, curriculum knowledge represents what Williams (1961) calls a "selective tradition." He distinguishes the "lived culture of a particular time and place, only fully accessible to those living in that time and place" (p. 49) both from the recorded culture of a period and from contemporary selections from the recorded culture, that is, the selective tradition. He reminds us that representations of the history and culture of a society will change over time because they reflect contemporary values and special interests. These representations are "a continual selection and interpretation . . . a continual selection and re-selection of ancestors" (p. 52). For example: Which authors and works of literature will students be asked to study? Which times, places, peoples, and cultures?

For two centuries public schooling has been seen as a primary means of building and maintaining loyalty to the nation. The purpose of the so-called common school of the nineteenth century was to transmit an emerging American identity to an increasingly non-Anglo population. Since the turn of the century the public schools have been charged with major responsibilities for the Americanization of the children of immigrants—even though some, like the Germans, resisted by setting up their own German-language schools.

By and large the public schools have been expected not only to teach basic skills and subjects but also to socialize and initiate the young into understanding, appreciating, and practicing good American citizenship. Conflict has emerged from differing visions of America and what constitutes the "good citizen" (recall Henry David Thoreau's essay "Civil Disobedience," for example) as well as from tensions between democratic ideals and everyday realities. Against such a backdrop, the apolitical pretensions of the neo-nativists, who claim to offer an authentic history most worth knowing, would appear to leave us few options.

How or on what basis curriculum knowledge is selected has been obscured by the so-called classic curriculum question, "What knowledge is of most worth?" which dates to an 1859 essay and subsequent book, *Education: Intellectual, Moral, and Physical*, by Herbert Spencer. "Worth," for Spencer, meant anything that contributed to the self-preservation of a people and its civilization. Although subject to varying definition, "worth" has been widely accepted or at least preferred as the primary criterion for selecting curriculum knowledge. That knowledge deemed most "worthy" or "worthwhile" was selected for inclusion in school programs. Framing the question of the selection of curriculum knowledge in this way gives the appearance of beneficence in the public interest. But it deflects questions of who, or which peoples, are left out "in the public interest."

For example, Charles Beard and William Bagley (1918) in *The History of the American People*, a textbook used in California schools during the early decades of the twentieth century, said that their plan for the text

> necessitated the omission of many of the staples of the textbooks. For example, the space given to the North American Indians has been materially reduced. They are interesting and picturesque, but they made no impress [sic] upon the civilization of the United States. In a history designed to explain the present rather than to gratify curiosity and entertain, Indian habits of life and Indian wars must have a very minor position. (pp. iii–iv)

Within and across school subject areas (and with respect to the subjects themselves), however, selection of curriculum knowledge has been shown to be less than coherent and more a result of tradition and politics than rational or other determinations of worth (see, e.g., Goodson and Ball 1984; Kliebard 1986; Popkewitz 1987; Reid 1990). And the decisions that are made are continually contested. Victories (and defeats) are rarely if ever complete or permanent.

Despite the historical record of conflicting values, interests, and traditions in curriculum policymaking, the "most worth" question holds continuing appeal. It not only gives the appearance of wisdom and good intentions but also carries the assumption of common interests and universality (of worth and perhaps truth) across time, place, and person.

Curriculum policymaking is more complex and contentious now than even a decade or two ago, given growing differences in social values and interests, increasing knowledge and specialization, and expanding state involvement (Cornbleth 1990). This contentiousness is exacerbated by ongoing efforts to devise national standards and assessment mechanisms in the school subjects recognized by former President Bush and the National Governors Association in their 1989 summit statement of national education goals, efforts reiterated in Bush's America 2000 education strategy statement of April 1991 and again in President Clinton's Goals 2000: Educate America Act of 1994. If curriculum knowledge is to be shaped at the national level rather than at state or local levels, the stakes are raised, and control is likely to be even more strongly contested.

Not solely academic or professional matters, then, but questions of curriculum knowledge are bound up with questions of interest and equity in the larger society. Curriculum contestation becomes problematic when the debate is limited to questions or participants or outcomes that are determined by only a few individuals and groups. To the extent that the debate is opened to include dissidents, curriculum stands a chance of being reinvigorated, and democracy of being strengthened.

The four chapters that follow in Part II present our case studies of the politics of education policymaking at the state level, of the battles for control over history and social studies curriculum knowledge in California and New York. The case studies clearly illustrate both how social issues and education policy are intertwined and how influence is exercised in the making of education policy.

Chapter 3 begins in California in 1987, when a new history–social science framework was adopted, and then we focus on the controversy surrounding the adoption of K–8 social studies textbooks in 1990. In Chapter 4 we turn to New York, beginning with the public uproar over a 1989 task force report, *A Curriculum of Inclusion*, and continuing with the saga of a second social studies review committee and report, *One Nation, Many Peoples*, and the related "Understanding Diversity" state policy. Chapter 5 stays with New York to examine the renewed public clamor generated by this second report, the formation of a new committee charged with incorporating diversity concerns into a broader education reform program, and the apparent outcomes in terms of more multicultural curriculum knowledge. In Chapter 6, we return to California three years after the controversial textbook adoption to glimpse what is happening in some San Francisco Bay Area school districts and classrooms, to see policy in practice at the ground level.

REFERENCES

Adler, Mortimer J. *The paedeia proposal: An educational manifesto.* 1982. New York: Macmillan.

Alterman, Eric. 1992. The triumph of the punditocracy. (*Image*), July 19: pp. 14–23.

Anderson, Benedict. 1991. *Imagined communities.* London and New York: Verso.

Anzaldua, Gloria. 1987. *Borderlands: La frontera: The new mestiza* (San Francisco: Spinsters/Aunt Lute).

Appleby, Joyce. 1992. Recovering America's historic diversity: Beyond exceptionalism. *Journal of American History* 79 (2): 419–431.

Appleby, Joyce, Lynn Hunt, and Margaret Jacob. 1994. *Telling the truth about history.* New York: Norton.

Baldwin, James. 1985. *The price of the ticket: Collected nonfiction 1948–1985.* New York: St. Martin's/Marek.

Banks, James A. 1987. The social studies, ethnic diversity, and social change. *Elementary School Journal* 87 (5): 531–543.

———. 1988. Approaches to multicultural curriculum reform. *Multicultural Leader* 1 (2): 1–3.

———. 1993a. The canon debate, knowledge construction, and multicultural education. *Educational Researcher* 22 (5): 4–14.

———. 1993b. Multicultural education: Development, dimensions, and challenges. *Phi Delta Kappan* 75 (1): 22–28.

Beard, Charles, and William Bagley. 1918. *The history of the American people.* Sacramento: California State Printing Office.

Berger, Peter, and Hansfried Kellner. 1981. *Sociology reinterpreted.* Garden City, N.Y.: Anchor/Doubleday.

Bernstein, Richard J. 1991. *The new constellation: The ethical-political horizons of modernity/postmodernity.* Cambridge: Massachusetts Institute of Technology Press.

Brinkley, Alan. 1992. The western historians: Don't fence them in. *New York Times* (September 20): 1, 22–27.

Carr, David. 1986. *Time, narrative, and history*. Bloomington: Indiana University Press.

Cherryholmes, Cleo H. 1988. *Power and criticism: Poststructural investigations in education*. New York: Teachers College Press.

Cornbleth, Catherine. 1990. *Curriculum in context*. London: Falmer.

Du Bois, W. E. B. 1935. *Black reconstruction*. New York: Harcourt, Brace.

Eagleton, Terry. 1983. *Literary theory: An introduction*. Minneapolis: University of Minnesota Press.

Ellsworth, Elizabeth. 1989. Why doesn't this feel empowering? Working through the repressive myths of critical pedagogy. *Harvard Educational Review* 59 (3): 297–324.

Erickson, Peter. 1992. Multiculturalism and the problem of liberalism. *Reconstruction* 2 (1): 97–101.

Foucault, Michel. 1970. *The order of things: An archaeology of the human sciences*. New York: Pantheon.

———. 1972. *The archaeology of knowledge*. London: Tavistock.

———. 1977. *Language, counter-memory, practice: Selected essays and interviews*, ed. D. F. Bouchard. Ithaca, N.Y.: Cornell University Press.

Fraser, Nancy. 1992. Sex, lies, and the public sphere: Some reflections on the confirmation of Clarence Thomas. *Critical Inquiry* 18: 595–612.

Fuchs, Lawrence H. 1990. *The American kaleidoscope: Race, ethnicity, and the civic culture*. Hanover, N.H.: Wesleyan University Press.

Fuentes, Carlos. [1964] 1987. *The death of Artemio Cruz*. New York: Farrar, Straus and Giroux.

Gates, Henry Louis, Jr. 1992. *Loose canons: Notes on the culture wars*. New York: Oxford University Press.

Gergen, Kenneth J. 1982. *Toward transformation in social knowledge*. New York: Springer-Verlag.

Goodson, Ivor F., and Stephen Ball. 1984. *Defining the curriculum: Histories and ethnographies*. London: Falmer.

Greene, Maxine. 1993. The passions of pluralism: Multiculturalism and the expanding community. *Educational Researcher* 22 (1): 13–18.

Greenfeld, Liah. *Nationalism: Five roads to modernity*. 1992. Cambridge, Mass.: Harvard University Press.

Gunn, Giles. 1992. *Thinking across the American grain: Ideology, intellect, and the new pragmatism*. Chicago: University of Chicago Press.

Harvey, David. 1990. *The condition of postmodernity*. Cambridge, Mass.: Blackwell.

Hill Collins, Patricia. 1991. Learning from the outsider within: The sociological significance of black feminist thought. In M. M. Fonow and J. A. Cook, eds., *Beyond methodology: Feminist scholarship as lived research*. Bloomington: Indiana University Press.

Jaenen, Cornelius. 1981. Mutilated multiculturalism. Pp. 79–96 in J. D. Wilson, ed., *Canadian Education in the 1980s*. Calgary: Detselig.

James, William. 1975. *Pragmatism: The meaning of truth*. Cambridge: Harvard University Press.

Kalantzis, Mary, and William Cope. 1992. Multiculturalism may prove to be the key issue of our epoch. *Chronicle of Higher Education* (November 4): p. B3.

Kessler-Harris, Alice. 1992. Multiculturalism can strengthen, not undermine, a common culture. *Chronicle of Higher Education* (October 21): B3, 7.

King, Joyce E. 1995. In press. Culture-centered knowledge: Black studies, curriculum transformation and social action. In James A. Banks and Cherry A. McGee Banks, eds., *Handbook of research on multicultural education*. New York: Macmillan.

Kliebard, Herbert M. 1986. *The struggle for the American curriculum, 1893–1958*. London: Routledge and Kegan Paul.

Kolchin, Peter. 1993. *American slavery, 1619–1877*. New York: Hill and Wang.

Limerick, Patricia Nelson, Clyde A. Milner II, and Charles E. Rankin, eds. 1991. *Trails: Toward a new western history*. Lawrence: University Press of Kansas.

McIntosh, Peggy. 1992. White privilege and male privilege. Pp. 70–81 in Margaret L. Andersen and Patricia Hill Collins, eds., *Race, class, and gender*. Belmont, Calif.: Wadsworth.

Minnich, Elizabeth K. 1990. *Transforming knowledge*. Philadelphia: Temple University Press.

Montero-Sieburth, Martha. 1988. Conceptualizing multicultural education: From theoretical approaches to classroom practice. *Equity and Choice* 4 (3): 3–11.

Morrison, Toni. 1992. *Playing in the dark*. Cambridge, Mass., and London: Harvard University Press.

New York State Education Department. 1991. *One nation, many peoples: A declaration of cultural independence*. Report of the Social Studies Review and Development Committee.

Olneck, Michael R. 1989. Americanization and the education of immigrants, 1900–1925: An analysis of symbolic action. *American Journal of Education* 97: 398–423.

———. 1990. The recurring dream: Symbolism and ideology in intercultural and multicultural education. *American Journal of Education* 98: 147–174.

O'Sullivan, Gerry. 1992. The PC police in the mirror of history. *Humanist* 52 (2): pp. 17–20, 46.

Popkewitz, Thomas S., ed. 1987. *The formation of school subjects*. London: Falmer.

Ravitch, Diane. 1990. Multiculturalism, E pluribus plures. *American Scholar* (Summer): 337–354.

Reid, William A. 1990. Strange curricula: Origins and development of the institutional categories of schooling. *Journal of Curriculum Studies* 22 (3): 203–216.

Rorty, Richard. 1991. *Objectivity, relativism, and truth*. Cambridge, England: Cambridge University Press.

Schlesinger, Arthur M., Jr. 1991. *The disuniting of America*. Knoxville, Tenn.: Whittle Direct Books.

Seller, Maxine. 1992. Historical perspectives on multicultural education: What kind? By whom? For whom? Why? *Social Science Record* 30 (1): 11–30.

Siegel, Harvey. 1993. Gimme that old-time Enlightenment meta-narrative. *Inquiry* 11 (4): 1, 17–22.

Sleeter, Christine E., and Carl A. Grant. 1987. An analysis of multicultural education in the United States. *Harvard Educational Review* 7: 421–444.

Slotkin, Richard. 1992. *Gunfighter nation: The myth of the frontier in 20th-century America*. New York: Atheneum.

Stimpson, Catharine R. 1994. A conversation, not a monologue. *Chronicle of Higher Education* (March 16): B1–2.

Swartz, Ellen, and Susan Goodwin. 1992. Multiculturality: Liberating classroom pedagogy and practice. *Social Science Record* 30 (1): 43–69.

Takaki, Ronald. 1993. *A different mirror: A history of multicultural America*. Boston: Little, Brown.

Taylor, Charles (and Amy Gutmann), ed. 1992. *Multiculturalism and "The politics of recognition."* Princeton, N.J.: Princeton University Press.

Tyack, David B., and Thomas James. 1985. Moral majorities and the school curriculum: Historical perspectives on the legalization of virtue. *Teachers College Record* 86 (4): 513–535.

West, Cornel. 1989. *The American evasion of philosophy.* Madison: University of Wisconsin Press.

———. 1993a. *Prophetic thought in postmodern times, vol. 1 of beyond Eurocentrism and multiculturalism.* Monroe, Me.: Common Courage Press.

———. 1993b. *Race matters.* Boston: Beacon Press.

White, Hayden V. 1973. *Metahistory: The historical imagination in nineteenth-century Europe.* Baltimore: Johns Hopkins University Press.

Williams, Raymond. 1961. *The long revolution.* New York: Columbia University Press.

Wynter, Sylvia. 1992. *Do not call us Negros: How "multicultural" textbooks perpetuate racism.* San Francisco: Aspire.

Zinn, Howard. 1981. *A people's history of the United States.* New York: Harper and Row.

NOTES

1. A related aspect of pragmatism is its interweaving or overlapping of theory and practice. Theory is seen to emerge from practice and to act back on it; theory has practical consequences. Further, there is no practice without theory, although operative theory may remain tacit knowledge for practitioners. Examples include theoretical knowledge of "how to" ride a bicycle or manage a classroom. It may well be that the hostility to theory associated with a crude form of pragmatism "usually means an opposition to other peoples' theories and an oblivion to one's own" (Eagleton 1983, p. vii).

2. Whereas our sense of critical pragmatism draws on critical theory, Cherryholmes (1988) creates a critical pragmatism primarily by association with linguistic post-structuralism, particularly deconstructionism. We leave it to interested readers to interpret the meanings and significance of our differing emphases.

3. The complexity of issues regarding values such as human dignity within the framework of a critical pragmatism is elaborated well by Cherryholmes (1988, pp. 172–177).

4. Pragmatists and others also might be uncomfortable with the language of fundamentalism, knowing that *fundament* derives from the Greek word for "anus."

5. In contrast to Gunn and others, we have purposefully avoided associating pragmatism with democracy or particular democratic institutions. While pragmatism and democracy can be mutually supportive and even constitutive, neither is dependent on a particular form of the other. To associate them, seemingly in an effort to justify pragmatism under a democratic banner, encourages taking current forms of democracy for granted rather than subjecting them to critical pragmatic scrutiny. In the ongoing America debate and multicultural education policy-making, the nature and future of U.S. democracy are very much in question.

6. Critical pragmatism as we have portrayed it here is compatible with, and can be seen to overlap, Sylvia Wynter's (1992) conception of a "black studies perspective." By this Wynter refers to an outsider perspective that challenges the existing order—mainstream beliefs and practices—on behalf of all who inhabit the margins and dominant group members as well.

7. For a proposal to blend ethnic and civic nationalisms in Canada under the umbrella of multiculturalism, see Taylor (1992).

8. For typologies of multicultural education, see, for example, Montero-Sieburth (1988) and Sleeter and Grant (1987).

9. While our conception of transformative multiculturalism is similar to that of James Banks (1987, 1988), it also draws on work in related fields dealing with what Kenneth Gergen (1982) called the transformation of social knowledge and Joyce E. King (1995, in press) called cultural knowledge and culture-centered knowledge. Also see Elizabeth Minnich (1990) on women's scholarship transforming, not merely adding to, extant knowledge and understanding, and Patricia Hill Collins (1991) on black feminist thought and the standpoint of the "outsider within" the university.

10. While our focus is on contemporary forms of multiculturalism, Banks (1993b) reminds us that "transformative academic scholarship" in the United States is more than 100 years old. It includes the work of late-nineteenth-century scholars of African American history whose studies "created data, interpretations, and perspectives that challenged those that were established by white, mainstream scholarship" (p. 26).

11. Morrison also suggests similar consideration of immigrant experiences.

12. Closely related to the canon—master narrative issues is the movement since the late 1980s toward national standards in core school subjects including history. National standards, or a national system of state standards and assessment, are considered in Chapter 7.

13. In this regard, it is curious that postmodernist views are gaining ground at the same time that women and racial-ethnic minority groups in the United States are looking to institutionalize their presence, for example, in history—social studies curriculum.

14. The concept of borderland, from Gloria Anzaldua's *Borderlands* (1987), refers to indeterminate and changing spaces along cultural boundaries where people from different cultures can come together. In a sense, the United States is or could become the world's borderland.

15. In the course of redefining the problem from inclusion to national unity, neo-nativists also have shifted attention away from structural inequities and group claims. By *structure* we mean the arrangement, pattern, or organization of elements in a system such as the U.S. education, political, or economic system. Structural inequity is discrimination that is built into the system, into the organized or established or institutionalized ways of doing things, such that some groups benefit (or are disadvantaged) more than others. It is a case of what McIntosh (1992) aptly calls unearned group privilege and conferred dominance. Instead, the neo-nativists adopt an individualist stance that leaves little or no room for cultural groupings or structural acknowledgments. On the "symbolic delegitimation of collective ethnic identity" and the "affirmation of the autonomous individual" as lasting effects of the early-twentieth-century Americanization movement, see Olneck (1989, p. 398; 1990).

PART II

Cases

3
California: Containing America

Nothing . . . renders a republic more firm and stable, than to organize it in such a way that the excitement of the ill-humors that agitate a state may have a way prescribed by law for venting itself.

> Niccolo Machiavelli, *The Prince and the Discourses* (New York: Random House, 1950), pp. 130–31

California is the place where new definitions of America are emerging. We have a possibility of creating a new model of ethnic relations, that I don't think exists in too many other places of the world. This is what makes our country kind of exciting, but at the same time is creating sources of tension.

> Ronald Takaki, UC-Berkeley Asian American Studies professor (1990, p. A12)

America cannot continue to be a mere echo of the Old World. It cannot depend on its cultural reference point to Europe [anymore]. It has to take as a concept something new in the world. Never before in the history of the world have you had . . . races and traditions . . . coming together to work out the problems of coexistence.

> Sylvia Wynter, Stanford University professor of African and Afro-American Studies (Interview, August 7, 1990)

During the last half of the 1980s a powerful top-down reform movement led by then–schools' chief Bill Honig succeeded in rewriting California's public school social studies curriculum. It created a blend of pluralism and nationalism rooted in a concept of America as a land of immigrants who have historically subscribed to a common set of ideals or values—a civic glue that has kept the nation together despite economic disparities and struggles over unfulfilled civil rights.

Having codified this immigrant concept into California's history–social science guidelines in 1987, state officials in 1989 and 1990 turned their attention to new social studies textbooks that were being submitted for state approval. Within the covers of these books, which publishers hoped would satisfy California's new guidelines, the story line of a Euro-immigrant America was embodied in print. Despite the multicultural appearance of the textbooks which ultimately won state approval, many people felt that their (and their forerunners') struggles for equality had been downplayed, their contributions mentioned only briefly—in other words, that the historical perspective was still that of European immigrants.

REFORM AND RESPONSE

The public uproar that greeted the textbooks was not only about content but also about deeper disputes, philosophical and emotional, over what it means to be American: Is there one common American culture that overrides the importance of group differences, or is democracy itself strengthened by racial and ethnic variety and maintaining—even celebrating—difference? Do we honor and study difference, or by doing that do we encourage separate enclaves?

That the textbooks were seen by many as failing to forthrightly respond to these kinds of concerns about democracy, difference, and conflict suggested the limitations of California's 1987 *History-Social Science Framework*. But the framework's drafters and supporters dismissed these concerns as they continued actively to promote it as a multicultural history curriculum model for the nation (Stage and Crabtree 1990a, p. 2; Leo 1989, p. 73; Alexander and Crabtree 1988; Cheney 1990, cited in Stage and Crabtree 1990b).

This propensity for promoting their professional product was a key element in the recent history of curriculum reform in California, a political consideration that sometimes detracted from the merits of the reform itself. As for the reform, in its report, *Conditions of Education in California 1990*, Policy Analysis for California Education (PACE) noted that the curriculum frameworks developed since 1983 in mathematics and science, history and social sciences, and language arts could be seen as both representing "bold new directions and breaks from past practice" as well as reflecting "emerging professional and nationwide consensus of what students should be taught in elementary, middle, and high schools" (p. 80). That may be a reasonable assessment, but in our view the road leading to the 1987 *History–Social Science Framework* left many critical voices, particularly those from ethnic and racial minority communities, crushed in the ruts of the framework promoters' wagon wheels west.

There are different ways of regarding California's highly diverse and expanding population: Some see the greater variety of peoples bringing new vitality to the state's economy, while others want to clamp a lid on further immigration, arguing that the growing population is a threat to natural and human resources. As the late Harvard historian and Afro-American Studies professor Nathan Huggins (1988) said:

> The question is whether the glass is half full or half empty—not a matter of values but one of ideological perspective. I do not think it is the historian's role to insist, for reasons of national interest, that the more positive perspective is more valid, while the other is mere cynicism. (p. 121)

Yet that penchant for celebrating perceived common values, while downplaying social inequities and the racial hierarchy that maintains them, characterized the attitude of key education officials when the time came in the state's seven-year adoption cycle to review new history–social studies textbooks. Within a few months the textbook adoption process became the subject of an unusual level of public debate and controversy. One effect of this, as the PACE report (1991) suggested, was closer public scrutiny of the framework itself, since the textbooks that were submitted supposedly were written to its guidelines. Earlier, the framework had gone through a drafting and approval process with hardly any attention from the media or the public. (PACE 1991, p. 82).

The criticism which greeted the textbooks focused almost entirely on a K–8 series by one publisher, Houghton Mifflin of Boston, primarily because this was the only complete series geared specifically to the framework's requirements. These were the only books which survived the state's initial review process, other than one eighth grade book from Holt, Rinehart and Winston.

Textbook Challenges

The most critical and detailed analysis of the textbooks, and of the framework, from any perspective was contained within an 88-page treatise written by Sylvia Wynter, a Stanford University professor with a joint appointment in African and Afro-American Studies and in Spanish and Portuguese. Her paper was finished too late in the adoption time frame to be used or cited by people who went to Sacramento to testify against the textbooks in July and September of 1990.

A prodigious effort of scholarship that Wynter worked on over the summer of 1990, her paper arrived at the California State Board of Education only a few days before the board's September 13 public hearing. By then the textbooks already had gone through initial review and were on the board's doorstep, recommended for approval by the Curriculum Development and Supplemental Materials Commission, the board's advisory body commonly known as the Curriculum Commission.[1] Education officials gave Wynter's critique hardly any formal notice. In their report to the board summarizing criticisms of the textbooks that had come in, Elizabeth Stage, chair of the commission, and Charlotte Crabtree, chair of the commission's history subcommittee, referred to it obliquely, without attribution, as a "lengthy condemnation of the California Framework" (Stage and Crabtree 1990b, attachment 1, p. 3).[2]

In her cordial covering letter to the board, Wynter faulted the text-books, and ultimately the framework itself, for promulgating an immigrant perspective of American history which, because of its focus, marginalized nonimmigrant Native Americans, African Americans, and Mexican citizens of the Southwest Territory who were incorporated into the United States by the 1848 Treaty of Guadalupe Hidalgo. While "an enormous creative effort has gone in to the preparation of these texts," Wynter (1990) wrote,

> and the effort to avoid ethnocentrism is plain on every page, the Euro-American scholars who have written these texts, because they write from *within* their own experience, necessarily ask questions of the past that are limited to that experience. To obtain an *American* view of the past, rather than an Euro-American, or Afro-American one, for that matter, one needs to bring together the perspectives from both Immigrant and non-Immigrant, Euro and non-Euro experiences; and which together consti-tute the lived, if not as yet the *narrated*, history of North America. (p. 3)

In their report to the state board, Stage and Crabtree (1990b) dealt with the charge—often heard during their commission's July hearing—that the texts were Eurocentric, by saying that the criticism was

> simply not supported by the facts. The texts in fact constitute a significant breaking out of the Eurocentric model and devote major emphases to world cultures, their history, achievements, and world view. (attachment 1, p. 4)

However, the textbooks submitted in 1990 did possess a narrative stud-ded with a Euro-immigrant American "implied reader," or "you." In Hough-ton Mifflin's fifth grade U.S. history text, *America Will Be* (Armento et al. 1991) for instance, the preface opens:

> The hunters shiver as an icy wind blows across the empty land. It is flat and treeless here, covered only with moss and small shrubs. Far away, the hunters can see a tall range of mountains covered with ice and snow.
>   So begins an imaginary account of the first humans who ever crossed over the ice from Asia to North America. . . . In Chapter 4 of this book, *you* will have the chance to read more about the ancestors of present-day Native Americans. (p. v; emphasis added)

Said Wynter (1992), "Clearly, had the 'you' of the text *included* today's Native American student body, the text would have read—'You will have the chance to read more about the ancestors of *some of us*, those of us who today call ourselves, Native Americans' " (p. 56). Or the author's imaginary sce-nario could have read something like, "*We* shiver in the icy wind," which would transform the "passive" shivering hunters into the "kind of active agents they must have been. They would have become, phenomenologically, 'our' ancestors—that is, of all of us who today inherit the continent they domesticated" (p. 57).

The eighth grade Houghton Mifflin U.S. history book, *A More Perfect*

Union (Armento et al 1991), also contained several "implied reader" narrative techniques conjuring up an image of a Michael J. Fox *Back to the Future*
observer:

> You are standing in the empty expanses of the Great Plains on a hot
> summer afternoon in the late 1600s. . . . Suddenly a thundering noise
> arises in the west, and black specks appear along the horizon. A few
> minutes later a herd of buffalo sweeps past you, followed by several men
> riding on the backs of strange beasts. With their hair streaming behind
> them, these men look like gods who have captured the wind. (p. 26)

Or, more to the Euro-immigrant point: "You're crossing the Atlantic Ocean
in the mid-1500s. Nearby you can hear the crew member on watch calling
out worried instructions to the man at the helm. . . ." (p. 16).

A More Perfect Union immediately establishes its immigrant perspective on
the title page to Unit 1, "A Land of Promise"—and dramatically so, when
one considers who is left out:

> America was different promises to different people. For Columbus, it was
> the hope of a faster trade route to Asia. For the Spanish explorers, it was
> an opportunity for fame and fortune. For the Pilgrims, it was a refuge
> from religious persecution. And for thousands of European settlers, it
> was a chance for political freedom and economic opportunity. Whatever
> the promise, the wilderness land that greeted these newcomers seemed
> as large and grand as their dreams. (facing p. 1)

Stage and Crabtree (1990a), however, refused to consider any criticism of
the textbooks that could be seen as an assault on the framework, which
Crabtree had co-authored. In their *Adoption Recommendations* report to the
board, they referred to the framework as the "final authority" (p. 7).[3] They
seemed to ignore the possibility that what was at issue was not the framework itself but how its multicultural scheme was to be interpreted or carried
out. In general, according to PACE (1991), frameworks in California

> are designed in part to identify the content to be covered, to provide an
> ordering of the subject-matter and sequence of topics, to identify themes
> with applicability across a range of issues and areas, and to suggest
> teaching strategies. The frameworks are not mandated for use by local
> districts, but since the onset of state education reform efforts in 1983,
> they have assumed greater importance and influence. (p. 74)

But far from focusing on the framework, most of the criticism of Houghton Mifflin's books specifically addressed disparate concerns about their treatment of race and ethnicity; of the Jewish, Christian, and Muslim religions; of
women; and about the total absence of gays and lesbians in a historical
context. The Curriculum Commission, which conducted the initial review,
reacted to each of these concerns differently; the existence of gays and
lesbians, for instance, was summarily dismissed as not being an appropriate
subject for discussion in the kindergarten through eighth grades, those cov-

ered by the textbook adoption. Moreover, said Stage and Crabtree in their "Summary of Public Comments" (1990b), "The Framework does not establish homosexuals as a minority or cultural group. Therefore, the criticism to identify and treat them as such is not within the scope of the adoption" (attachment 1, p. 14). Women's issues, perhaps because few critics had raised them during public hearings before the commission, were not addressed at all in their report. Concerns raised by Jews and Muslims scored the best success, in terms of the editorial corrections and revisions they sought and obtained from the commission and Houghton Mifflin—perhaps because commissioners and state staff were highly concerned about how the textbooks portrayed the sensitive subject of world religions, which the new framework required for the sixth and seventh grades.

Issues involving religion were relatively easily resolved; race and ethnicity proved more nettlesome to the commission, precisely because they represented the most direct challenge to the underlying ideology of the framework—its viewing of the glass as being half full by trumpeting the upside of pluralism while giving scant attention to historic racism. Appreciation for cultural "difference" is addressed in the framework, but it is subsumed by an overriding emphasis on "national identity." The message seems to be that difference is of value, but only if it is contained.

The critiques raised by racial and ethnic groups varied. The concerns of Chinese Americans were focused on seeking more inclusion in the textbooks befitting their standing in California's history, beginning just prior to 1850—including their role in the gold fields, their contributions to California agriculture, the pervasive discrimination they suffered (see Chapter 1), and other areas untouched by the textbooks. Stage and Crabtree (1990b) responded, in part, that "with the great diversity of cultures and ethnic groups represented in California, it is impossible to mention each group's contributions or involvement at a particular period in history and to the extent that group might like" (p. 8). On the other hand, African Americans critical of the textbooks, while interested in similar omissions and distortions, were primarily concerned with a more basic restructuring of the immigrant ethos underlying the textbooks— which Stage and Crabtree may or may not have recognized: "Many critics of these texts have made clear their fundamental opposition to the basic multicultural approach of the California Framework and their opposition to materials written for the Framework necessarily follows from that opposition" (p.3), they said in response to African American critiques.

Public Culture, Prescriptive Rules

Wynter's analysis is worth reviewing in some depth to better understand the conceptual differences and, by extension, the political divisions which separated the various textbook critics from Curriculum Commissioner Charlotte Crabtree, a UCLA professor of education, and other state education officials. Recall that the terms *multicultural* and *multiculturalism* until the mid- to late 1980s referred usually to an approach which was considered an alternative or challenge to mainstream education policy. By the 1990s, after

?5 years of unprecedented immigration from Asian and Latin American countries, multiculturalism had become transformed into a far vaster rubric encompassing the arts, society, politics, even business—a buzzword and, to some, a code word carrying negative connotations of extremist, separatist thinking. In California the education establishment incorporated multiculturalism into the *History–Social Science Framework* as "cultural literacy"—and as such it became one of 12 "strands" or spokes in a curriculum "wheel" (alongside such other spokes as "historical literacy," "ethical literacy," "economic literacy," and "civic values"). Multiculturalism also was subsumed within the "national identity" strand; earlier, during development of the framework, some such as Curriculum Commissoner Joyce E. King—then professor of education at Santa Clara University—had argued unsuccessfully that the "national identity" strand more aptly should be labeled "multicultural identity."

As Wynter wrote in her critique, the prescriptive rules that determine who and what are to be included or excluded in or from American social and political life, the canon, and education policy are predetermined by a native model of the "public culture" which evolved in America. She cites (1990) the Eritrean anthropologist Asmarom Legesse:

> One of the many prescriptive rules in America is the classification of human beings into Blacks and Whites. These are mutually exclusive categories in the sense that one cannot be both Black and White at the same time. One cannot but be impressed by the extreme rigidity of this native model. It denies the fact that Blacks and Whites do marry and enter into elaborate illicit sexual liaisons. The myth of the two races is preserved by the simple rule that all the offsprings of interracial unions are automatically classified as Black. (p. 3)

The brand of multiculturalism espoused in the framework and carried out in the textbooks, says Wynter (1990), actually perpetuates perspectives that nurture racism because it "does not move outside the conceptual field of our present essentially EuroAmerican cultural model" (enclosure 1, pp. 13–14).

As have other black intellectuals, such as Cornel West and bell hooks, Wynter says the consequences of this model stretch far beyond the classroom. She asks:

> How did the dispossession of the indigenous peoples, their subordination and the mass enslavement of the people of Black African descent . . . come to seem "just and virtuous" actions to those who effected them? And secondly: How does the continuance of this initial dispossession, in the jobless, alcohol-ridden reservations, the jobless drug and crime ridden inner city ghettos and barrios, still come to seem to all of us, as *just*, or at the very least, to be in the nature of things? Thirdly, why is this contemporary fate so lawfully and extremely visited upon the three non-Immigrant alter ego groups, i.e., the Reds, the Blacks and the native

Chicano, and correlated with their also relatively low test-performance scores and high school drop-out rate? (enclosure 2; p. 59)

What deters classroom teachers and students from addressing these questions, assuming they even think to ask them, is that under California's immigrant schema those actions still seem to have been inevitable and don't seem to *need* to be questioned—a form of what King (1991) has called "dysconscious racism . . . an *impaired* consciousness or a distorted way of thinking about race," a form of racism that "tacitly accepts dominant White norms and privileges" (p. 135). Because the framework stresses chronology, American history becomes a continuum of inevitability—of development, of progress, of "destiny"—starting with European arrival and colonization, the inevitable if unfortunate conquest of Native Americans, the inhumane enslavement of Africans to replenish and replace the original Native American slaves, and the development of democratic institutions based on the Judeo-Christian, European tradition. America today thus becomes a pluralistic society built by immigrants who fought, struggled, and ultimately came to subscribe to one commonly held set of democratic values. Looking at American history in this way reduces blacks to just another immigrant group. As University of Wisconsin-Parkside education professor Christine Sleeter (1992) and others have written, it is a way of generalizing the white ethnic experience to encompass enslaved blacks, indigenous Native Americans, more recent immigrant Koreans, Muslims from India and Pakistan, Nicaraguans, and political refugees from Cambodia, Laos, and Vietnam—*everyone*.

The effect of an immigrant model is to reduce racism to prejudice. Instead of recognizing it as a dominant factor in American history, racist behavior toward non-Europeans—Native Americans, blacks, and Mexicans of the Southwest—is likened to the troublesome but eventually surmountable ethnic prejudice encountered by immigrants from Poland, Italy, Germany, and Ireland.

Although only a partial representation of American history, this immigrant perspective is presented as if it were the universally valid one, says Wynter (1990), who suggested that the authors of the history textbooks were not even aware of their own cultural blinders. In the obverse, "Any recognition of the centrality of the history of Black America to the history of America necessarily challenges the conception of the United States as a 'nation of immigrants' " (enclosure 2, p. 25). Since the roles of blacks and Native Americans are restricted and contained, or marginalized, it's not possible for students to develop any real empathy for them, assuming that empathy is a goal of education. "Liberal pity replaces empathic identification," says Wynter (p. 34).

An example of this emerged during the debate over the textbooks among members of the Curriculum Commission. Joyce King, the commissioner who first raised concerns from her perspective as a black educator and parent, cited among other things the "Moment in Time" illustration of an "Escaping Slave" in the fifth grade text, *America Will Be*. Its description of the young black man's eyes, feet, whiplashed back and clothing, she said, were "more akin to the description of an animal than of a human being." King said her two teenage youngsters reacted to the drawing in the same manner, without any prompting from her. But Daniel Chernow, another commissioner, said he had puzzled over King's complaint but could not agree. Chernow said he had "tried to be as sensitive as I could be, tried to see what Joyce saw, and I couldn't. I thought this [the drawing] evoked some empathy" (Waugh 1990b, p. A9).

If empathy is a goal of the framework, then its attainment is problematic when black students, like King's children, react in one way and white adults, like Chernow, in another. Empathy is generated when stories are told through the eyes of the participants, and a note of understanding is struck. Alex Haley's *Roots* was a book that created widespread empathy, said Wynter, who heard tales of black youngsters stealing copies of *Roots* in order to read it. "The genius of *Roots* was it was the first time Americans identified empathetically with Blacks," she said. "That's what I find lacking in these [Houghton Mifflin's] books. You won't see black kids stealing these books" (interview, August 7, 1990).

In her critique Wynter argued that the horizontal plain of the "common ground" offered by the textbooks was an idealized ground, since American society is a vertical hierarchy built on racial divisions and prescriptive rules. She called for a "reconception of the United States . . . based on reciprocal recognition, rather than on hierarchy" (1990, enclosure 2, p. 10). Such a reconception might bring Americans closer to realizing the ideal of racial equality than would the assimilationist myth of the American melting pot.

California's conception of revisionist multiculturalism is rendered remarkably well in Chapter 1 of *America Will Be*. Entitled "A Tale of One City," this chapter focuses on New Orleans as a melting pot of many cultures:

> New Orleans is made up of people from many backgrounds. This kind of culture is called *pluralism,* or a pluralistic culture. In a pluralistic culture, life is exciting. People work, join together, struggle, learn and grow. (p. 6)

A few pages later:

> Maybe the hardest problem in a pluralistic culture is *prejudice,* disliking a person without knowing anything about them. You will learn how immigrants, Native Americans, and blacks have met with prejudice. (p. 21)

Placing the example of New Orleans at the beginning of the text, says Wynter (1990),

> imposes a narrative beginning able to "center" the immigrant story of history [and to] substitute the representation of cultural pluralism in place of the reality of a hierarchy of *races,* and of cultural prejudice in place of the reality of *racism.* (enclosure 2, p. 16)

It is not until 470 pages after the reference to prejudice in the 1990 review version (actually copyrighted 1991) that fifth grade readers finally encounter the word *racism*. Why was the milder term, *prejudice*, used to introduce students to the concept of racism against blacks? Textbook co-author Gary Nash, a UCLA historian with what one reporter described as "impeccable left-liberal credentials" (Reinhold 1991, p. 46), said that to him the words *racism* and *prejudice* mean essentially the same thing (interview, August 15, 1990).

This conflation would seem consistent with the tendency to generalize the white ethnic immigrant experience—to equate the prejudice encountered by Poles, Slavs, Irish, Italians, and other European immigrants with the racial discrimination experienced by African Americans, Chinese, Japanese, and Filipinos—as if to say that racism, like prejudice, is something that will cease to be a major problem as soon as one learns to speak English and moves to the suburbs.

BUILDING A NATIONAL IDENTITY

The need to define the nation as a coherent whole obliges one to obliterate or subordinate those particular groups who would lay claim to an independent or an alternative generalization. The nation-state came about by subsuming the many into the one; and it succeeds best when individual groups are able to submerge themselves comfortably into the large abstraction of the nation.

Nathan I. Huggins (1988, p. 118)

Revising the Framework

The approach taken in the Houghton Mifflin textbooks fit in nicely with the framework's emphasis on national identity and common values, what some have referred to simplistically as a "common culture." Together, the framework and the textbooks represented a major accomplishment for those historians and educators who saw the need to incorporate and contain California's and America's increasingly diverse populations. Both the framework and the textbooks could be hailed as blueprint and building blocks for a redefined American nation, and most of the media did just that.

This neo-nativist achievement in California owed much of its success to the fortuitous confluence of University of California-Los Angeles education professor Charlotte Crabtree and state Superintendent of Public Instruction Bill Honig, who rode into office in 1983 on a campaign to reform the schools. In 1986 he received assistance from some educators and historians who wanted to replace social studies with a curriculum centered on history and geography. A few who would become increasingly active later in the national standards effort came to California to work with the committees that Honig formed to draft a new history–social science framework. They included Diane Ravitch, then an adjunct professor at Teachers College, Columbia University, and Paul Gagnon, then a professor of European history at the University of Massachusetts-Amherst.

The framework drafting committee's 20 members were teachers, school principals, social studies specialists, and university professors of history, geography, or education. Almost all of them where white. An 18-member "blue ribbon advisory committee" including some who would later serve on the drafting committee met first to discuss current research and needs in history–social science education, and to offer suggestions to the framework committee. A first draft of the framework was compiled by Matthew Downey, a University of California-Berkeley history professor (who later bid for a National Endowment for the Humanities grant to establish a history center at Berkeley and lost out to UCLA's proposal, awarded to Charlotte Crabtree by NEH chair Lynne Cheney in 1988). The draft was circulated for "field review" to educators and policymakers in California and elsewhere, resulting in more than 1,700 responses. The draft was taken over by Crabtree and Ravitch, who produced a second draft. Although they were assisted by Diane Brooks, manager of the state Department of Education's history–social science unit, Crabtree and Ravitch were identified in the final version as the "principal writers" (Framework 1988, p. xii).

In an interview conducted by NEH chair Lynne Cheney for the magazine *Humanities* (1990), Crabtree recalled development of the framework:

It began in 1985. Diane Ravitch was on the initial framework committee; I was not. And for about a year they struggled. Many did not want to see any change from the existing curriculum, and they made no bones about it. I was called in to present a speech on what elementary school students should learn, and after I had done that, I was asked to do the same for junior and senior high, which I did, and I found myself on the framework committee. Very quickly, Diane and I joined forces. We had some strong support from several other members, and we began to work toward the curriculum that is there now.

During the process, 1,700 reviewers participated. They sent in elaborate reviews of specific sections of what we submitted, and we worked very closely with the state board of education. I flew to Sacramento sometimes three times a week, to keep the revision process moving. (p. 6)

Joyce King, who was appointed to the Curriculum Commission in 1986 at the same time as Crabtree, was among those who wrote a field review. Although she found the second draft much improved from the standpoint of requiring a multicultural approach, she said that it, too, failed to give central importance to the pluralistic nature of American society and the vital link between "our pluralistic heritage, national identity and constitutional heritage." Much later, after the textbooks were adopted, King (1992) wrote:

The concerns I raised about the textbooks were the same ones that I raised in 1987 about the inclusion of diverse perspectives when early drafts of the Framework were circulated for public input and review. Even though the Framework writing committee incorporated some of

the changes I suggested into the final version of the document, the textbooks the state ultimately selected following this curriculum guide mir-
rored its fundamental conceptual flaws and biases. (p. 322)

The framework, unanimously adopted by the state board of education
in July 1987, had several elements which distinguished it from past curriculum guides and which posed problems—or challenges, depending on
one's point of view—for publishers. It introduced the teaching of world
religions—Judaism, Christianity, Islam—in sixth and seventh grade world
history courses. It called for an end to "dumbed down" writing and for
lively, inspired narrative: a "story well told." It replaced the traditional
"expanding environments" approach with history and geography, encouraging teachers to move far beyond the child's neighborhood, into old myths
and folk tales from many other countries. History and geography assumed
a central place, and history itself was carved up into segments: Instead of
repeating a survey course, U.S. history now was to be taught in three
segments, in the fifth, eighth, and eleventh grades. World history would be
taught in the sixth, seventh, and tenth grades. The six history courses
doubled what was called for in earlier frameworks.

The 1987 framework was a product of the times. Pearl M. Oliner (1988),
a professor of education at Humboldt State University, described it as

a "no nonsense" document . . . marked by straightforward identification
of content, developed sequentially and presented chronologically within
the parameters of clearly defined courses and identified themes and
events. In some fundamental sense, it calls for a modernized version of
the McGuffey readers—an emphasis on national heritage, myths and
fables, history and geography as literature, ethics and morals and above
all, exciting, dramatic well written texts. (p. 27)

The new framework stood in contrast to the previous framework.
Whereas the 1981 framework acknowledged both diversity and conflict, the
1987 framework portrayed American society as "pluralistic, yet in harmony
and balance, with a consensus on fundamental values," one educator observed (Maxey 1988, p. 33). In 1987 conflict was understated, as Maxey
demonstrated with a passage from the new framework: "Yet even as our
people have become increasingly diverse, there is broad recognition that we
are one people. Whatever our origins, we are all Americans" (Framework
1988, p. 20).

The 1987 framework mentions conflict here and there but then briskly
moves along, leaving it entirely up to the individual teacher's knowledge of
specific historical conflicts and judgment as to whether and how to examine
them—such as the controversy over whether Father Junipero Serra saved
the California Mission Indians or helped destroy their way of life forever.

Maxey (1988) noted further the "emphasis on consensus rather than
conflict" in another passage from the framework, describing the 1870s in the
fourth-grade California history course:

As California became home to diverse groups of people, its culture reflected a mixture of influences from Mexico, the Far East and Pacific regions, and various European nations. With cultural diversity, however, came elements of tension. Students can compare the many cultural and economic contributions these diverse populations have brought to California and can make the same comparisons for California today. (p. 49)

And, from a description of the eleventh grade, twentieth century U.S. history course: "In a world riven by ethnic, racial, and religious hatred, the United States has demonstrated the strength and dynamism of a racially, religiously, and culturally diverse people, united under a democratic political system" (*Framework*, p. 102). It is difficult to see, as Maxey wonders, whose story is being told here, and how California's young people could relate to it.

Thus the framework may not be as "no-nonsense" as Oliner suggests; it is socially and ideologically constructed. S. G. Grant (1991) contends that the framework is aimed more at "manipulating textbooks" (p. 219) through its call for improvements in textbook writing and presentation than it is at promoting teacher autonomy, teacher professionalism, or even teacher knowledge. "Far from seeing teachers as integral to curricular change, the Framework has been designed around them, undercutting their autonomous decision making and disregarding their professional knowledge" (p. 220).

While Crabtree, Ravitch, Cheney, Honig, and others persistently lauded the virtues of the framework, contrary opinions did and do exist, held by educators both inside and outside California. The Rochester, New York, school district, for instance, examined the framework in 1989 as part of its search for what Ellen Swartz, the Rochester district's multicultural project coordinator, described as a "theoretical focus and practical application of a truly representational and integrated curriculum based on the inherent inclusivity of diverse sources of knowledge and on the highest standards of academic integrity and scholarship" (personal communication, April 4, 1990). Swartz continued: "At first glance, the California plan appears to be multicultural, in that men and women of diverse cultural groups are included. Actually, it is this inclusion, or 'mentioning' which is the basis of the plan's shortcomings." California would include Native Americans in its curriculum, she said, "but the realities of colonial land theft, cultural disruption and destruction, and genocide are sanitized and thus suppressed" (p. 1).

The framework says that African Americans should be presented in textbooks as "contributors" to historical events, but the framework does not "integrate" their experiences "into the American drama." And while the framework contains tones of moral outrage when discussing treatment of the Holocaust, it lacks that tone when discussing how the history of slavery should be taught, Swartz said (pp. 2, 3).

California's approach, "the mentioning of the previously unmentioned," Swartz said, "presents itself as equitable treatment, but actually restricts the possible integration of culturally diverse bands of knowledge" (p. 4).

While E. D. Hirsch uses the term *cultural literacy* to describe his ideal mind-bank of facts and dates about Western culture, this term has a much different meaning to others, including educators, parents, and students of color, for whom cultural literacy would encompass the forgotten and suppressed knowledge of the "other"—their own histories. All too frequently, racial and ethnic minority students graduate from high school being, in this sense, culturally illiterate. University of California-Berkeley student Gloria Chun, for instance, was typical of Asian Americans who grew up not reading in school of their ancestors' roles and struggles in American history and didn't discover what they'd missed until college, usually in an ethnic studies class. "It makes me angry. It also makes me sad," said Chun. "I feel cheated. I've had this truncated kind of education. Only now I'm finding out what I have been missing all along" (Kang and Waugh 1990. p. A1).

For over a half-century African Americans and other ethnic minorities have waged an unsuccessful struggle to get their voices and perspectives included in the schoolbooks. Significant gains were made in terms of eliminating overtly racist stereotyping, but there were still significant lapses. In 1970, for instance, the American Indian Historical Society criticized the author's dedication page in one 1957 book, which said, "For all boys and girls who like Indians and Animals" (1970, p. 102). Twenty years later the same book with the same dedication intact was included on Houghton Mifflin's trade book list.

Students, if you ask them pointedly, often are aware of what's excluded as well as included in their curriculum. In a survey of San Francisco high-school seniors conducted by the *San Francisco Examiner* in early 1990, nearly 1,800 seniors, or about 44 percent of the graduating class, responded to questions about such things as how much they felt they had learned about other cultures, how they felt about themselves, and whether their textbooks had portrayed their ethnic group accurately. The district—with 20 percent Latino, 18 percent black, 48 percent Asian, and 14 percent white students—is among the most diverse of California's large school districts. Native Americans, blacks, Chinese, Japanese, Latinos, Koreans, Filipinos, Vietnamese, and other Southeast Asians—everyone except white students—responded that it was equally important to be seen both as an American and as a member of one's own ethnic or racial group. Typical was the response from one female aware of this Du Bois–like duality: "I'm a Chinese American. I'm an American citizen, but I'm of the Chinese race. Some things I do are American and some are Chinese" (Ramirez 1990, pp. A1, 8).

When it came to textbooks, only 17 of the 149 black seniors surveyed felt that their history had been adequately treated, and only seven said their textbooks were accurate. By contrast, 83 percent of the white seniors said whites were treated adequately in textbooks, and 29 percent felt they'd been "very accurate." But six out of 10 white students also said they had not learned enough about other groups (Ramirez 1990, pp. A1, 8).

Berkeley historian Matthew Downey, who had taken subcommittee suggestions and compiled the first draft of what became the 1987 framework, ended up thinking the final framework was a "pretty good" document (interview, January 8, 1990). He agreed it was "very strongly" weighted toward an emphasis on developing in students a sense of national identity in contrast to examining more deeply the nation's pluralistic culture and various ethnic histories. The framework process, he pointed out, was inevitably the result of compromise. "What it comes down to is, do you like the trade-offs made? I think there are certain areas where it's Eurocentric, it has a Western focus, that many people would have liked to have seen otherwise" (interview, January 8, 1990).

Others were satisfied with the framework's handling of multiculturalism. Todd Clark, executive director of the Constitutional Rights Foundation of Los Angeles and a former high school teacher, served on both the blue-ribbon advisory committee and the full framework committee. Clark, whose primary interests lay in promoting youth participation in civic affairs, said that 1987 framework achieved a greater integration of all concerns than did the 1981 framework, which emphasized ethnic-group identification much more distinctly:

> I think there are people who probably don't think there is enough there, multiculturally, but if you like the extent to which it's integrated, it's probably more effectively integrated than it's ever been. It's not spelled out and separated out as something you do independently, but as something you do throughout, with attention being given in the content of some instructional areas to information on the origins of various cultures and ethnic groups, so that a kid can see in the context of learning content that there is a reason to feel pride in one's heritage. (interview, February 9, 1990)

The framework edition copyrighted and published in 1988, listing 20 members of the drafting committee, actually omitted one important participant—Jack Hoar, who served as the committee's chair. Hoar, a history–social sciences consultant for the Long Beach school district, wrote to Bill Honig asking *not* to have his name on the list. As Hoar explained in an interview two years later (August 21, 1990), the framework draft was taken from the committee and given to a subcommittee of the Curriculum Commission, where it was rewritten by Crabtree and Ravitch, before the drafting committee had had a chance to hold public hearings on their document. His account:

> We had hoped to have hearings around the state for additional input, but the timeline was decided by others. . . . My understanding was that would happen, and it didn't, and I was irritated about that. That's when I asked that my name not appear on the document.
>
> Interestingly enough, the hearings [by the drafting committee] didn't happen, but there was a whole series of orientation meetings and so forth, that in a sense accomplished what I think could have happened if the hearings had proceeded.

Hoar remembers only one occasion when committee members actually took a vote; most of its decisions were made instead by consensus. As he puts it:

> We talked—maybe that's why they [the Curriculum Commission] got tired of our process—we talked and talked and finally the decision emerged.

Hoar also sees the 1987 framework as being in many ways a result of the times in which it was written. The 1981 framework, for instance, was

> what I called the "diversity" framework: it was [written] when multiculturalism, pluralism, diversity—there was a strong emphasis there. It was a conceptual framework. This [1987] Framework I'd characterize as the "bicentennial" framework. It was developed during the time of the Bicentennial of the Constitution, [so development of] democratic understandings is underlined even more than you would expect it to be in a document dealing with history.

PUTTING EVERYONE IN THE COVERED WAGON

I saw the Liberty Bell today. It's got a big crack in it—right through the word "liberty."

> Joyce King, in Philadelphia on the day the California State Board of Education adopted the history textbooks she'd opposed

The 1990 Evaluation and Adoption of History Textbooks

Just as the implications of the framework were not clear to the public at large until the history textbooks embodying its precepts came along in 1990, the degree to which the framework's architects would go toward bolstering it didn't become completely evident until the textbook adoption process began. The textbooks came at a time when a national debate in the mass media and academic journals was swirling around questions about a common American identity. Old-line liberals like Arthur Schlesinger Jr. were joining neo-conservatives like William Bennett in assaults on what they perceived as multiculturalism; a 1989 New York State Minority Task Force report, *A Curriculum of Inclusion*, and a 1990 Atlanta conference on infusion of African and African American content into the curriculum, in particular, took heavy hits from academics and media pundits who saw them as omens that the common cultural glue was failing to contain ethnic separatists bent on "balkanizing" the nation. It was within this context that the new Houghton Mifflin textbooks—picturing a covered wagon on its fifth-grade U.S. history book's colorful blue, red, and gold cover, its pages graced with paintings of ancient American Indian villages and portraits of black inventors— arrived in California for review in early April 1990.

Because of the new framework, far fewer publishers submitted books for state approval in 1990 than in the previous adoption year of 1983—nine, compared to 22. Only Houghton Mifflin submitted an entire K–8 series. (California does not have an adoption process for high-school textbooks other than putting all books through a routine "legal compliance" review; local districts choose their own books for grades 9 through 12 and thus have more choices than they do for the K–8 grades.)

The Houghton Mifflin textbooks, which ultimately won state approval, became the only textbook option available to districts for grades K–7 (another history text was also adopted for grade 8 in addition to Houghton Mifflin's). One of its co-authors was UCLA historian Gary Nash, an associate of Charlotte Crabtree at UCLA, who was in a key position on the Curriculum Commission as chair of its History–Social Science Subject Matter Committee.

Crabtree and Nash had been directly associated with each other at least since 1988, when the National Endowment for the Humanities awarded a $1.5 million, three-year grant to establish a National Center for History in the Schools at UCLA. Crabtree and Nash were the center's director and associate director, respectively. Despite this closeness, Crabtree said that she only became aware of Nash's contract with Houghton Mifflin in December 1989, a few months before the adoption process began (interview, July 27, 1990).

Under California's Political Reform Act, public officials are required to disclose any financial interest that could cause conflicts in matters requiring their vote. Crabtree's financial statement (June 17, 1987) disclosed none. Under state law, therefore, she was not required legally to disqualify herself from her role in the adoption of textbooks authored by her associate. When questioned about her association with Nash and her role on the Curriculum Commission following its July 1990 vote recommending approval of the Houghton Mifflin textbooks, Crabtree insisted that "there was not a single time, not one, when Gary Nash and I discussed any of these materials—ever." She added:

> If you put a caveat on participation on the basis of people knowing one another, we couldn't do the job. The critical point is whether we [the Commissioners] treat them like we treat any other author. Those are criteria I can absolutely assure you were followed to the letter. (Waugh 1990c)

But Crabtree did not treat Nash like any other textbook author; she regularly extolled him on occasions that were inappropriate, such as before the panel of teachers and university professors assembled by the California State Department of Education to review the textbooks. For instance, during the March 1990 orientation and training session, before the panelists had seen the textbooks, Crabtree described Nash as a "magnificent historian at UCLA." One of Nash's co-authors, geographer Christopher Salter, also came in for praise from Crabtree. None of the authors of textbooks from other publishers were mentioned in such glowing terms by her. One of the panelists, Gloria Ladson-Billings (1992), in a paper which does not use the names of the participants, refers to a commissioner whom we infer was Crabtree:

> She regularly referred to two of the authors as the "best" in their field. They may just be. However, the constant reiteration of their names *before* the panel members saw the textbook submissions was wrong. (p. 10)

Ladson-Billings, who served on the subpanel reviewing history texts for the fourth, fifth, and eighth grades, said she thought that the high school teachers on her panel "were definitely swayed by who they were told the 'best' were. When these materials arrived at their homes or schools with these authors' names on them, I believe their judgment was compromised" (p. 10). She also noted that a couple of the teachers on the 4-5-8 subpanel knew Nash from having participated in workshops with him at the UCLA history center.[4]

Crabtree exercised her influence in other ways, too. Commission member Joyce King, who had clashed previously with Crabtree over diversity issues, had suggested using materials by well-known multiculturalist James Banks, an education professor at the University of Washington, Seattle, for the pre-review presentation to the panelists on how to judge textbooks from the criteria of the framework's cultural literacy strand. Crabtree rejected the suggestion, saying that Banks was a "separatist" (interview with King, October 20, 1992). Some of Crabtree's compatriots, on the other hand, turned up as presenters—including Paul Gagnon, who had served on the framework drafting committee, and Gilbert Sewall, director of the American Textbook Council and a former associate of Diane Ravitch and Chester Finn at the Educational Excellence Network.

King ended up making the presentation on evaluation of cultural diversity, using criteria developed by the Curriculum Commission; it included a slide show and lecture focusing in part on scholarship dealing with the contributions and influence early Africans had had on Western culture and thought, and on Native Americans. King did not discuss the more controversial claims made by some Afrocentrists. Yet, when King had finished, Crabtree spoke up. She began by observing that "controversy among historians also needs to be reviewed and understood" by students (tape of Instructional Materials Evaluation Panel training session, March 1990).

Crabtree continued (remember, this is in March, a month before the panelists have even seen the textbooks): "History, as Gary Nash puts it, is an inquiry with the past, in which new perceptions and developments in today's world bring new questions for historians to rethink and relook at the historical record." The degree of cultural exchange in the ancient world— King had cited Martin Bernal's groundbreaking work, *Black Athena*—was still in dispute, said Crabtree. "The amount of historical backing for all of the new work that is being proposed is not entirely clear," she said, cautioning that such work would be settled eventually by "good solid historical scholarship" (tape of IMEP training session, March 1990).

Crabtree's caveat, although lacking the neo-nativists' hyperbole, reflected their allegations, in New York and elsewhere, that multiculturalists were promoting a revised history based on substandard scholarship. State schools chief Bill Honig also took their tack, accusing critics of wanting their children to learn only positive things about their own particular group, and nothing negative. On ABC's nightly news broadcast with Peter Jennings, Honig asserted that the textbook critics "deny that there are common, basic principles of democracy or ethical ideas that are valid across all groups" ("Person of the Week," September 14, 1990). In Honig's view, the textbooks were adopted not *for* political reasons but "in spite of intense political pressure to reject them" (Honig 1991, p. 179).

But the public pressure to reject them did not come until after the panelists had finished their review and made their recommendations to the Curriculum Commission. The panel—known as the Instructional Materials Evaluation Panel (IMEP)—conducted its review over the course of five days during the last week of June 1990, at the Sacramento Holiday Inn. It was five days of hard work, with the panelists meeting in groups during the day to discuss the textbooks and often working into the evening hours to write detailed evaluations of the 26 separate textbooks for the nine grade levels that had been sent to the panelists' homes two months earlier.

Each textbook was to be judged on the basis of 18 criteria that had been determined by the Curriculum Commission. Among the criteria were narrative style, inclusion of civic values and democratic principles, cultural diversity, critical thinking, ethical issues, religion, primary sources, how well the book presented controversial issues, and how well it aligned over all with the framework. The criteria were weighted differently; narrative style was worth four times as much as cultural diversity, for instance. A book could get a maximum of 100 points for narrative style but a maximum of only 25 points for cultural diversity—or, for that matter, for inclusion of civic values and democratic principles. (A minimum of 735 points out of a possible 1,050 was required for IMEP recommendation.)

At the IMEP's March training session King had argued that the inclusion of cultural diversity was a criterion implied throughout the framework. She urged panelists to consider a book's multicultural perspective in conjunction with the other criteria, "so [that] this is not something that is set off to the side." In practice, in the review session during IMEP Week in late June, each of the criteria was taken up separately; cultural diversity was treated as only one of the 18 criteria. But it was this criterion which became the focus of much of the criticism that later erupted over the Houghton Mifflin textbooks.

The March training session represented to King the "culmination of a long struggle I had had on the Commission trying to get the definition of that particular criterion [cultural diversity] articulated in a way that made sense to me." The process in King's view was somewhat "backwards," in that each of the criteria was assigned a numerical weight before criteria definitions were written. "When you get to the definition stage, you've already been constrained by a point structure. I don't think that that was planned necessarily, it was just how it worked out," said King. King recalled that she and

Crabtree debated for an hour at one commission session over nuances of wording in the cultural diversity definition (interview, October 20, 1992).

The Houghton Mifflin textbooks received only moderate scores for cultural diversity. Using a scale of 1 to 5, with 5 being the highest rating for adhering to each of the criteria, panelists ranked the Houghton Mifflin books roughly in the middle, at 3, for inclusion of cultural diversity. (Out of the publisher's nine K–8 books, five were ranked moderate for cultural diversity, one was ranked low, and three received the high rating.)

There were other problematic aspects to the evaluation process. One had to do with juggling of scores and another with the ethnic makeup of the panel. In addition to the numerical scoring of criteria, the panelists were also to take a "consensus" or "holistic" vote. In the subpanel evaluating the K–3 books, the Houghton Mifflin first and third grade textbooks received consensus approval but both fell short of the required 735 points on the numerical scoring. Francie Alexander, an associate superintendent under Honig, went into the room and told the commissioner in charge of that subpanel to have the panelists "revisit" their scores to bring them in alignment with the subpanel's consensus or holistic approval. The commissioner in charge refused. Department of Education staff members asked the panel's facilitator, a commission member, to "revisit" the scores to bring them into alignment. She refused, she later said at a commission meeting, explaining that the distinction between the two scoring methods had not been made clear and that the request had come late in the week, when her panel was due to finish its work. Francie Alexander, an associate superintendent, then led the panelists through a review of their scores. They voted to modify their numerical scoring for the first grade textbook but balked at adjusting the scores of the third grade text. As a result, the Houghton Mifflin third grade book ultimately went to the commission and won approval without meeting the minimum requirement of 735 points.

Although reportedly distraught at the time over the adjustment of the first-grade scores, the commissioner acting as a facilitator for this subpanel (who later abstained from voting on the books in question) seemed to acquiesce to Crabtree's conclusion at the committee's meeting in July, during which Crabtree and Alexander opined that the two scoring systems—numerical and holistic—apparently had not been adequately communicated to the panelists. Crabtree said:

> So that nothing is interpreted, misinterpreted here, by publishers or the public, that some kind of fancy dancing with the recommendations, it apparently was a lack of common shared understanding as to the, bringing those two [scoring methods] into sync. (transcription of proceedings July 19, 1990)

The commissioner who abstained subsequently declined several requests for interviews to discuss the matter. Several months later, before the end of her term, she quietly resigned from the Curriculum Commission.

A high-ranking person who was inside that subpanel's meeting room the day the scores were "revisited," and who preferred not to be named, later wondered: "We had high standards going into this. But, the other side of it is, did we adhere to our high standards, or did we deviate just to bring some textbooks on?"

The representative of a publisher whose eighth grade textbook was rejected broached the scoring controversy delicately during the public hearing. Noting that his book actually had scored higher than the Houghton Mifflin book that was approved with a below-minimum score, he said dryly, "Perhaps there are some technical difficulties in the scoring process." And when it came time to vote, five of the commissioners showed their distaste for the apparent score rejuggling in a most indirect way: They abstained from voting on the IMEP's recommendation to reject the textbooks of the seven other publishers.

The other problematic aspect of the proceedings—the racial-ethnic makeup of the IMEP—was raised by King and Ladson-Billings, among others. They were concerned that the Department of Education staff had not pursued an opportunity to increase minority representation on the panel by appointing those who were available as alternates. Department staff, who argued they had made three recruiting attempts to broaden representation, said they decided to save the state the extra expense involved in naming alternates to fill out the panel, which resulted in 53 members rather than the originally intended 60. Although the overall panel had minority representation of about 30 percent, the makeup on the critical 4-5-8 subpanel reviewing U.S. and California history textbooks was only five minorities out of 19. How the outcomes of this or the other panels might have been affected by a greater presence of minority panelists is conjecture, but observations and objections made by two relatively vocal members of the 4-5-8 subpanel (one African American and the other Native American) seemed to carry much weight with the other, white panelists. On the other hand, an Asian American panel member spoke hardly at all—at least in the group session—during the two days that were observed, making it difficult to judge what effect her presence might have had overall.

The Great Divide

I am not trying to get anyone to change their vote. I am just stating flatly that these books have problems.
    Joyce King (1990)

As already illustrated, Joyce King played a key role in the textbook controversy, primarily by raising critical questions about the books' incorporation and portrayal of African Americans. Her experience before and during the textbook controversy sheds light on the depth of the issues and their wider ramifications, both for education policymaking and the America debate.

Joyce Elaine King grew up in a working-class family in Stockton, in California's San Joaquin Valley. She was the only one in her family to go to a prestigious college like Stanford University; she has cousins her own age who don't know how to read. It wasn't until she left the United States that King learned about the heritage and achievements of black people. There had been nothing in her Stockton school books. She was a junior participating in Stanford's student-abroad program, in Italy, when she learned about the Harlem Renaissance and read the poetry of Countee Cullen and Claude McKay in Italian.

For many years she lived on a quiet, gently curving street with stucco and wood California bungalow and ranch-style houses in East Palo Alto, a community that was incorporated relatively recently and that in many ways is still a backwater of black and Hispanic families which has failed to attract revenue-producing electronics or other industries as have surrounding communities in the Silicon Valley. Squeezed between the mudflats of San Francisco Bay on the east and the freeway, State Highway 101, on the west, with Palo Alto unfolding farther to the west toward the flat expanse of Stanford University and the oak-dotted hills beyond, East Palo Alto in 1992 had the unfortunate distinction of racking up the highest homicide rate in the nation; intensive police work reduced the rate dramatically in 1993. The city does not have its own high school; its teenagers go to schools in neighboring cities, where their dropout rate is much higher than the average. King, who until Fall 1994 was a professor and director of teacher education at Santa Clara University, a 20-minute drive south on Highway 101 from her home, worked for five years during the 1980s with a group of mothers organizing other parents in East Palo Alto for improvements in the schools; she sent her two children to after-school programs that emphasized African and African American cultural themes and activities.

King had lived in East Palo Alto since 1967. She moved there when she was a sophomore at Stanford and encountered racial discrimination at the dorms. Receiving permission to move off campus—lower-division undergraduates then were expected to live within the campus compound—she began working with black students in East Palo Alto's public schools, at a time when students at Stanford, at UC-Berkeley, and elsewhere were forging movements that would lead to the establishment of ethnic studies classes and departments. Part of the alchemy that many of the students hoped to achieve was a bond between the university and Third World communities. This variation on town and gown, the attempt to focus black scholarship on the root causes of community problems, which nearly disappeared during the ensuing two decades, has recently been revived as a necessary pursuit by numerous black intellectuals. But some, like King, maintained a focus on community. As a product of the '60s, her sense of the importance of that time shaped her idea of the public intellectual as someone who "tries to make a bridge between what we do as academics and what people need" (interview, March 14, 1992).

That issue, what people need, proved to be a crucible for King during her four-year tenure on the state's Curriculum Commission, from 1986 to 1990, during which time she argued with other members of the commission over concepts of multicultural inclusion and ways of meeting the needs of California's diverse student population. By her account it was a difficult four years, and she nearly didn't make it: In January 1990, several months before the textbook adoption, King had decided to resign. She planned to announce her resignation at the January meeting. But she changed her mind:

I had been sick for two years, really sick. I couldn't really admit to myself that the Commission had anything to do with it, I just didn't see myself as a person who was inflicted with stress, you know. But I was talking to one of the other Commissioners and saying that I was going to resign. . . . [She] said to me that they had said to her, and they apparently had had a discussion about this, that if they could keep me away from the history books, they would really be happy. And this Commissioner was saying to me that she hoped, in fact she pleaded with me not to resign. She said, "Please don't do that, that's what they want; they want to keep you away from the history books." And I hadn't even thought about the history adoption per se, as something problematic. I mean, I'm just going along step by step, encountering disagreements and viewpoints that—I was basically naive, you know, thinking "How can these people possibly be doing this?" and to have someone say to me, "They're anticipating having to contain your influence, and to keep you from having any effect on this process"—then I had a different view of what was going on. And that influenced my decision not to resign. (interview, October 20, 1992)

After nearly four years of having her ideas and views often rebuffed by most of the other commissioners and the state board, King took a different tack. A few days before the commission's July 1990 public hearing and vote on the IMEP's recommendations, King distributed a memo outlining her opposition. She sent her July 11, 1990, memo listing her reasons for opposing the textbooks to, it seemed, everyone but the media. In addition to sending it to all the members of the Curriculum Commission and Board, King also sent it to black state legislative leaders and to nearly two dozen black university professors and educators around the country—people King considered her "family." In the memo she struck a tone that later was imitated by some black supporters of the textbooks, who used virtually her same language by referring to themselves, as she did, as a "citizen, educator and African American parent."

It was almost by accident, during a telephone call, that Waugh learned of King's memo; he wrote an article about it in the *San Francisco Examiner* (1990a, p. A1).[5] The newspaper stories that followed catapulted King and her views into the public eye and, more important, helped bolster groups of African Americans, Asian Americans, Muslims, and others around the state who had their own concerns about the textbooks.

The Muslim groups, mostly from the Los Angeles area, and a group of black parents and educators from the Sacramento area calling themselves TACTIC (Taxpayers Association Concerned about Truth In Curriculum), actually had organized themselves before the July public hearing and before they knew of King's memo. And King in fact had not met the organizers of these groups until the day of the July public hearing. "They didn't even know about my memo, and I didn't know about them," said King. "I mean, I felt so relieved when I saw them, but the Muslims had been organized for months!"

King said she had not intended the memo to be an organizing tool, but simply a personal statement:

> I look at the experience on the Curriculum Commission from a four-year perspective, and I was dug in with them for a long time, battling over things, it was like constant struggling to move just one small inch forward. So for me, the memo that I wrote was a release. It was cathartic, rather than a beginning point to open up something. For me, it was like leaving the plantation and, you know, thumbing your fingers at the ol' massa. You know, "I'm gone."
>
> . . . [T]his process of what I call "anointing" these books, with what I saw were serious flaws, it's like, you as a person feel like you are being compelled to . . . give [it] legitimacy. There's no way to participate with integrity. Because by participation, you are lending the authority of your own experience and reputation to a flawed outcome. . . . I didn't know whether or not they would adopt the books, I mean there's no way to know that. But I know that they were not going to be able to use my vote to do that. (interview, October 20, 1992)

King's July 11 memo (1990), addressed to Crabtree and Stage, stated her unwillingness to support a recommendation to adopt the Houghton Mifflin or the Holt, Rinehart and Winston textbooks. "Although aspects of these books are a great improvement over existing materials, I feel an ethical and moral responsibility to oppose the adoption of instructional materials which violate the dignity and worth of people in any way," she wrote, and continued:

> I have attached selected but representative examples from several books which illustrate the most egregious racial stereotyping, inaccuracies, distortions, omissions, justifications and trivialization of unethical and inhumane social practices, including racial slavery, that I, as a citizen, educator and African American parent, feel compelled to condemn. . . . As a result of such shortcomings, these books fail to meet the standards set by the California framework for cultural diversity, ethical literacy, historical accuracy, opportunities to examine controversial issues and to develop critical thinking and democratic social participation skills. These standards should not be compromised by content that distorts the diverse histories, cultural backgrounds and experiences of men, women and children.

The examples King (1990) cited were under three categories: "racial stereotyping," "inacurracies, distortions and omissions," and "justifications and trivialization of unethical and inhumane social practices, namely racial slavery" (attachment, p. 6).

In the context of this public controversy, which the Curriculum Commission certainly hadn't expected and which would not have been as heated without King's memo, the argument raised by King and likeminded critics in California, New York, and elsewhere was often reduced by their opponents to something separatist, centric, and cranky. King was discouraged by this response, but she decided that what it signified was that more work had to be done to educate the public.

In retrospect, King's decision to cite specific textual examples reflected an inherent problem faced by textbook critics: Policymakers, teachers, parents, news editors, all want to know what is wrong with a textbook, and invariably they want to have chapter-and-verse citations, which effectively shifts attention away from the overall narrative perspective and down to comparing pictures and paragraphs. King's opponents picked off each of her examples one by one, without addressing the broader challenge to perspective that Wynter elaborated in her critique.

This was true also of a far larger body of examples that originated from the Rochester, New York, school district, where teachers had reviewed the fifth grade Houghton Mifflin textbook, *America Will Be*. Ellen Swartz, coordinator of the Rochester school district's multicultural project, sent to the Curriculum Commission a critique citing 62 examples in which *America Will Be* failed to meet the Rochester district's multicultural criteria. Gary Nash, the book's co-author, responded to King's and Swartz's examples, rejecting most of them. Moreover, Nash complained that many of the specific examples were taken out of context and that the concerns raised were addressed elsewhere in the series. For instance, when Chinese American critics said there was no mention of the Chinese during the California Gold Rush in his eighth grade U.S. History textbook, Nash said there was plenty about the Chinese in California in his fourth grade book—missing or ignoring the obvious point that many students might not have had access to his book during the fourth grade. Nash also noted that "the critics fail to mention the positive and extensive treatment of the Chinese in grades 6 and 7" (Stage and Crabtree 1990b). Nash didn't mention that these grades offer world history courses and do not deal with the Chinese in America.

While both King and Nash were constrained by the particularism of example citation, Nash was able to use it to his advantage. He did not have to deal with the criticism of perspective raised by Wynter; as for the specific examples—68 in all from *America Will Be*—in most cases Nash ruled: "Text verified as accurate." (One of the few citations Nash and Houghton Mifflin agreed to change was one stating that John Wesley Powell and his men were the first to travel down the Colorado River the entire length of the Grand Canyon. The reference was amended to the "first white men.")

Crabtree dealt with the larger question of Eurocentric bias at a press conference on the day the textbooks were unanimously adopted by the state board by stating that that accusation was "simply not supported by the facts."

Nash, during the course of the controversy, became increasingly frustrated, and in public forums he took to introducing himself as the one-time UCLA faculty chairman of the Angela Davis Defense Committee, in order to remind people of his liberal credentials. His academic reputation had been established with books like *Red, White, and Black*, a study that examined colonial America through the convergence and experiences of the three races. In the introduction to the second edition (1982), Nash voiced the same criticisms that would haunt him in 1990. American historians, he wrote,

> have tried to provide a corrective to the white-oriented, hero-worshipping history of the high school textbooks. But in the main their efforts have amounted to little more than a restocking of the pantheon of national heroes with new figures whose skin is not so pale. . . . But has American history been rewritten if the revisionism consists primarily of turning a monochromatic cast of characters into a polychromatic one with the story line unchanged? . . . What is revisionist about a history that still measures all events of our past in terms of the values of white society, that views American history through an Anglo-American lens, and that regards Indians and Africans in the colonial period as inert masses whose fate was wholly determined by white settlers? (p. 2.)

In an August 1990 interview, Nash noted what he referred to as the "irony" of the situation:

> I've been attacked a lot from the other side for making too much of race, and for not including in what I write enough of the solid white well-known personages in our history books. So this is a little new for me, too, being attacked from the other side for downplaying race.

To the critics, the irony was that he did not fulfill the promise of *Red, White, and Black* in the school textbooks. But Nash said he was willing to "bear the full brunt of criticism" since he had had "full input" into the historical content of the textbooks. "I came in quite early in the process, early enough so the structuring of chapters, and the whole architecture of the book, was my responsibility," he said (interview, August 15, 1990).

Despite critiques by King and others, and a last-ditch request from the state's legislative Black Caucus to delay the vote in the slim hope that better textbooks could be found, the textbooks were recommended for adoption by the Curriculum Commission on July 20, 1990, by a 10–3 vote. Joining King in voting against recommendation were Roger Tom, director of curriculum for the San Francisco school district, and Charles Jackson, director of instruction for the Los Angeles Unified School District.

The vote was a foregone conclusion. King recalled one of her first commission meetings in Sacramento in 1986, when commissioners went out for dinner and King happened to sit next to Crabtree, who was also a new member but already actively involved in the development of the history–social science framework. "We sat next to each other, and she was telling me all about the Framework and how it was coming along and how great it was," said King:

> She mentioned this thing about immigrants. How the United States was a nation of immigrants. This was my first conversation with Charlotte. And I said, "But Charlotte, the United States isn't a nation of immigrants."

And she said, "Oh, but in Los Angeles we have all these Hispanic students and they're in the majority." And I said, "Well, regardless of who's
in the majority, African Americans are not immigrants and neither are
Native Americans."

It was just dinner conversation, and I didn't have a clue that this was
like a founding, cement block, that was being resurrected here [in 1990],
that would never be removed. Now I can look back and see that was
either part of the plan, or it was all working together for good, from their
perspective. The same thing when we had the trainers, when people [the
IMEP panelists] came to Sacramento for their training and here's Gil
Sewall, and [Paul] Gagnon—I had no idea that this was a network of
folks. (interview, October 6, 1992).

A GATHERING OF NEO-NATIVISTS

*A stress on "common culture" turns history into a tool of national unity,
mandated principally by those anxious about national order and coherence.*
  Nathan I. Huggins (1988)

The criticisms raised by King, Rochester's Swartz, and others were
met by an onslaught from neo-nativists and their sympathizers in the media.
Crabtree drew support from NEH head Lynne Cheney, her framework co-
writer Diane Ravitch, and the American Textbook Council—Gilbert Sewall's
operation, based in New York, which gained remarkably easy access to the
multicultural debate (see Chapter 1).

When the Los Angeles school board later approved the same textbooks,
Sewall (1991) gleefully reported in his *Social Studies Review* that the decision
in favor of Houghton Mifflin "leaves activists twisting in the wind and their
orchestrated attack on California's effort to improve the history curriculum
and social studies textbooks in shambles" (p. 11). California, he wrote, had
"demonstrated that cultural anger, group intimidation, and flimsy kinds of
historical revisionism do not necessarily sway steady minds" (p. 11).

Sewall also had little truck with multiculturalism and attempts to diver-
sify the canon or include more racial-ethnic representation in curriculum or
textbooks: "Weasel words like multiculturalism, self-esteem, canon, sensitivity, and diversity are no longer shining verbal talismans" (p. 10). Sewall
dismissed as passe the concerns of minorities such as those Chinese American teachers and parents in San Francisco who were despairing over the
continued failure of U.S. history textbooks to get beyond merely mentioning
that Chinese laborers contributed mightily to building the transcontinental
railroad. In an interview on March 8, 1990, he said:

No matter has received more attention than representation and balance
and inclusion of groups of formerly under-represented or ignored than
during the last 10 or 15 years. The issue is not a new issue. It is not an
issue of the '90's by any means. . . . I sometimes become weary of all the

attention paid to group representation in textbooks, and wish the general public, not to mention interested journalists, wanted to pay more attention to good writing, literary quality, and the issues that concern us all as Americans.

A week before the board's public hearing in September 1990, an Op-Ed Page commentary urging approval of the textbooks appeared in the *Los Angeles Times,* written by Diane Ravitch. Asserting that something happened that actually didn't, and implying that she'd been there to see it (she hadn't), Ravitch (1990) wrote of the critics who had appeared at a previous hearing in July before the Curriculum Commission: "Time and again, the refrain was heard that racial, religious and ethnic groups should have the power to judge and veto what is written about them." Ravitch called the textbook critics "special interest groups," an epithet that Honig also used dismissively (p. M5).

Ravitch joined the NEH's Lynne Cheney and Chester Finn, among others, in writing letters of support for the Houghton Mifflin series to the state board. Finn likened the issue facing the board to a virtual Armageddon.

> It is one thing to tell the "whole story," as I believe the California framework mandates and as the Houghton Mifflin books do with reasonable success. It is quite another to fragment the society into warring tribes. This is going to be the most contentious issue in American education in the 1990's, bar none. (Stage and Crabtree 1990b, Finn letter, August 7, 1990)

In her letter, Cheney said she had "used every opportunity to praise the new California Framework for the Study [*sic*] of History and the Social Sciences. It is, in my opinion, the best history/social science curriculum in the nation." As for the textbook adoption, she said that "what happens in your state will settle once and for all whether or not we are going to be able to teach our children history as it should be taught" (Stage and Crabtree 1990b, Cheney letter, September 13, 1990). For Cheney and others, California clearly became a rallying point.

Ravitch chastised textbook critics for pursuing "censorship and lies." She warned, "Today the loudest voices are those who have no sense of the common good, who want only to divide our nation into antagonistic racial and ethnic groups" (Stage and Crabtree 1990b, Ravitch letter, August 7, 1990).

All of these letters were attached to the Curriculum Commission's submission to the board. The submission contained no letters in opposition. King received several from prominent black scholars around the country, but copies apparently were never sent to the commission.

Three statements may sum up the disparate views that swirled around the textbook adoption. One came at the board's public hearing, from Jessea Greenman, co-chair of the Gay and Lesbian Alliance Against Defamation: "When we read your books, it is like looking in a mirror and not seeing ourselves reflected" (Stage and Crabtree 1990b, statement, September 13, 1990).

Another came from Henry Der, executive director of Chinese for Affirmative Action, a San Francisco civil rights organization:

> While, in comparison to existing textbooks, the recommended textbooks make progress in promoting student understanding of the fundamental issues and ethical dilemmas that have contributed to the development of our nation, to a large extent, these textbooks maintain a dominant, Eurocentric perspective at the exclusion of some racial, ethnic groups like Chinese Americans. (letter of September 7, 1990 to Joseph Carrabino, president of the California State Board of Education)

The third statement was released by Crabtree at a news conference an hour before the board's September hearing: "The materials recommended by the Commission represent a new generation of materials that are far superior to those in wide use throughout the nation."

In the context of this controversy, the gap between the views expressed by textbook critics and Crabtree was perhaps irreconcilable; it was Crabtree's position that prevailed. Crabtree, however, could not have succeeded without the support of Honig, others on the commission, and members of the board itself, nearly all of whom were appointed by the governor. The extent of this support became very clear at the news conference held an hour *before* the board's 1 P.M. public hearing September 13, 1990. The news conference was hosted by President Joseph Carrabino, Crabtree, another board member, two other members of the Curriculum Commission, two Houghton Mifflin textbook authors, a Houghton Mifflin representative, and two African American Studies professors flown in by Houghton Mifflin from East Coast colleges to testify in favor of the textbooks. The purpose of the news conference, said Carrabino, was to describe to reporters the neutrality and thoroughness of the review process and to demonstrate how superior the Houghton Mifflin books were in their inclusion of cultural diversity compared with textbooks then in use. Peach, green, pink, and blue sheets were passed out, each briefly highlighting examples showing how the Houghton Mifflin textbooks handled slavery and diversity, and contrasting the number of pages dealing with such topics in the Houghton Mifflin books with the number of pages in other texts then in use. For instance, with regard to slavery, the blue sheet noted that Houghton Mifflin had "at least 34 pages devoted to the topic of slavery in grade 5," contrasted with other texts: "Pages devoted to slavery in various texts are 3 pages, 12 pages, 14 pages." On Native Americans: "35 pages devoted to an in-depth study of history related to Native American Indians in grade 5," contrasted to then-current texts: "pages devoted to Native American Indians in various texts: 5 pages, 17 pages."

As Crichlow, Goodwin, Shakes, and Swartz (1990) observed: "The quantifiable approach is the most comfortable for publishers and educators who seek to compensate for longstanding omission and misrepresentation. . . . [It] masks itself as social justice in the curriculum" (pp. 102–103).

The 70 or so textbook critics who came to testify at the hearing an hour later went through the motions, but some who were aware of the news conference realized they were wasting their breath: "It becomes very suspect when the Board holds a press conference in advance of the hearing to say that they like the textbooks," said Henry Der. "That renders comments at the public hearing moot and inconsequential" (October 14, 1990, p. B5).

Apple (1991) has observed the evolution of state control in the South through the process of an *accord:* "historic compromise in which dominant groups maintain much of their economic, political, and cultural power by incorporating under their own leadership parts of the perspectives of competing or dispossessed groups" (p. 20). But in California there was no accord, or compromise, entered into voluntarily by the hundreds of people who actively opposed the textbooks in Sacramento and later in local districts around the state. What was compromised was a vision that could lead to a transforming of America. In its place was incorporated a modest multiculturalism, representing an outright co-optation, disenfranchisement, and apparent victory by the neo-nativist enthusiasts in their effort to contain and control the future course of California's social studies curriculum and textbooks—and perhaps of those beyond the state's borders as well.

King saw the state's victory as a limited one. "The most important issues were not the books themselves; the most important issues are the concepts that produced the problems with the books," she said in October, 1992:

> And Sylvia's essay [Wynter's critique] makes an alternative way to understand these concepts available to people in a really visceral way, that once you understand it, you can't go back to blitheness and unawareness. People got informed and participated on the basis of that new level of information, and that's education, and it can't be stopped, it can't be turned around.

REFERENCES

Alexander, Francie, and Charlotte Crabtree. 1988. California's new history–social science curriculum promises richness and depth. *Educational Leadership* (September): 10–13.

American Indian Historical Society. 1970. *Textbooks and the American Indian.* Rupert Costo, editor, and Jeannette Henry, writer. San Francisco: Indian Historian Press.

Apple, Michael W. 1991. Regulating the text: The socio-historical roots of state control. Pp. 7–26 in *Textbooks in American Society,* Philip G. Altbach, Gail P. Kelly, Hugh G. Petrie, and Lois Weis, eds. New York: State University of New York Press.

Armento, Beverly J., Gary B. Nash, Christopher L. Salter, and Karen K. Wixson. 1991. *A more perfect union.* Boston: Houghton Mifflin.

———. 1991. *America will be.* Boston: Houghton Mifflin.

Crichlow, Warren, Susan Goodwin, Gaya Shakes, and Ellen Swartz. 1990. Multicultural ways of knowing: Implications for practice. *Journal of Education* 172 (2): 101–117.

Grant, S. G. 1991. The California history–social science framework: A study in the de-professionalization of teachers. *Journal of Curriculum and Supervision* 6 (3): 213–221.

History-Social Science Curriculum Framework and Criteria Committee. 1988. *History-Social Science Framework.*

Huggins, Nathan I. 1988. American history and the idea of common culture. Pp. 115–123 in *History in the schools: What shall we teach?* Bernard R. Gifford, ed. New York: Macmillan.

Humanities magazine. 1990. A conversation with . . . Charlotte A. Crabtree. As interviewed by Lynne V. Cheney (November–December): pp. 4–8.

Kang, K. Connie, and Dexter Waugh. 1990. Minority students feel like outsiders who were robbed of their past. *San Francisco Examiner* (May 6): pp. A1, 14.

King, Joyce E. 1990. Memo to California Curriculum Development and Supplemental Materials Commission (July 11): attachment, pp. 1–6.

Ladson-Billings, Gloria. 1992. Distorting democracy: An ethnographic view of the California history–social science textbook adoption process. Paper presented at meeting of the American Education Research Association.

Leo, John. 1989. On education. Teaching history the way it happened. *U.S. News & World Report* (November 27): p. 73.

Machiavelli, Niccolo. 1950. *The prince and the discourses.* New York: Random House.

Maxey, Phyllis F. 1988. The California history framework: Whose story? *Social Studies Review* 28 (1): 31–37.

Nash, Gary B. 1982 *Red, white, and black: The peoples of early America*, 2d ed. Englewood Cliffs, N.J.: Prentice-Hall.

Oliner, Pearl M. 1988. What's wrong with the new framework? Some preliminary thoughts. *Social Studies Review* 28 (1): 27–30.

PACE (Policy Analysis for California Education). 1991. Conditions of education in California 1990. Berkeley: University of California, School of Education.

Ramirez, Raul. 1990. Students feel unprepared for life in a multicultural society. *San Francisco Examiner* (May 7): pp. A1, 8.

Ravitch, Diane. 1990. The troubled road to California's new history textbooks. *Los Angeles Times* (September 2): p. M5.

Reinhold, Robert. 1991. Class struggle. *New York Times Magazine* (September 29): pp. 26–29, 46–47, 52.

Sewall, Gilbert. The multiculture watch. *Social Studies Review* (Spring): 10–11.

Sleeter, Christine E. 1992. The white ethnic experience in America: To whom does it generalize? *Educational Researcher* (January–February): 33–36.

Stage, Elizabeth, and Charlotte Crabtree. 1990a. Adoption recommendations of the Curriculum Development and Supplemental Materials Commission to the State Board of Education. 1990. Sacramento: California State Department of Education.

———— and ————. 1990b. Summary of public comments, to members of the State Board of Education (October 5).

Takaki, Ronald. 1990. Quoted by Dexter Waugh in North Beach in transition: Influx of Chinese producing hostility. *San Francisco Examiner* (February 19): pp. A1, 12.

Waugh, Dexter. 1990a. Official rips textbooks under review. *San Francisco Examiner* (July 18): p. A1.

————. 1990b. Special interests criticize state textbooks. *San Francisco Examiner* (July 19): p. A9.

————. 1990c. Questions raised in textbook vote. *San Francisco Examiner* (July 29): p. B3.

Wynter, Sylvia. 1990. Letter to California State Board of Education members, September 9. Enclosure 1: America as a "World": A black studies perspective and "cultural model" framework, pp. 1–26. Enclosure 2: A cultural model critique of the textbook *America will be*, pp. 1–62.

———. 1992. *"Do not call us Negros": How "multicultural" textbooks perpetuate racism.* San Francisco: Aspire Books.

NOTES

1. California's textbook adoption process for history–social studies textbooks followed criteria for evaluating instructional materials that were included in the *History–Social Science Framework* adopted by the state board of education in July 1987. The board's curriculum commission "produced an evaluation instrument that incorporated both analytic and holistic judgments on criteria which reflected the distinguishing characteristics" of the framework. In 1989 the commission developed "quality indicators consisting of descriptors differentiating materials that showed exceptionally high correlation with these criteria, those that showed moderate correlation, and those with poor correlation." The commission then screened and appointed 53 educators and academics to the Instructional Materials Evaluation Panel (IMEP), of which approximately 30 percent were racial and ethnic minorities. The IMEP underwent a training session during the third week of March 1990. Each panelist received review copies of all textbooks submitted for adoption beginning in April. In May panelists attended publishers' presentations, "where a formal information exchange occurred between the evaluators and publishers' representatives." During the week of June 24–29, the IMEP met to review and recommend or reject the publishers' textbooks. The three subpanels (K-3; U.S. history 4-5-8; and world history 6-7) produced one consensus report for each grade-level program, detailing the panel's findings and rationale for recommending or not recommending each textbook. The IMEP report then went to the Curriculum Commission, which held a public hearing and voted in July; the commission's recommendations went to the state board in September, when a public hearing was held, and a final board vote was taken in October (all quotes from Stage and Crabtree, 1990a, pp. 4–6).
2. Wynter's critique reappeared in 1992, published by John Templeton's Aspire Books: *"Do Not Call Us Negros": How "Multicultural" Textbooks Perpetuate Racism* (1992).
3. As elsewhere in the field of education policy, nothing is "final" in California: Frameworks have been routinely updated or drastically revamped every seven years or so since the 1950s, and the *History–Social Science Framework* was to undergo review again in 1994.
4. Kirk Ankeney, a classroom teacher from the San Diego Unified School District who was on Ladson-Billing's 4-5-8 subpanel, had a different reaction: "When I heard the whole [Houghton Mifflin] series was driven by Gary Nash, and Gary Nash works with Charlotte Crabtree, I said, 'Hell, this guy ought to know more than anybody what these books ought to look like.' There's nothing wrong with that." Ankeney said he "never heard" Crabtree mention Houghton Mifflin "as an example of a company doing a lot for the new framework. She'd mentioned Nash once in a while because she considers him a pre-eminent historian, and I'd say he probably is one of the top colonial historians" (interview, July 1990). Ankeney later became a member of the Curriculum Task Force of the National History Standards Project co-directed by Charlotte Crabtree and Gary Nash.

5. Because the *Examiner* had spent a significant amount of money on the survey of high-school seniors mentioned previously and its editors had made a commitment to follow the entire 1990 textbook adoption process, the story of King's memo received better news play, on page 1, than it might have otherwise, since commission activities rarely if ever received media attention. The story's prominence might have influenced decisions by other news media to begin covering the textbook controversy.

4
New York:
Extending America

Since the 1960s . . . a profound reorientation of the self-image of Americans has been underway. . . . Previous ideals of assimilation to an Anglo-American model have been put in question and are now slowly and sometimes painfully being set aside. . . . many in the United States—from European and non-European backgrounds—have been encouraging a more tolerant, inclusive, and realistic vision of American identity than any that has existed in the past.

This identity, committed to the democratic principles of the nation [is evolving] toward a new model marked by respect for pluralism and awareness of the virtues of diversity. This situation is a current reality, and a multicultural education, anchored to the shared principles of a liberal democracy, is today less an educational innovation than a national priority.

. . . Two centuries after this country's founders issued a Declaration of Independence . . . the time has come to recognize cultural interdependence. *We propose that the principle of respect for diverse cultures is critical to our nation, and we affirm that a right to cultural diversity exists. We believe that the schoolroom is one of the places where this cultural* interdependence *must be reflected.*

One Nation, Many Peoples: A Declaration of Cultural Interdependence (1991), pp. xi–xii

In the four years between the summers of 1987 and 1991 New York State education policy with respect to K–12 social studies curriculum changed significantly in the direction of transformative multiculturalism despite substantial opposition within the state and on the national scene. The reform movement was initiated and sustained by the new Commissioner of Education, Thomas Sobol. Without his persistence it is unlikely that New York would have taken what, at the time, were seen as bold steps toward teaching more of the stories of more of America's peoples to New York's students. There were three phases of policy activity associated with three statewide appointed committees:

1987–1989   Task Force on Minorities produces *A Curriculum of Inclusion*

1990–1991   Social Studies Review and Development Committee produces *One Nation, Many Peoples*, leading to adoption of the "Understanding Diversity" policy

1992–1994   Social Studies Curriculum and Assessment Committee produces learning outcome statements [renamed "Content and Performance Standards"] and a revised curriculum framework for New York's social studies program, based on "Understanding Diversity" and the state's education reform program, "A New Compact for Learning"

After briefly recounting the controversy surrounding *A Curriculum of Inclusion* (1989) as prologue, we focus on the experience of the Social Studies Review and Development Committee, commonly known as the Review Committee, as a case of policy-in-the-making. Our story highlights the political process and the intersection of the broader America debate with the policy deliberations. The third phase of New York's multicultural politics and policy activity is taken up in Chapter 5.

In 1987 the official New York State policy with respect to multiculturalism was expressed in the Regents' Goals for Elementary and Secondary School Students (Regents Action Plan 1984). That policy can be characterized as individualistic. It called for individual student knowledge, understanding, appreciation, and respect for "the diversity of cultural heritages" (goal 3.6); "political, economic, and social institutions and procedures in this country and in other countries" (goal 4); and "people of different race; sex; ability; cultural heritage; national origin; religion; and political, economic, and social background, and their values, beliefs and attitudes" (goal 6). Individual knowledge and respect for other individuals are to improve human relations; we are to get along better if not love one another and live happily ever after. There is nothing explicit here about structural inequalities or institutionalized racism—or about what history is to be taught or how it is to be taught.

In a less well publicized and not yet fully implemented policy statement about at-risk students, the regents also mandated that "Educational programs, services and staff must respect and represent the cultural, racial, social, economic and language background of the students served" (Youth Placed At-Risk 1989). This policy statement begins to recognize that increasing numbers of students represent the "others" whom the 1984 Regents' Goals say "we" are to become knowledgeable about and to respect. It is not until the 1991 policy statement, "Understanding Diversity," that the "we" is extended to include all Americans in our considerable diversity and that structural inequities are acknowledged and addressed.

While the "Understanding Diversity" policy adopted in July 1991, based on the *One Nation, Many Peoples* report quoted above, has not yet been put into operation, its existence became a potentially powerful symbol, and the

highly publicized process by which it came into being sensitized both educators and the general public to the issues—and contributed to polarizing
opposing factions. There is evidence that local schools and districts acted to
make their social studies programs more multicultural independent of state-
level policy initiatives as well as in anticipation of state policy implementation. What follows is the often-turbulent story of that policy-in-the-making.

PROLOGUE: CREATING *A CURRICULUM OF INCLUSION*

In 1987, about the time that California's new *History–Social Science
Framework*, refined by Diane Ravitch and Charlotte Crabtree, was being
adopted by the State Board of Education, New York's Board of Regents was
appointing a new Commissioner of Education to head the New York State
Education Department (SED).[1] This was the bicentennial year of the U.S.
Constitution as well as the year in which the Bradley Commission on History
in Schools was formed, E. D. Hirsch published *Cultural Literacy*, and Ravitch
and Finn published *What Do Our 17-Year-Olds Know?* based on a survey of
students' knowledge of history and literature supported by the National
Endowment for the Humanities.

The appointment of Thomas Sobol, then superintendent of schools in
Scarsdale, Westchester County, did not please those legislators and others
who had pushed for a "minority" commissioner. One of Sobol's first acts,
"partly in response to questions and criticisms by minority legislators and
others" ("Understanding Diversity," 1991, p. 1), was to create the Task Force
on Minorities, chaired by Hazel N. Dukes, president of the New York chapter
of the National Association for the Advancement of Colored People (NAACP).
The task force was charged with reviewing department personnel policies and
practices as well as the state's syllabi and instructional materials to determine
how well they reflected the pluralistic nature of American society.[2] As with
California's frameworks, New York's syllabi are guidelines for school districts
and teachers that are not mandatory but generally are followed because state
tests are based on them.[3] Unlike California, New York does not adopt textbooks on a statewide basis.

Two years later, in July 1989, the minority task force produced what was
to become a hotly debated report, *A Curriculum of Inclusion*, which addressed
the second part of the charge, with a focus on social studies education. Its
principal author was task force member Harry L. Hamilton, then of the
Department of Atmospheric Sciences, State University of New York (SUNY)
at Albany.[4]

A Curriculum of Inclusion noted improvements in New York's syllabi
and instructional materials toward meeting the regents' call for understanding, respect, and acceptance of diverse people and cultures. It found,
however, that the materials failed to "adequately and accurately reflect
the cultural experience in America" (Task Force on Minorities 1989, p.
16). Most of the report's nine recommendations addressed materials and

staff development necessary to realize "inclusion," which was symbolized as a round table:

> European culture is likened to the master of a house ruling over a dinner table, himself firmly established at the head of the table and all other cultures being guests some distance down the table from the master, who has invited the others through his beneficence. . . . the new model is likened to the fabled Round Table of King Arthur, with all cultures offering something to the collective good, each knowing and respecting others, and each gaining from the contribution of others; no culture is master of the new table. (p. iv)

Ignoring the reference to English mytho-history, the neo-nativist critics said that the round table implied that all cultures had contributed equally to America, which they then said was a distortion of fact. *A Curriculum of Inclusion* drew the same sort of complaints and dire warnings of balkanization as those heard in California a year later. California's schools chief Bill Honig joined in too, calling the New York report "nothing but racism" (Fiske 1990), while Gilbert Sewall's *Social Studies Review* (1990) called it "an angry, ignorant, polemical document" (p. 11).

The furor in both the public media and professional circles stemmed from one or more factors, including:

1. Its so-called inflammatory language; for example: "African Americans, Asian Americans, Puerto Ricans/Latinos, and Native Americans have all been the victims of a cultural oppression and stereotyping that has characterized institutions—including the educational institutions—of the United States and the European American world for centuries." (p. 6)
2. The composition of the 17-member task force (one white member and no historians).
3. The perceived threat of social fragmentation inferred from the report's four separate appendices, each of which presented an analysis of New York State syllabi and other instructional materials from the point of view of a different group—African Americans, Asian Americans, Puerto Ricans/Latinos, Native Americans.
4. The retention by the task force of controversial Afrocentric spokesperson Leonard Jeffries as one of four consultants.
5. The unwillingness of critics to take seriously the report's legitimate claims and conclusions.

In the conservative political climate of the late 1980s *A Curriculum of Inclusion* came to be seen as another attack on traditional American history and historians, and on the so-called canon of Western civilization. It clearly challenged the version of cultural literacy and the vision of America espoused by national figures such as William Bennett, Lynne Cheney, Chester Finn, Diane Ravitch, and Arthur Schlesinger Jr. by calling on students to learn a wider range of "facts" and to consider various different perspectives.

The report, as its title indicates, was a call for inclusion foremost, but in that inclusion could be seen the beginnings of a transformation. It is not clear what most upset those who objected to the report—the assertive language, the call for inclusion, or the hint of a transformation into a new America— all of which demanded responsive change. A number of historians and educators in New York seemed interested in maintaining the status quo—or, as they would say, preserving the nation—in the face of a rapidly growing immigrant population.

A Curriculum of Inclusion appeared at a time when the eastern bloc and Soviet Union were disintegrating, when large numbers of Asian and Central American immigrants were entering the United States, when U.S. students were faring poorly in international comparisons of achievement test scores, and when the U.S. position in the world economy was slipping. For those who already felt threatened by social, economic, and demographic changes, *A Curriculum of Inclusion* was anathema. For the report's authors and support-ers, the status quo was anathema. Both sides engaged in a rhetoric of crisis, doom, and salvation.

Sobol's attempt to improve the state's education programs for elementary and secondary school students as well as to gain "minority" support for his efforts created a maelstrom, especially in the state's opinion centers from Long Island to Albany. Faced with sometimes-vicious opposition from neo-nativists, newspapers such as the *New York Post*, and conservative state legis-lators, Sobol and the Board of Regents bided their time. The *New York Post*, for example, opened an editorial on August 4, 1989 as follows: "Pronounce-ments from the office of State Commissioner of Education Thomas Sobol are beginning to sound more and more as if they were written by Angela Davis."

In reflecting on these events three years later, Sobol commented that, because urban and minority students had not been well served by the public schools of New York State, he thought it was desirable to "let a lot of voices be heard," including those that created *A Curriculum of Inclusion*, before proposing any statewide education policy changes. As a result, he said, he incited the wrath of the "politically right [sic]." *A Curriculum of Inclusion* was an advisory report that resulted in the press "beating up on us," he said, for something SED had not in fact done. Indicating the extent of opposition from the press, he referred specifically to a meeting with the *New York Times* editorial board at which he was chastised "for having permitted this out-rage." He should have repudiated the report, they said. Now, Sobol contin-ued, they were holding him responsible for the angry debate, for upsetting people (interview, August 4, 1992).

In fact, Sobol had been upsetting New Yorkers who were content with the status quo for some time before the appearance of *A Curriculum of Inclu-sion*. Annually, New York's education commissioner submits "A Report to the Governor and Legislature on the Educational Status of the State's Schools," which is largely a statistical profile. In his preface to the report submitted in December 1988, after his first full year as commissioner, Sobol echoed the Kerner report (*Report of the National Advisory Commission on Civil*

Disorders, 1968) in highlighting the divided condition of New York's public
school system:

> The picture which the report's data display is one of two contrasting
> systems—one largely suburban, white, affluent, and successful; and the
> other largely urban, of color, poor, and failing. The many individual
> exceptions do not dispel the pattern. It is a situation which all people
> must view with alarm. (*New York, The State of Learning* 1988, p. i)

Sobol continued by citing a "pattern of failure," most evident in New
York's large cities and poor rural areas, a pattern characterized by failure to
acquire the knowledge and skill needed to function in U.S. society, by drop-
ping out of school, and by consignment to a "socioeconomic underclass"
where young people "face dismal personal lives and constitute a growing
threat to the well-being of the total society." This pattern, he noted, is

> clearly associated with poverty and with race. The students whom our
> system fails are disproportionately poor and minority. . . . And yet, these
> students most in need frequently lack access to an equitable share of the
> State's educational resources.
>   Ever since my appointment as Commissioner a year and a half ago, I
> have been warning of the crisis that impends in our failure to educate
> alarmingly large numbers of our children, particularly in our cities. . . .
> [At which time he said] A civilized people cannot tolerate this waste of
> human lives. Twenty years ago the Kerner Commission warned that we
> were becoming two societies, separate and unequal. That threat is just as
> real today. (p. i)

And Sobol has continued to reiterate this theme.[5] When *A Curriculum of
Inclusion* appeared in July 1989, many New Yorkers apparently saw it as
more unwanted bad news from the commissioner, and they personalized
their opposition by labeling it, disparagingly, "the Sobol report." Among the
few visible signs of support for more multicultural curriculum knowledge in
New York social studies programs were an October 1989 resolution of the
New York State School Boards Association calling for increased attention to
multicultural studies in the schools and a November 1989 resolution of the
New York City Board of Education calling for development of a comprehensive multicultural education plan.

TRANSITION: 1989–1990

Shortly after the report's release in July 1989, Sobol proposed a plan
for statewide review of *A Curriculum of Inclusion* and for regents action by
January 1990. Instead, little or no public action was taken by the commissioner's office until February 1990, when the regents approved Sobol's recommendation that he and his staff develop a plan for increasing students'

understanding of American history and culture, of the history and culture of the diverse groups which comprise American society today, and of the history and culture of other peoples throughout the world. (memo to Board of Regents, February 2, 1990, p. 2)

In a subsequent public memo, Sobol officially distanced himself and the regents from some of the report's language, assertions, and recommendations, while standing behind its "central message" that the schools should be more inclusive in teaching about American and world history and cultures. He denied that his plan of action entailed rewriting or distorting history or would "diminish the importance of our western heritage and values," or would "lead to a fragmentation of our society" as claimed by his critics (memo to Interested Persons, February 22, 1990, pp. 4–5).

The seemingly moderate tenor of this memo and subsequent statements from the commissioner's office is well captured in the following excerpt from his memo of February 22, 1990:

We cannot understand our complex society without understanding the history and culture of its major ethnic and cultural components. We face a paradox: only through understanding our diverse roots and branches can we fully comprehend the whole. Only by accommodating our differences can we become one society. Only by exploring our human variations can we apprehend our common humanity. (p. 2)

In April 1990 the Board of Regents announced a second round of social studies syllabus review and revision that would be "thoughtful, scholarly, and apolitical" ("Item for Action," April 16, 1990, p. 1). With one major exception, a research-development-dissemination model of curriculum change, similar to that typically employed by SED, was proposed. That exception was the composition and means of selection of the Review Committee. It would be larger than usual, would include "scholars and teachers who represent the ethnic and cultural groups under consideration" (p. 2), and, unlike most prior SED committees, would be approved by the Board of Regents. An intricate process for selecting this second committee began in May 1990.

In June, before the appointment of the new Review Committee, Diane Ravitch and Arthur Schlesinger Jr. co-authored a "Statement of the Committee of Scholars in Defense of History," which originally appeared in *Newsday* and subsequently was reprinted elsewhere.[6] In their statement, which was signed by 26 other scholars, they expressed their concern about "the proposed revision of the State of New York's history curriculum" and their intent to "constitute ourselves as a professional review committee to monitor and assess the work of the Commissioner's panel." In other words, they set "scholars" like themselves as the proper authorities to judge what constitutes appropriate knowledge for inclusion in history–social studies curriculum.

The Committee of Scholars' concerns were based on their interpretations of *A Curriculum of Inclusion*—substantially different from Sobol's—as well as the lack of a historian among its authors and the possibility that the new review committee "might end up with only one historian." Illustrative of their rendering of *A Curriculum of Inclusion,* the Committee of Scholars asserted:

> The report, a polemical document, viewed division into racial groups as the basic analytical framework for an understanding of American history. It showed no understanding of the integrity of history as an intellectual discipline based on commonly accepted standards of evidence. . . . We condemn the reduction of history to ethnic cheerleading on the demand of pressure groups. . . . We have further concern: The commissioner of education's task force contemptuously dismisses the Western tradition. . . . And little can have more damaging effect on the republic than the use of the school system to promote the division of our people into antagonistic racial groups.

These assertions represent a curious mix of scholarly indignation and self-interest—indignation that their views were not reflected in the report and interest in seeing more historians, presumably historians who shared their views, involved in shaping curriculum knowledge. The statement may well have had an influence on the selection of members of the Review Committee (four university historians were appointed, including Schlesinger, who agreed to serve as a consultant to the committee, but not as a regular member).

The statement also reflected a seeming contradiction in the position of neo-nativists. On the one hand they argued that the selection of curriculum knowledge should have historical integrity and represent high standards of historical scholarship. "We steadfastly oppose the politicization of history, no matter how worthy the motive." On the other they urgently appealed for a curriculum that unites America's peoples—presumably also a political act, no matter how worthy. Ravitch, for example, is reported to have told an American Federation of Teachers audience in 1991:

> A historic mission of the public school is to teach civic virtue and citizenship and to create a community and common culture for people of varied backgrounds. Appeals to race consciousness, group pride and a multiracial, multi-ethnic society are socially divisive. (Ravitch, cited in AFT 1991)

And Schlesinger (1991) warned in *The Disuniting of America,* a critique of Afrocentrism and New York's multicultural efforts: "The national ideal had once been *e pluribus unum.* Are we now to belittle *unum* and glorify *pluribus?* Will the center hold? or will the melting pot yield to the Tower of Babel?" (p. 2) In contrast to Ravitch, however, he did acknowledge that this "debate about the curriculum is a debate about what it means to be an American. What is ultimately at stake is the shape of the American future" (p. 3).

The Committee of Scholars issued no further statements. Ravitch and Schlesinger continued to be highly visible in opposition to the work of the Review Committee and multiculturalism in general. Earlier, Ravitch herself had complained about knowledge becoming politicized, fearing that truth would depend on who is in power" (Berger 1990).

Meanwhile, in July 1990, with the advice of Sobol and his staff, the Board of Regents selected a review committee of "eminent scholars and educators . . . distinguished scholars and teachers in relevant fields who represent a diversity of views and backgrounds" (press release, July 27, 1990, p. 1) from more than 300 nominees.[7] The committee's charge was

> to review existing State social studies syllabi and to make recommenda-
> tions to the Commissioner designed to increase students' understanding
> of American culture and its history; the cultures, identities, and histories
> of the diverse groups which comprise American society today; and the
> cultures, identities, and histories of other peoples throughout the world.
> (Social Studies Review and Development Committee Charge, September
> 1990)

Seemingly in an effort to clarify the committee's role, the charge ended with the statement that committee "recommendations to the Commissioner will be made public and will be given great weight. However, final authority for making policy decisions on these matters remains with the New York State Board of Regents."

Since it is this committee's report, *One Nation, Many Peoples*, that resulted in the new state multicultural education policy, "Understanding Diversity," in July 1991, and it is this committee of which co-author Cornbleth was a member, our account of this part of the New York story is largely an insider's participant-observer view—that is, close up, more detailed, and necessarily personalized.[8]

CREATING *ONE NATION, MANY PEOPLES*

Buffalo is far removed from New York State's opinion centers along the Albany–Long Island axis, although less than 300 miles actually separate Albany and Buffalo—and the canal towpath is used regularly by hikers and bicyclists. From downstaters' perspective, Buffalo might as well be part of Ontario or Ohio. Although Buffalo is New York's second-largest city, with significant economic and social problems that refuse easy resolution, the scale of problems is much smaller and the pace of everyday life much slower than in New York City.

For these reasons and perhaps also because Buffalo has only one daily newspaper, the downstate multicultural wars have appeared as occasional skirmishes in western New York. An African and African American History Infusion Project has been under way in the Buffalo public schools for several years, and the University at Buffalo (UB, the State University of New York system's largest and "flagship" campus) has established undergraduate courses in American Pluralism and World Civilization without major protest. In part because multiculturalism has been a less pervasive, less angry issue in

Buffalo, its contentiousness elsewhere in New York State has been quite striking.

By May 1990, after four years in New York on the faculty at UB, Cornbleth had read *A Curriculum of Inclusion* and had heard that there was to be a second, more cautiously selected social studies committee. Given her background in social studies education, her work on curriculum practice and change, and her growing interest in New York State's education politics, she intended to follow the policy process from a distance with more or less scholarly detachment. Instead, she was appointed to the Review Committee—as one of two representatives from western New York, the only university faculty member working full time in education rather than in history or one of the social sciences, and the only female full professor.

The committee selection process was significant insofar as it illustrated the caution of Sobol and the regents following the hullabaloo occasioned by the prior Task Force on Minorities and the effort to make this second committee something special. The aura and feeling of specialness was intended, it seems, both to foster more positive public response to the Review Committee's work and to encourage committee members to take their charge seriously and carry it off successfully. Playing up the committee was evident in the deference with which nominees and then members were treated by SED staff and in SED press releases, which called them "eminent scholars and educators," "distinguished scholars and teachers," and "recognized experts" ("Board of Regents Selects Committee to Oversee Project for Understanding Diversity," SED press release, July 27, 1990).

Cornbleth's direct involvement began with a phone call on May 16, 1990, from SED's Social Studies Bureau asking if she would agree to be one of the bureau's nominees for the Review Committee. She agreed. The chief of the bureau explained that this was only a nomination and that a steering committee would sort through the nominees and select three names per position on the eventual committee of about 20 to submit to the Commissioner and Board of Regents. (The positions were described as elementary-, middle-, and high-school social studies teachers; social studies supervisors; school administrators; university-level teacher educators; and university scholars in history and the social sciences.)

Nearly two months and several phone conversations later, the Board of Regents appointed Cornbleth to the Review Committee along with 22 others. On August 3, 1990, a letter followed from Commissioner Sobol. It described the committee's

> vital and central role in the Regents project to strengthen students' understanding of one another, of U.S. history and culture—including the parts played by the diverse racial and ethnic groups in our society—and of the history and culture of other nations of the world. (p. 1)

Among the most prominent university scholars who attended at least one of the committee's meetings were sociologist Nathan Glazer of Harvard, psychologist Edmund Gordon (then) of Yale, historian Kenneth Jackson of

Columbia, political scientist Ali Mazrui of SUNY at Binghamton, and historian Arthur Schlesinger Jr., then of CUNY. Historian Paul Gagnon and sociologist Lloyd Rogler withdrew from the committee; educational psychologist Asa Hilliard of Georgia State was unable to attend meetings but did not formally withdraw.

Overall, five of the 13 university members of the committee were from public universities (SUNY or CUNY), and four were female. In contrast, four of the seven teachers but none of the four supervisors or administrators were female; only one elementary or secondary representative was from a private school. Half of the 24 were European Americans (compared with one of the 17 members on the prior minority task force); six were African American, four were Hispanic, and the group also included one Asian American and one Native American. The nine European American males were the largest subgroup. All the members were school or university people; there were no representatives of government, business, the general public, or professional organizations. So, in composition, this was a broadly representative committee of educators and scholars.

The commissioner and regents hoped that a highly touted "blue ribbon" committee would be respected and that its recommendations would be taken seriously. This would both continue the process of making social studies curriculum more multicultural and ward off criticism from a range of actual and potential opponents. A slow, deliberate, and "apolitical" process presumably would allow time for tensions to ease and a wise course of action to emerge.

The neo-nativists, however, were not reassured. Before the first of the committee's seven meetings, in September 1990, several members received copies of a book chapter authored by a conservative British academic ten years earlier that was highly critical of committee member Ali Mazrui. Attached to the copy was a printed card reading "Compliments of Diane Ravitch." On August 12 Albert Shanker, president of the American Federation of Teachers, reprinted the June 29, 1990 "Statement of the Committee of Scholars in Defense of History" in his paid "Where We Stand" column in the *New York Times* under the heading "Remaking New York's History Curriculum." In an August 13 letter to Review Committee members about the Shanker column, Sobol commented that

> making America's ethnic and cultural diversity the asset it can be is a difficult but crucial undertaking. I agree with Professors Ravitch and Schlesinger that the state history curriculum should "reflect honest and conscientious scholarship and accurately portray the forging of this nation from the experiences of many different groups and peoples." This end will be more readily accomplished when we are prepared to listen well to one another and to acknowledge the good faith of those involved in the effort. (p. 2)

Sobol's wish was not to be realized. A harbinger of that came during dinner at the committee's first meeting, when consultant Schlesinger commented

that there was no significant connection between American blacks today
and African history or culture. He dismissed the African legacy as "tribalism,
slavery, and tyranny."

That first committee meeting, September 16–17, 1990, was noteworthy
for the serious tone that was struck—in large part by Sobol's opening remarks at the first evening's dinner and Ed Gordon's presentation about
cultural diversity and hegemony—and the efforts of co-chairs Gordon and
Fran Roberts to encourage all of the committee members, with their diverse
positions and concerns, to feel welcome and to learn from one another, to
create a new path rather than push their various perspectives.[9] Also significant in retrospect were various efforts to get to know one another. It was not
yet time to roll up one's sleeves and get to work.

One instance of getting to know one another and looking for connections
was a result of Cornbleth's having learned that the sister of one of her UB
colleagues also had been appointed to the Review Committee. She and
Susan Sagor, a history and literature teacher at The Brearley School in
Manhattan, sought each other out that first evening and sat talking after
dinner, about Susan's knowing Tom Sobol through her friendship with his
wife, Harriet, and about apparent divisions within SED and the Social Studies Bureau regarding proposed program revisions.[10] Sobol sat down with
Sagor and Cornbleth as the group was breaking up, asking "How are we
doing?" and then his assistant, Celia Diamond, also joined the group. They
talked for a few minutes, agreeing that the change in Schlesinger's Kennedy-
liberal outlook—as indicated by his recent writing and his dinner comment
about African "tribalism, slavery, and tyranny"—was disappointing. A key
impression from this brief and somewhat careful conversation was that
Sobol was sincere about the Review Committee's charge. While he might
well have hoped that this committee would help him politically, he also
seemed to believe strongly, as he would say, that New York's social studies
programs should tell more of the story of more of the people.

Three themes that would dominate the Review Committee's meetings
and work emerged at this first meeting. The least controversial concerned
supporting teachers in making desired changes, whatever they might be.
Support in the form of education (preservice and inservice), teaching materials, and a manageable program (one not overloaded by too much to teach in
the time available) were emphasized; later, compatible forms of assessment
and other supporting conditions were added to this list. A second theme was
whether and how to address directly African American experience and racism in the United States. The third and most contentious theme concerned
questions regarding a "common culture" introduced early on by Schlesinger.
These questions as they emerged were

- Do Americans have or share a common culture?
- If so, what is it?
- How much emphasis (time and space) should it receive in school curric-
  ula compared with cultural diversity?

During the committee's first working session Schlesinger said that U.S. history as the making of a single nation with a common culture should be basic to the committee's deliberations. While Americans have not appreciated the diversity of other "contributions," he continued, the origins of the United States were primarily European—racially and culturally—and he for one was tired of "West bashing." Despite problems, he concluded, the West has been the major force for democracy. In response, Virginia Sanchez Korrol, a historian and professor of Puerto Rican studies at Brooklyn College, referred to a common culture but from a different perspective, asking, "Where do we fit?" Mary Carter, a social studies teacher at a Long Island junior high school, expressed discomfort with "jumping into" common culture when various groups have been left out and the history being taught needs to be corrected. And Nathan Glazer pointed to the English language and the U.S. Constitution and system of government as what Americans have in common. In a similar vein, John-Paul Bianchi, an elementary social studies supervisor from the Bronx (the district in which Glazer attended public schools many years ago) questioned whether Americans share a common culture or whether what is shared are common understandings and beliefs. And Diane Glover, a social studies teacher at a Queens elementary school, noted that people need a better understanding of who they are before they can relate well to others. Ali Mazrui concluded this first conversation about common culture by pointing to what he called "two sociological myths" of shared ancestry and of collective purpose. If we are going to engage in ancestor worship (for example, the Founding Fathers), he said with a smile, we need to be more inclusive about our ancestors. Second, we need wider participation to justify the claim to collective purpose. The committee did not then or later endorse Schlesinger's notion of a common culture.

A concluding observation from this first meeting was that Sobol and the co-chairs' messages about learning from one another and creating consensus did not merely reflect their self-interest in getting the job done. These messages also communicated, at least implicitly, a key political democratic (and critical pragmatist) belief in coming together to work things out—a belief that dialogue and compromise, though not always from equal positions, is the preferred means of conflict resolution, if not the democratic way. This aspect seems a crucial component of the American sociopolitical system, one that seemed to be taken for granted in the committee's deliberations about America and what we share or have in common as Americans.

Taken together, subsequent meetings of the Review Committee can be characterized as a roller coaster in slow motion—with highs and lows, twists and turns, but moving slowly and occasionally doubling back on itself. The October meeting was spent in redefining the committee charge—coming to general agreement about what the committee would do and how—and hearing out those who wanted to speak, especially those such as Gary Van Cour, a global studies teacher in an upstate secondary school, who had participated in the last round of syllabi revision and preferred things pretty much as they were. The November meeting was devoted to hearing grade-by-grade results of committee members' reviews of the social studies syllabi. It ended with the co-chairs creating two subcommittees to draft statements for discussion: a conceptual foundations group co-chaired by Nathan Glazer and Jorge Klor de Alva, an anthropologist at Princeton; and a pedagogy and supporting conditions group co-chaired by Lloyd Elm, principal of the Native American magnet elementary school in Buffalo, and Cornbleth.

The January 1991 meeting was spent working in the subcommittees and then reporting to the group as a whole. March featured an arranged "conversation" between Klor de Alva and Schlesinger (in lieu of Glazer, whose flight was canceled, keeping him from the meeting); the dialogue was intended to address differences expressed in a December–January exchange of memos between Klor de Alva and Glazer. This meeting represented a pause if not a step backward and circling around in an apparent effort to bring as many members as possible around to supporting a revisionist if not transformative multiculturalism. In March the chief of the Social Studies Bureau, who defended the existing syllabi, took early retirement. By this time it was clear that most of the committee would recommend major changes in New York State syllabi and social studies programs to recognize recent scholarship and the experiences of America's peoples and their multiple perspectives. The April and May meetings were long and intense as the committee worked to complete a report that most if not all could agree upon. In June the report, *One Nation, Many Peoples,* was presented to the Board of Regents. New York and its education commissioner, Tom Sobol, were again catapulted into the news for ostensibly escalating the so-called multicultural wars.

In addition to the issues with which committee members wrestled, particularly important in this case of policy-in-the-making were the evolving group dynamic and continuing awareness of the political sensitivity of the work and its likely misunderstanding or misrepresentation. The group dynamic and political awareness provided background and context for the committee's dealing with the substantive issues.

E PLURIBUS UNUM

A sense of *e pluribus unum* came to characterize the committee—even though the media focused attention on the dissents of Schlesinger and Jackson, whose statements were included in the committee's report. The Review Committee's emerging group identity came to override most school level, racial-ethnic, gender, and political-ideological tensions.

The "specialness" accorded the committee and its members already has been noted. It probably is fair to say that most members both appreciated the positive attention (such as an elegant catered dinner at the Sobol's home in May, just as the committee's report was being completed) and were aware of its political intent. As a consequence of the effort to enhance the committee's status, and the skill of the co-chairs, members who attended regularly took the task seriously and, despite substantial initial differences in some cases, worked toward agreement.[11] By April the effort to accommodate and incorporate was palpable, and the pull to "come on board" was strong. Increasingly a "we" feeling was evident, and individuals appealed to the good of the group in urging agreement.[12]

For example, Syracuse-area social studies supervisor William Fetsko, who earlier had expressed doubt that the syllabi were in need of much revision, seemed to be pulled in by the emerging consensus, and he became a strong supporter of the committee's direction (and a strong critic of Jackson and Schlesinger, who were present less than half the time). Midway through the committee's lifetime, Fetsko argued the desirability of reaching consensus. Like Elm, he said, he'd changed his mind on some things. When co-chair Gordon invited Schlesinger, Glazer, and a few others to write a conceptual statement to which "they and we" could agree, he was candid in saying that he wanted consensus. Fetsko added that such a statement had to be one that Glover, Klor de Alva, and Mazrui would accept as well. "Dissenting opinions will kill us," he said. (Schlesinger did not draft any statements for committee consideration.)

Early divisions within the committee—between school and university representatives, for example—seemed to fade over time.[13] The appearance of sexism was complicated by most of the committee's conservatives being male. What seemed to be catering to male committee members, by the co-chairs' allowing them more time to speak, for example, probably was less sexism than an effort to hear out and bring in those who were less than enthusiastic about change in multicultural directions. By April four of the committee's eight women emerged as a visible and vocal coalition in support of the committee's work: Mary Carter, Susan Sagor, Virginia Sanchez Korrol, and Cornbleth (two school and two university representatives, one African American, one Puerto Rican, and two European Americans).[14]

Especially noteworthy with respect to the group dynamic and the coming together of diverse individuals over the course of many committee meetings was the emergent collaboration of Nathan Glazer and Jorge Klor de Alva. Separated by several decades in age and national boundaries of place of birth, they moved through memos and conversations to understand each other at least partially and to reach a position with which they both could be comfortable. Elaboration here is warranted to illustrate how the committee process itself was significant in demonstrating some of the give-and-take of dialogue and compromise. Some of that give-and-take was made possible by norms of politeness or civility that, with occasional lapses, were very much in evidence during committee proceedings. The Review Committee, according to an experienced SED staffer, came together as a group and tried to work out differences much more than most such committees.[15]

An emerging professional relationship between Glazer and Klor de Alva was evident by the third Review Committee meeting in November 1991, when, several times, Klor de Alva deferentially prefaced his remarks with reference to Glazer's prior statements. By the end of that meeting co-chairs

Gordon and Roberts had created the conceptual and pedagogical subcommittees, and Glazer and Klor de Alva had agreed to co-chair the former.[16]

The Glazer–Klor de Alva letters were their authors' efforts, as subcommittee co-chairs, to draft a conceptual or philosophical statement for the eventual
committee report. While one newspaper account portrayed the exchange of
letters as part of the committee's emotional exchange of diametrically opposed views (Hildebrand 1991), it also can be seen as illustrative of efforts to
reach or create a meeting ground from very different starting points. Glazer
began December 4, 1990 by suggesting that the subcommittee seriously consider the existing preamble to *Charting a Course: Social Studies for the 21st
Century* (National Commission on Social Studies in the Schools 1989) and his
additional comments (for example, about the role of history and geography,
central themes, balance) "as a basis for discussion and to find out where we
disagree and how we should proceed." He said:

> I have been, in addition to other things, struggling with the promised
> "philosophical" statement. Reading the Preamble to the report, "Chart-
> ing a Course: Social Studies for the 21st Century," that had been distrib-
> uted to us, I could not, however, for the life of me see what more I had to
> say. I would just be repeating language that had been hammered out by a
> committee that had done a good job. (p. 1)

With apologies for his delay, Klor de Alva responded in January 1991
that

> I have taken the suggestions . . . very seriously and have searched for
> ways to make them my own. However, although I am quite sure that a
> common ground will eventually come into view, I must respectfully
> submit that it is not yet fully in sight. Why?
>   First, I do not think that the Preamble to "Social Studies for the 21st
> Century" is appropriate for our purposes. While obviously well-inten-
> tioned, it betrays the very insensitivity we might wish to remove from
> the syllabi. (p. 1) [The disputed segments read as follows: "This diver-
> sity enriches *our* nation even as it presents a new challenge to develop
> social education that integrates all students into *our* system of demo-
> cratic government and helps them to subscribe to the values from *our*
> past—especially *our* devotion to democratic values and procedures."
> And "The coexistence of *increasing diversity and cherished tradition require*
> social studies courses in our schools to cultivate participatory citizenship
> and encourage the growth of independent, knowledgeable young adults
> who will conduct their lives in accord with democratic and ethical
> principles." (p. 5, emphasis added)]

Klor de Alva continued with a detailed critique of the preamble, the gist of
his critique being that:

> Quite apart from the uncharitable comparisons, which contrast, for in-
> stance, *"increasing* diversity" with *"cherished* tradition" . . . what bothers

me is the exclusionary (really, ethnocentric) and hegemonic use of "our" in the first paragraph. . . .

Transforming our students into Euro-Americans by devaluing their own memories and cultural values will hardly build the world we want for them in the future. Instead, the Preamble I support is one that begins by drawing from the past of the U.S. its greatest strength: its commitment to majority rule through the exercise of democratic procedures. With that in place we can face the twenty-first century safe in the knowledge that the children of today's immigrants will become the new defenders of these democratic values, especially as the Euro-American minority begins its retreat from them and from the cherished guarantees found in the Constitution. (p. 2)

Regarding Glazer's own comments, Klor de Alva responded with agreement on some points and disagreement on others. For example:

I am less sanguine about the general march of U.S. history progressing [as Glazer had suggested in his letter] toward "greater inclusion for all." The history of tolerance in the U.S. has not been linear, does not always move forward . . . and it is not inevitably on the way to the "fulfillment" of the "original promise of equal opportunity for all." Indeed, all forward progress in the U.S. (as anywhere else in the world) has been bitterly resisted, has had to be fought for, is always being challenged, and is frequently lost. (p. 4)

He ended with:

What we must attempt to guarantee our students is a sound background in historical studies and the social sciences. This background should include, not hide, opposing viewpoints, presented so that the merits of the data that supports [sic] them, as advanced by their scholarly advocates, can be debated in class. In this way intellectual honesty is not only served but p[r]omoted as a pedagogical end worthy of pursuit. If some historical lines have a greater base of consensus, then there will be little argument; where this does not exist, the arguments themselves will be the best educational exercise. In short, we need to create thinkers more than we need to impose historical dogmas. (p. 5)

Because we are all on the same side, a consensus will surely be reached; but open and informed debate is very much a part of the process of consensus building. We must encourage it among ourselves and our students. It is with this in mind that I share the above. (p. 5)

A key part of Glazer's February 1 rejoinder was his statement that "It has been eye-opening to me to see what other readers, from other perspectives, might consider insensitive" (p. 1). He continued:

I see nothing "uncharitable," for example, in the [disputed Preamble's] contrast of "cherished traditions" and "increasing diversity." There is no suggestion that the first challenged the second; or that the "cherished traditions" do not themselves include respect for and appreciation of diversity.

I detect a nuance in your reference to "majority rule" that I would find objectionable. Majority rule is certainly one element of democracy, but an equally important element is respect for rights, regardless of the numbers who claim them. The implication of your reference to "majority rule" is that with the change in the "majority," the new "majority"—the children of today's immigrants—will have to sternly resist the "retreat of the Euro-American minority from the cherished guarantees found in the Constitution." (pp. 1–2)

Glazer goes on to clarify further points of disagreement and agreement with Klor de Alva, ending with:

I fully agree we should "guarantee our students a sound background in historical studies and the social sciences" . . . and it should "not hide opposing viewpoints." That language presents no problem. But how now are we to settle disagreements over some central issues, as to whether the history of the United States is one of a steadily wider inclusion of all, regardless of religion, race, ethnic background, language, sex? That does seem to be one central point on which we weigh things differently.

We will have to take these matters up in future meetings. (p. 4)

Neither Glazer nor Klor de Alva could attend the January Review Committee meeting; the conceptual subcommittee, substitute-chaired by Sanchez Korrol, worked from their initial letters and reached agreement on a number of general points—for example, that the United States has seen increasing inclusion but that movement has not been steady, without opposition, or completed. Agreement on specifics was more difficult to reach. The exchange of views between the two men continued in a collegial manner through the March–May meetings to a report both could support.

Political Sensitivity

A second aspect of the background and context of the Review Committee's deliberations was continuing awareness of the political sensitivity of its work and the likelihood of the eventual report's being misunderstood or misrepresented by the press and public. The overriding interest of the committee was to be understood, not to be credited or, more likely, blamed for saying something that had not been said. The experience of the prior committee and its report, *A Curriculum of Inclusion,* and the attacks on Commissioner Sobol provided ample grounds for concern.[17] In the political milieu of 1990–1991, whatever the Review Committee said would be subjected to intense scrutiny. Political sensitivity was manifest in repeated reviews of committee language to eliminate "red flags" and any appearance of extremism. More conservative committee members seemed to have played on this concern to push their positions.

While some committee members may have exaggerated the public's opposition to multiculturalism, the expectation and appearance of misrepresentation by the media and external critics did contribute to group cohesion. The decision by SED staff to say little or nothing officially to the press or directly to the public before the committee's report may have been a mistake. Their circumspection fanned fears and imaginings of what was happening. For example:

- After the Review Committee's first meeting, in a piece entitled "Group Divided on Mixing Cultures," the *Binghamton Press & Sun-Bulletin* (September 24, 1990) quoted only two committee members—who held divergent views—and nonmember Diane Ravitch as saying that "the committee is going to be struggling with a phony problem. The curriculum as it stands now is not racist or biased."
- A guest column by John R. Howard in the Gannett Westchester Newspapers (October 28, 1990) claimed that "Arthur Schlesinger quit a follow-up panel [that is, the Review Committee] charged with generating a new set of recommendations." Schlesinger did not quit; he agreed to serve as a consultant to the committee, not as a full-time member.
- In his *U.S. News & World Report* column (November 12, 1990) John Leo stated: "Jeffries, perhaps the major figure in the Afrocentric movement in New York State, is frankly racist. . . . He serves on the state multicultural curriculum development committee." Jeffries did not serve on any of the committees.
- A *New York Post* editorial (November 15, 1990) entitled "Sobol's Obsession (Cont'd.)" asserted: "It's a shame that state Education Commissioner Thomas Sobol remains bent on his bizarre quest to impose an 'Afrocentric' curriculum on the state's schools. . . . Last year, the commissioner appointed Jeffries, the professor who teaches African racial superiority in his City College classes, to write what came to be known as the 'Sobol Report' on New York curricular reform—a widely unbalanced, pro-Afrocentric, quasi-illiterate document." Sobol had not supported, let alone attempted to impose, any form of Afrocentrism, and he did not appoint Jeffries to write *A Curriculum of Inclusion*.

The last two examples illustrate either simple ignorance or a guilt-by-association tactic, a nonexistent association with Afrocentrism and the demagoguery of Leonard Jeffries.[18] As a tactic, it continues to be employed by critics and opponents of a more inclusive multiculturalism (see note 17).

Within the committee it was agreed early on that individual members were free to speak for themselves and to share their views publicly but not to speak for the committee. At the October meeting Sanchez Korrol noted that the press continued to be negative. She urged that SED and committee members counter the negativism in the media and elsewhere so that the climate of opinion would not work against the committee's efforts. Mary Carter reported that Albert Shanker had spoken at a meeting she had attended and that his account of what New York State was doing with respect to multiculturalism was "slanderous." She argued that the committee needed to counter the notion that inclusion means distortion of history.

Although several committee members strongly endorsed these suggestions and similar ones made at the January meeting, SED did not follow through with an organized public relations effort. After the initial hoopla promoting the committee, Sobol spoke publicly on a few occasions, but otherwise SED was silent about the committee's work. At the committee's first meeting in September 1990, Sobol said that he "had to call in a few chits" to keep the press away that evening, but committee members were free to say whatever they chose. Subsequent meetings saw a few visitors (such as SED staff and members of the Board of Regents) but no members of the press. While few outsiders attended Review Committee meetings, the committee felt itself in (or about to enter) the spotlight.

By November, as the committee began to consider writing its report, co-chairs Roberts and Gordon strongly urged creating a conceptual base for recommendations so that thoughtful people including skeptics could deal with, rather than dismiss, the report as a political statement. Here and at other times Diane Ravitch was cited as an example of the thoughtful skeptic or critic to whom the committee was attempting to appeal. While not physically present, Ravitch was an influence on the Review Committee, and by the time the committee's report was presented to the Board of Regents, Ravitch was perceived much less favorably by committee members. The change is attributable to her continuing public statements against an inclusive multiculturalism in general and against New York's activities in particular. Examples of such statements include her October 1990 pieces in *The Chronicle of Higher Education* (1990d) and the Educational Excellence Network's *Network News & Views* (1990c) and her exchange with Molefi Kete Asante in the spring 1991 issue of *American Scholar*.[19]

In response to Lloyd Elm's concern that the committee "say what needs to be said," Ed Gordon reiterated that he was "talking about saying radical things" in moderate, sensible ways, adding that there was a "rising tide of people who ought to know better" opposing the committee. Gordon was referring to knowledgeable people like Ravitch who should have known, he thought, that the committee was not endorsing any "centrism," Afro- or other, that inclusion was more unifying than exclusion, and that students should learn to think critically about the information they encounter (not merely acquire information for regurgitation on an exam or quiz show).

The Review Committee's relation to the prior minority task force and its report, *A Curriculum of Inclusion*, was discussed early in the March meeting. Because the Review Committee was viewed by many as a continuation of the prior group or as a next step, it seemed important not to "get caught up in that" (co-chair Roberts) while not criticizing or demeaning *A Curriculum of Inclusion* (co-chair Gordon). By April, attention to the language of the report and how it might be misrepresented was evident throughout the meeting. In the course of reviewing a very rough draft of the eventual report, Ken Jackson reminded committee members to be aware of the larger politi-

cal context, which he characterized as a growing backlash (against multiculturalism). To reach people in the middle, Jackson urged paying attention to
language and being positive wherever possible, rather than negative. His
more specific suggestion, to add a phrase saying that there have been efforts
to close the gap between ideals and realities in America, and his later suggestion for a compromise statement where there had been disagreement, were
accepted. Overall, Jackson was looked to with some deference (Glazer, Gordon, and Schlesinger—the "elder statesmen"—were not present at this
time), and he played an important "senior" role during the first day of the
April meeting (he left at the end of the afternoon session) by suggesting
specific compromises and offering to draft alternative statements.

Also at the April meeting, Ali Mazrui shared an unsigned flyer that had
been distributed on his SUNY at Binghamton campus and his response to it.
The flyer, a particularly ugly bit of racism, defamed Martin Luther King, Jr.,
Nelson Mandella, and especially Ali Mazrui, who was described as "a genu-
ine dirtbag shit-for-brains street nigger." In his response to what he called
"racism and anonymous venom," Mazrui observed (April 1991):

> What was distinctive about Nazi Germany was that it was an *extreme* case
> of something much more widespread in the Western world—racism and
> a sense of cultural superiority. Hitler was the *worst* case of something
> which—in milder forms—is still rampant in the Western world. Racial
> and cultural arrogance. Fortunately many Westerners are fighting it. Let
> us join them in the crusade.
>
> Why do we need diversity and multiculturalism on our campuses? In
> order to produce future generations of Americans to whom odious docu-
> ments of this kind will be as bizarre as are medieval documents of witch
> trials to us. . . . Every method of cultural intolerance is a form of tyranny.
> Every racial insult is a vulgarization of our shared humanity.

In the meantime, charges and countercharges of political correctness
were being traded on university campuses and in opinion journals. Houghton Mifflin's elementary social studies textbook series was being advocated
and challenged and then adopted in California. Lamar Alexander had been
appointed secretary of education, President Bush announced his America
2000 education strategy, and NEH director Lynne Cheney chaired the History Task Force of the National Council on Education Standards and Testing.
Articles about multiculturalism, cultural diversity, and "America" were ap-
pearing in, for example, the *Wall Street Journal* (Solomon 1990), the *New
Republic* (Sullivan 1990), and the *New York Times* (Campus Forum on Multiculturalism 1990) as well as in *Education Week* (Viadero 1990) and weekly
newsmagazines including *Time* (Tifft 1990; Clarke and Tifft 1991), *Newsweek*
(Alter and Denworth 1990), and *U.S. News & World Report* (1990), which
carried John Leo's vituperative columns.

The May meeting was the committee's last. It was the last group opportunity to reach agreement on the report to be submitted to Commissioner
Sobol and the Board of Regents in June. Glazer was present after missing

three meetings, Jackson was not, and Schlesinger appeared for a few hours on the second day. (Schlesinger apparently took with him second or next-to-last drafts of the report, including the May 10 Klor de Alva and Mazrui draft statements of what became a preamble, on which he apparently based his dissent—rather than the actual, further revised version.) Anticipating that the Review Committee report, like *A Curriculum of Inclusion*, might become the target of debate generating more heat than light, committee members very carefully reviewed and revised the draft report, especially the recently added preamble based on statements prepared by Klor de Alva and Mazrui, and considered the question of minority reports or dissenting statements (examined in the next section). Whereas Jackson had played the conciliator role at the April meeting, in May the role was shared by Glazer, Klor de Alva, and Mazrui. They raised most of the questions and suggested compromise alternatives to resolve differences, including their own.[20]

A final political note here concerns publication of the Review Committee report, *One Nation, Many Peoples: A Declaration of Cultural Interdependence*. Committee members received their copies about 10 days before its presentation to the Board of Regents at a June 20, 1991 press conference. The committee had been asked not to release or comment on any of the report publicly before then. Jackson and Schlesinger disregarded this request, if not directly then by allowing their dissenting "reflections" to be released by others. While most committee members who were contacted by the *New York Times*, for example (including Cornbleth, Gordon, and Fetsko), declined to discuss the specific content of the report before the press conference, what became known as the Jackson and Schlesinger dissents were released earlier and were quoted in a *Times* article that appeared on June 20 *before* the press conference. The early release was a major factor prompting Cornbleth, Sanchez Korrol, and Sagor to prepare a written statement supportive of the report that was distributed at the June 20 press conference and was quoted in the *Times* on June 21 at the end of an extensive front-page article, "Plan to Emphasize Minority Cultures Ignites a Debate." According to the *Times* (June 21, 1991), which printed part of the brief statement:

> Most members of the committee said today that they strongly endorsed the report's conclusions, and three of them took the unusual step of issuing their own written rebuttal to the dissents from Professors Schlesinger, Kenneth T. Jackson of Columbia University and Paul Gagnon of the University of Massachusetts at Boston.[21]
>
> "Given the diverse backgrounds of the committee members, the consensus that was reached represents well the strengths inherent in diversity and the unity which can emerge," wrote Catherine Cornbleth, an education professor at the State University of New York at Buffalo; Susan Sagor, teacher at the Brearley School in Manhattan, and Virginia Sanchez Korrol, chairwoman of the Department of Puerto Rican Studies at Brooklyn College.

"The report balances diversity and commonality in ways that benefit all our people, not some at the expense of others."

The middle part of the statement, omitted by the *Times*, read:

Our report, "One Nation, Many Peoples: A Declaration of Cultural Interdependence," is the constructive outcome of a participatory democratic process.

It would have been preferable had individuals like Jackson and Schlesinger chosen to work within the democratic process that guided the committee throughout its work rather than to stand apart and criticize later. Perhaps if they had, they would better understand the spirit of the committee's efforts. The dissenting statements would seem to confirm the need for the revisions that the commissioner has initiated and this report suggests—to extend *unum* to encompass *pluribus*, to include all our peoples.

Constructing Consensus and Individual "Reflections"

As suggested already, the emergent group dynamic and continuing political sensitivity of the Review Committee contributed significantly to widespread consensus among members. That consensus was constructed or crafted, especially by the co-chairs; it did not simply happen. The turning of threatened minority reports or dissents into supplementary "reflections" included *in* the report (this inclusion might not have been recognized from many media accounts) provides a key example of consensus construction. *All* committee members agreed to the *form and format* of the "reflections" section of the report—even those like Jackson and Schlesinger who participated in the reflections in order to disagree with some of the report's substance or seeming implications. In other words, they agreed to work within the system and to play by the rules of the political democratic game.

By November 1990 it seemed likely that the Review Committee would recommend more inclusive New York State syllabi and social studies programs—inclusive in the sense of the experiences, cultures, histories, and perspectives of the varied groups and individuals who constitute America, not merely inclusive of their contributions to a pre-existing Anglo- or Euro-mainstream. Further, that inclusion was to an America framed by our secular trinity: the Declaration of Independence, the Constitution, and the Bill of Rights—and subsequent constitutional amendments and Supreme Court decisions. There was continuing disagreement about the emphasis to be placed on American ideals vis-à-vis realities, the extent to which the gaps between them had been narrowed or closed (and how and by whom), and what came to be symbolized as *pluralism and unity*.

The extreme unity position, most clearly expressed on the committee by Schlesinger, equated unity with sameness or standardization and characterized pluralism as tending toward if not causing separatism. The committee's eventual strong endorsement of inclusion and multiple perspectives, neither Euro- nor Afro-centric, drew fire before it was made public. For example, Whittle Communications published Schlesinger's *Disuniting of America* (1991), replete with colorful Federal Express ads, a few weeks before the Review Committee report was presented to the Board of Regents in June 1991. The monograph, free copies of which were sent to Review Committee members via Federal Express, roundly criticized Afrocentrism and multicultural efforts such as New York's, which were portrayed as Afrocentric.

The question of minority reports arose at the Review Committee's second meeting in October 1990 when Lloyd Elm expressed his doubts that the committee would reach consensus about the syllabi, implicitly suggesting that he would write a minority report. Co-chair Gordon said privately that he had suggested to individuals that, if they could not endorse whatever the majority agreed to, they could write minority reports. At the January meeting Gordon twice remarked that there would be space in the report for dissenting opinions; he also commented that consensus adds strength. At the April meeting Diane Glover made clear that she didn't want her ideas watered down, although they could, she said, "be prettied up." Gordon responded that they (Gordon and Roberts with the assistance of two graduate students working with Gordon, and Sobol's assistant, Celia Diamond) would try to represent her views adequately in drafting the report but that she could have her own voice. Elm later asked about room for minority reports, to which Gordon responded as he had to Glover. At this point it seemed that several committee members would write minority reports largely to assuage their constituencies as well as their own concerns. By May, as the press for consensus gained momentum, the openness to minority reports changed.

The morning after a contentious evening committee session in May, Gordon said he felt "troubled" the previous night given that there appeared to be a "great amount of agreement" underneath the differences that had been expressed rather heatedly (mostly about individual committee members speaking on behalf of the groups they represented in ways that might undermine the committee's report). Wanting to maintain wide consensus, Gordon suggested the possibility of multiple attachments to the report for views "not fully expressed in the main document," rather than a collection of minority reports or dissents. He referred to Lloyd Elm as an example of a person who represented a community (Native American–Onondaga) for which he felt he must speak.

In the discussion that followed, committee members agreed that the report should encompass the multiple perspectives it advocated as reflecting the larger society. They also agreed that people who had been appointed to the committee but had not attended any meetings were not entitled to such statements (Paul Gagnon and Asa Hilliard were mentioned in this regard.)

Later Elm asked to return to the question of commentaries. (Note that the issue had become one of "commentaries" instead of minority reports; in the final report the term *reflections* was used.) Susan Sagor asked people who might write commentaries to say what they would write. Gordon followed by asking people to declare themselves, saying that he (or he and co-chair Roberts) would write an opening commentary about the commentaries. In addition to Gordon and Roberts, four committee members indicated that they would write commentaries: Elm, Glover, Mazrui, and Susan Wong Ostrofsky, an elementary teacher in Dobbs Ferry and the only Asian American on the committee. Although Wong Ostrofsky ultimately did not write a commentary, the other three did, as did Glazer, Jackson, Schlesinger, and Elleni Tedli, director of the Cultural Center at Colgate University.

Elm said that his statement about cultural genocide was not a dissent; it would enhance the report. Glover reassured the committee that "whatever I write will enhance" the report. Mazrui, who earlier in the day warned against engaging in self-censorship, now talked about "how we can make a virtue of this," referring to the committee as a multicultural experience and to members' agreement as indicative of the viability of a multicultural approach. Bill Fetsko urged positive, supportive language to avoid arousing opposition or providing ammunition to opponents, and John-Paul Bianchi called for statements to enhance the report. In effect, potential minority reports had been redefined as commentaries that extended the main body of the report (Elm, Glover, Mazrui, and Tedla); that counseled caution (Glazer); or that expressed reservations or dissent (Jackson and Schlesinger). Everyone's voice was included. The circle had been enlarged, but not without considerable efforts to convince Jackson and Schlesinger to make their reservations and dissents part of the report. Much of this effort went on behind the scenes in private phone conversations between the co-chairs and Jackson and Schlesinger.

Mazrui, caricatured by the local press as an extremist, not only spoke to his constituencies in his reflection but also worked with the group—in hammering out the preamble, for example; and he played the conciliator in urging Jackson to stay with the group at the very end. Responding to Jackson's May 28 memo asking that his name not be associated with the report unless changes were made to give more attention to commonality and unity, Mazrui wrote on June 8, 1991:

> I too have reservations about the Report as it stands. But I have not withdrawn my name. Instead I have submitted a personal annex to the report. I do very much hope Ken Jackson will do the same, if the two Chairs would extend the deadline for him. [They did.]
>
> We all worked wonderfully well together for many months. We must not break up in disarray at this late hour. Kenneth, please close ranks—and write a separate annex if there is still time. But annex or not, please remain with us. Democracy means being outvoted from time to time—without withdrawing from the system!

Jackson did add a dissenting reflection to the report.

RACISM AND COMMON CULTURE

The three dominating themes of the Review Committee's deliberations were (1) supporting teachers in making desired changes, (2) whether
and how to address African-American experience and racism in the United
States, and (3) the nature of and emphasis to place on a common or shared
American culture. A fourth recurrent topic was the actual review of New
York's social studies syllabi and how much of that review to include in the
report. While the specifics were important to support general conclusions,
they could be (and were) taken out of context, misinterpreted, and trivialized by others—not dissimilar to what occurred when specific objections
were raised by textbook critics in California.

As noted already, the theme of supporting teachers was not controversial. Including the specifics of syllabi review in the committee report was
more important to teacher than to university members of the committee, in
part because the teachers had done most of that work. However, with few
exceptions, the specific problems noted with the syllabi were not points of
contention among committee members. The questions and debate regarding a common culture have been sketched in previous sections. Here, they
are reconsidered in conjunction with the committee's dealing with racism
and African American experience.

Racism as a problem of U.S. history and contemporary society was
treated gingerly at first by committee members, probably to avoid confrontation, since at the time charges of racism often were taken as "fighting
words." For example, racism was characterized cautiously by one committee
member as an unconscious product of ignorance among many teachers and
students. Syllabi and materials that distinguish "us" and "them" were characterized as racially biased if not racist. As the committee coalesced, more
attention was given to both individual and institutional racism, and the
language of culture was specified as including or referring to race, ethnicity,
and gender. Although disagreement became tense over whether the treatment of Africans during the Middle Passage and enslavement in America
amounted to a holocaust (as claimed by Glover and Mazrui), portrayal of
genocide against African Americans, Hispanics, and Native Americans was
less an issue.

A one-page statement about multicultural history education—
formulated and endorsed by the executive board of the Organization of
American Historians in January 1991 and shared with the Review Committee at its March meeting—may have influenced committee members to take
a bolder stand. This was the first instance to reach the committee's attention
of professional historians' taking a public position in support of multiculturalism (OAH Executive Board 1991).

> The history curricula of public schools should be constructed around the
> principle that all people have been significant actors in human events.
> Students should therefore understand that history is not limited to the

study of dominant political, social, and economic elites. . . . A primary goal of history education is to foster mutual understanding and respect among people of different backgrounds and traditions. Historical studies should proceed first from the clear acknowledgement that no major group or society has a wholly singular and static cultural heritage. On the contrary, the cultures of all people have become intermingled over time, often in subtle and complex ways that historians are still exploring. . . . a history that asserts or implies the inherent superiority of one race, gender, class, or region of the world over another is by definition "bad history" and should have no place in American schools.

. . . Whether the people of the United States regard themselves as one nation or many, or as some combination of both, most Americans will probably recognize that they share certain common traditions, values, and experiences arising out of their common humanity and their interactions with one another. These include our political and economic institutions, however imperfect, a mass culture that affects everyone, and a common entitlement to freedom, equality, and dignity. A successful history education should help students understand what binds Americans together while simultaneously promoting respect for America's pluralism and diversity. (p. 6)

By April, when Gary Van Cour suggested omitting a section of the draft report on racism, he was met with a chorus of "NO'S" and several members spoke for keeping the statement. African Americans Mary Carter and Elleni Tedli spoke more often and more forcefully than they had at earlier meetings, and most committee members responded positively to what they said. At the May meeting, for example, Carter made an eloquent statement in support of maintaining the committee's focus on racial-ethnic diversity and experience. She called on the committee not to dilute its efforts by listing a number of discriminated-against groups (for example, homosexuals), which in effect would provide loopholes so that teachers could deal with diversity and avoid dealing with race and racism. Tedla suggested that categories such as physical disability and sexual orientation cut across the four groups identified as underrepresented minorities in New York (African Americans, Puerto Ricans/Latinos, Asian Americans, and Native Americans).

In the Review Committee's final report, *One Nation, Many Peoples,* racism is mentioned in the first two of the seven principles suggested as guides to social studies curriculum, and other *-isms* are mentioned by way of reference to a New York City position statement.

1. *Democracy:* Bridging the gap between reality and the ideal.
   . . . That racism, which has marred U.S. society since its founding, has been a formidable obstacle standing in the way of making the democratic ideals of America a reality for all. (p. 8)
2. *Diversity:* Understanding and respecting others and oneself.
   The social studies curriculum should help students to make sense of a multicultural world and their place in it. This includes respect for

and appreciation of the cultures of others as well as their own. Although the Committee regards racism as the fundamental schism in
American society which the curriculum must address, it shares the
view, adopted by the New York City Board of Education in November
1989, that multicultural education should also help students to deal
with human differences based upon "linguistic diversity, gender, socioeconomic class, religion, sexual orientation, age, and the perspective
and contributions of the physically challenged." (p. 9)

In retrospect, a strong element of the committee's resistance to "common
culture" was the emergent agreement to iterate the legacy of individual and
institutional racism that has limited the participation of too many Americans
in mainstream culture.

Beyond political democratic values, principles, and institutions, the notion of what Americans share in common was not specified. Even the common culture that Schlesinger had argued for remained unspecified beyond
democratic ideals of European origin. During one committee discussion
Schlesinger stated that he was referring to common political ideals, not
cultural values. When a committee member noted widespread agreement
among U.S. citizens about some democratic political values (such as government by consent and due process) but not about cultural or social values,
Schlesinger agreed. While acknowledging that "unifying ideals" have kept
America from the factional struggles occurring elsewhere, he cautioned that
the "bonds of cohesion" are fragile. But he did not explain or elaborate on
the claimed fragility.

Later he commented that America's "national identity [is] in [a] constant
process of redefinition." At this point there appeared to be little disagreement between Schlesinger and the committee majority. However, when he
went on to say that the problem or challenge was "how to keep a highly
differentiated society sound and whole," he did not explain how diversity
challenged either soundness or wholeness.

While Schlesinger said that he accepted multiple perspectives or narratives in principle, he went on to say that they were not feasible in elementary
or secondary schools. He did not spell out his objection, but said that it
would be difficult enough in college. Even college students, he implied,
would be confused by examining more than one account of an event, person, group, time period, or other historical phenomenon. The committee
disagreed, and a key section of *One Nation, Many Peoples* strongly recom-
mends making multiple perspectives available to students:

> Because of the diversity of American society and in order to prepare
> students to understand and influence the world of which they are a part,
> we should strive to teach social studies from a multicultural perspective,
> regardless of whether the school community is itself diverse or whether
> the local student population is drawn predominantly from one cultural
> group. . . . A multicultural perspective, then, means that all the applica-
> ble viewpoints of the historical and social protagonists should be ex-
> plored, paying special attention to the ways in which race, ethnicity,

gender and class generate different ways of understanding, experiencing, and evaluating the events of the world. Because interpretations vary as experiences differ, a multicultural perspective must necessarily be a multiple perspective that takes into account the variety of ways in which any topic can be comprehended. (p. 7)

One Nation, Many Peoples goes beyond affirming multicultural and multiple perspectives to explicitly acknowledge racism (as indicated, for example, in the previously quoted excerpts) and to call for students to examine systematically the continuing struggle to realize democratic ideals in everyday life, racism, and such questions as "What is an American?" "What holds us together as a nation?" "What can I and others do to promote greater economic fairness and equity?" (p. 9) "How have the people with whom I share a cultural heritage contributed in the past, and how do they contribute in the present, to the making of the U.S. and the world?" "What are our civic values? Or, what should they be?" "How do we evaluate historical events that have contradicted or opposed the ideals of pluralism, fair play, equality and justice for all?" (p. 10).

Rather than offering answers in the form of California's "a story well told" (History–Social Science Curriculum Framework and Criteria Committee 1988, p. 4), New York opted to deal with complexity: "The curriculum should provide students with the resources to understand the social divisions that affect them and the overlapping loyalties that form the intricate social web linking them to others" (p. 11). In so doing, the New York position recognized structural inequities in American society. Pluralism was not contained as in California, and diversity was not trimmed to fit the European-immigrant experience. Yet the conventional story of America was not directly challenged. *One Nation* was not a radical document—but it could be seen as undermining the conventional heroes-and-contributions approach to school history that in effect keeps minorities on the margins (from which location they can offer contributions to the mainstream), and as a counterpoint to California's grand immigrant narrative. Instead of directly confronting the conventional story of America with an alternative narrative, *One Nation* called for a social studies curriculum that involves students in systematically examining questions such as those just cited.

The New York report also stands in contrast to California's 1987 framework with respect to how it came into being. It was, as indicated by its sometimes-ponderous prose, written by a committee, not by the Albany equivalents of UCLA's Charlotte Crabtree and consultant Diane Ravitch, who reworked a committee draft and became the "principal authors" of California's framework (see Chapter 3). Also, recall co-chair Gordon's reassurance to Glover that the drafters would try to represent her views but that she could have her own voice. And while the co-chairs urged and worked toward consensus, there was no New York equivalent of Crabtree's captaining of the social studies textbook review process in California. The neo-nativists actively tried to influence the policymaking process in both states. While they were insiders who closely controlled the process in California, they were outsiders who stirred public opinion but wielded less direct influence in New York.

UNVEILING *ONE NATION, MANY PEOPLES*

Early in the afternoon of June 20, 1991, at a press conference in Albany, the Social Studies Review and Development Committee report, *One Nation, Many Peoples*, was presented formally to Commissioner Sobol and the New York State Board of Regents. The room was crowded with regents, SED staffers, Review Committee members, reporters, and lights and cameras. Sobol and co-chairs Gordon and Roberts sat at one end of a large conference table; committee and SED staff members sat in rows behind them. Sobol offered an introductory statement in which he characterized the report as "thoughtful, scholarly, constructive" and deserving of a thoughtful rather than a quick response. Consequently, he said, he would submit his recommendations, stemming from the report, to the Board of Regents in July. (The month's pause also would enable him to gauge political, professional, and public reaction.) Sobol noted three reasons why he was happy with the report: its tone, which he said elevated the discourse; its incorporation of a broad area of consensus, which he said showed that *pluribus* and *unum* are complementary; and its reflection of the diversity of thought about the issues. The Review Committee, Sobol observed, was a microcosm of American society that demonstrated how a new unity could be forged.

Once again, Sobol's high hopes were not to be realized—yet, neither were they dashed. The report's appearance ushered in another round of battles in the so-called multicultural wars. In a July 12 memo entitled "Understanding Diversity," Sobol presented his recommendations—which followed *One Nation, Many Peoples* closely—to the Board of Regents. Despite the controversy, to be described in the next chapter, those recommendations were adopted by the regents, in a 12–3 vote, and became New York State education policy. The 322 pages of news clippings dealing with the controversy over multiculturalism, compiled in five booklets and subsequently distributed by SED's Office of Communications, were one indicator of the intensity of the renewed debate in New York. Beyond that, they illustrated the variety of interests and questions about what it meant to be an American in the 1990s and what kind of America would enter the twenty-first century. In Chapter 5 we turn to "Understanding Diversity," the ensuing debate, and the next round of state policy activity.

REFERENCES

Alter, Jonathan, and Lydia Denworth. 1990. A (vague) sense of history. *Newsweek* (Fall–Winter; special issue): pp. 31–33.
American Federation of Teachers. 1991. Multicultural education: Which direction? *On Campus* 11, no. 1 (September 11): p. 7.

Berger, Joseph. 1990. Now the regents must decide if history will be recast. *New York Times* (February 11): p. E5.

Campus Forum on Multiculturalism. 1990. Opening academia without closing it down. *New York Times* (December 9): p. E5.

Clarke, Breena, and Susan Tifft. 1991. A "race man" argues for a broader curriculum. Interview with Henry Louis Gates Jr. *Time* (April 22): pp. 16, 18.

Fiske, Edward B. 1990. Lessons. *New York Times* (February 7, 1990, p. B5).

Gates, Henry Louis, Jr. 1992. *Loose canons: Notes on the culture wars.* New York: Oxford University Press.

Hildebrand, John. 1991. Rewriting history? *Newsday* (Long Island ed., June 18).

History–Social Science Curriculum Framework and Criteria Committee. 1988. *History–Social Science Framework.* Sacramento: California State Department of Education.

Hogeboom, Willard L. 1992. Letter to the editor. *Social Science Record* 30 (1): 107–109.

Hughes, Robert. 1992. The fraying of America. *Time* (February 3): pp. 44–49.

Leo, John. 1990. A fringe history of the world. *U.S. News & World Report* (November 12): pp. 25–26.

National Commission on Social Studies in the Schools. 1989. *Charting a course: Social studies for the 21st century.* Washington, D.C.: National Council for the Social Studies.

New York State Education Department, Information Center on Education. 1989. *Annual educational summary 1988–89.* Albany: Author.

———. 1988. Commissioner's preface: A house divided, pp. i–ii. *New York, the state of learning. A report to the governor and the legislature on the educational status of the state's schools.* Albany: Author.

Organization of American Historians, Executive Board. 1991. History education in the public schools. *Organization of American Historians Newsletter* (February): p. 6.

Ravitch, Diane. 1990a. Diversity and democracy: Multicultural education in America. *American Educator* 14 (1): 16–20, 46–48.

———. 1990b. Multiculturalism, E pluribus plures. *American Scholar* (Summer): 337–354.

———. 1990c. Multiculturalism redux. *Network News & Views* 9 (10): 77–81.

———. 1990d. Multiculturalism yes, particularism no. *Chronicle of Higher Education* (October 24): p. A44.

———. 1990. Multiculturalism: An exchange (with Molefi Kete Asante). *American Scholar* (Spring 1991): pp. 272–276.

Schlesinger, Arthur M., Jr. 1991. *The disuniting of America.* Knoxville, Tenn.: Whittle Books.

Sewall, Gilbert. 1990. Noted with interest. *Social Studies Review* 3: 11.

Social Studies Review and Development Committee. 1991. *One nation, many peoples: A declaration of cultural interdependence.* Albany: New York State Education Department.

Solomon, Jolie. 1990. Learning to accept cultural diversity. *Wall Street Journal* (September 12): pp. B1, 8.

Sullivan, Andrew. 1990. Racism 101. *New Republic* (November 26): pp. 18–21.

Task Force on Minorities. 1989. *A curriculum of inclusion.* Albany: New York State Education Department.

Tifft, Susan. 1990. Of, by and for—whom? *Time* (September 24): pp. 95–96.

Viadero, Debra. 1990. Battle over multicultural education rises in intensity. *Education Week 10* (13): 1, 11–13.

NOTES

1. In New York State the policymaking body for education is the 16 member Board of Regents. Regents represent varying regions (one member from each of 12 judicial districts and four at-large members) and are appointed to seven-year terms by the state legislature. The regents, in turn, appoint the commissioner of education, who heads SED and serves at their pleasure. The independence of the regents and commissioner from the governor's office has not been appreciated by New York governors for some time.

2. A May 1988 report addressed the first part of the charge, recommending improvement in SED affirmative action practices. Most of those recommendations have been acted upon, creating some dissatisfaction within SED's bureaucracy.

3. Secondary social studies syllabi had been under revision before 1987; grades 7–12 social studies syllabi revised as of 1987 still are labeled "tentative."

4. Leonard Jeffries, then chair of Africana Studies at the City College of New York, was one of four consultants retained by the task force, and he prepared initial drafts of portions of the report; he was not an appointed member or author of the report, as media accounts and commentators have claimed.

5. Statistics for 1990–1991 show the pattern continuing as reported in G. Scott Thomas, "Grading Western New York School Districts," *Business First* 8 (47), September 7, 1992, pp. 1, 10–12.

6. The statement was reprinted, for example, in *Education Week*, August 1, 1990; in Albert Shanker's paid advertisement column in the Sunday *New York Times*, August 12, 1990; in Shanker's "Where We Stand" column in the *New York Teacher*, September 3, 1990; and in the American Historical Association's newsletter, *Perspectives*, October 1990.

7. Before the Review Committee's first meeting, one member died in an auto accident, and two additional members were appointed, for a total of 24.

8. Cornbleth kept detailed field notes of each meeting and an archive of correspondence and documents distributed to the committee. Unreferenced quotations in what follows are from her field notes. Quotations from individual interviews are noted as such. Other sources are specified.

9. Francis Roberts had been superintendent of schools, Cold Spring Harbor, Long Island, since 1983. Previously he had served as assistant director of the National Endowment for the Humanities and as president of the Bank Street College of Education.

10. Reportedly, the bureau chief resented the whole chain of events, both the critique of syllabi that he had played a major role in creating and the review process that was taken out of his and his bureau's hands. So, interestingly, Cornbleth's nomination to the committee came from one of the more conservative blocs within SED. Dissension within SED, occasioned in part by Sobol's acting on the affirmative action recommendations of his minority task force, was noted later by a seasoned SED staffer.

11. The co-chairs' skill was evident in their moving slowly, retracing steps, setting additional subgroup meetings, and occasionally playing good cop, bad cop (purposefully or inadvertently) in order to bring and keep most if not all members on board. Particular effort was directed toward Schlesinger and Jackson. While Schlesinger came to be seen as a lost cause, Jackson's "defection" was a surprise to some. "Who got to Ken Jackson?" was how a key SED staffer put it.

12. The growing group cohesion was also, in part, a response to external "enemies" as described below.

13. At first it seemed as though several university representatives treated the teacher representatives with artificial respect as if they were exotic creatures. Later several teachers jokingly but firmly distanced themselves from the "high-falutin' " language of some of the university faculty (e.g., Ed Gordon's *hegemony* and *communocentric*). Importantly, both groups came to respect and/or accept the other and to defer to each other's areas of expertise (e.g., the conceptual and pedagogical subgroups were weighted heavily toward university and school people, respectively).

14. Three of the four (Carter was not present) would issue a statement at the June press conference at which the committee report was submitted to the Board of Regents. Also, of the nine review committee members who were appointed to the successor Social Studies Curriculum and Assessment Committee, the four women were these four.

15. He attributed the difference to this committee's being external (not chaired or otherwise led by SED staff, including non–New Yorkers as members) and having overnight meetings (more time together may have contributed to collegiality).

16. Having co-chairs of these subcommittees appeared to be a second thought which turned out well politically and substantively—with Klor de Alva, and Cornbleth on the pedagogical subcommittee, as the seconds. The subcommittees worked largely from the December to February Glazer–Klor de Alva exchange of letters and Cornbleth's January outline.

17. As late as fall 1992, more than three years after the appearance of *A Curriculum of Inclusion*, presumably respectable essayists were misrepresenting Tom Sobol and the authorship and message of that report. For example, retired Long Island social studies teacher William L. Hogeboom wrote in the fall 1992 issue of the Journal of the New York State Council for the Social Studies, "CCNY's [City College of New York's] Leonard Jeffries *is said to* have written most of the final report" (p. 107, emphasis ours). Earlier, in the February 3, 1992 issue of *Time*, Robert Hughes referred to the Portland African-American Baseline Essays and how "they are popular with bureaucrats like Tom Sobol, the education commissioner of New York State—people who are scared of alienating black voters or can't stand up to thugs like City College professor Leonard Jeffries. Their implications for American education are large, and mostly bad" (p. 48).

18. In *Loose Canons* Henry Louis Gates Jr. refers to Jeffries—along with Alan Bloom—as a "vulgar cultural nationalist" (1992, p. xvi).

19. The *Chronicle* piece was one of several that reiterated Ravitch's strained but oft-quoted pluralism-particularism distinction that appeared earlier in the *American Scholar* (1991) and the AFT's *American Educator* (1990a). The EEN piece was a sharp statement of self-defense against perceived insult at the hands of SED's minority task force, and the Board of Regents—and of disapproval of some members of the Review Committee who "enter the process with strong views": Hilliard, Elm, and Cornbleth were mentioned.

20. From both political and substantive angles, the exchanges among these three very different men were fascinating. Of vastly different backgrounds and different generations, they also shared experiences as discriminated-against newcomers to the United States and as distinguished faculty members at high-status universities.

21. Gagnon, who never attended a Review Committee meeting, had withdrawn from the committee and was not officially associated with the report.

5

New York: Muting Multiculturalism?

Resolution: *Resolve to perform what you ought; perform without fail what you resolve.*

Benjamin Franklin, *The Autobiography of Benjamin Franklin* (1940), p. 95

I t's early February 1992, Groundhog Day, at a hotel near the Albany airport. Inside, the decor is colonial "American," and the doorman wears breeches and a white wig that has seen better days. Joining the Social Studies Curriculum and Assessment Committee at its first meeting, New York State Education Commissioner Thomas Sobol urged the group to bring the social studies syllabi up to date. The "door is pretty much wide open," he said. And, because of the extensive debate and public misunderstanding of the State Education Department's (SED's) position on multiculturalism, he reviewed some recent history. Then, thanking the committee in advance for its work, he noted that "the whole world's watching."

Later during that meeting one committee member, a social studies supervisor, made it clear that another curriculum revision was the last thing that the teachers he knew needed or wanted. An administrator member of the committee admonished the group to keep practicality in mind—what could and could not be done in schools like his. Thus, from the start, various tensions between tradition and change, between ideals and realities, characterized the committee's work and efforts to translate New York's multicultural curriculum policy into practice. The nature of these tensions and how they played out are examined in this chapter, against the background of the renewed America debate that followed *One Nation, Many Peoples* (Social Studies Review and Development Committee 1991) and the "Understanding Diversity" policy in 1991.

POLICY AND DEBATE

"Understanding Diversity"

The only new state policy since 1987 directly addressing social studies curriculum knowledge was contained in the July 1991 "Understanding Diversity" document, which called for (1) reaffirmation of a longstanding Board of Regents policy "to promote the understanding of both our common democratic values and our multicultural origins, along with the development of a global perspective on our own and other societies" (p. 4); (2) revision of social studies syllabi; and (3) provision of support for social studies teaching and learning (for example, teacher education, staff development, instructional materials, and compatible assessment programs).[1]

Syllabus revision was to occur within the following guidelines, which, in effect, mute the transformative potential of *One Nation, Many Peoples:*

1. *Establish balanced goals*—including "understanding and appreciation of the democratic and moral values of our common American culture," "understanding and appreciation of the history and culture of the various major ethnic and cultural groups which comprise American society," and developing "students' capacity to think critically about societal issues, drawing on historical knowledge, contemporary information, and points of view from many sources."
2. *Adopt sound principles*—including democracy, diversity, and economic and social justice.
3. *Emphasize understanding*—depth more than breadth, reasoning as well as information acquisition.
4. *Cultivate "multiple perspectives"*—to help students perceive and understand phenomena from different points of view.
5. *Teach our common traditions*—including democratic values and "the political, legal, and cultural roots of our society in England, in Europe, and in the traditions of the West." (p. 7)

   "This common tradition, the tradition which unites us and makes our diversity possible, must be taught to all our children. We must be honest, and acknowledge that we have not always lived up to our ideals— egregiously not, in some cases. And we must show how this tradition has been further shaped and enriched by Americans from all continents. But as we make our curriculum more inclusive, we should not lose sight of what we are including people in." (p. 8)
6. *Include examples of the experiences of many peoples*—not an "encyclopedic list of every contribution by every person and group" (p. 8) but appropriate examples so that all students "find in the curriculum reason for believing that they and their ancestors have shared in the building of the country and have a stake in its success and . . . learn more about those who are different from themselves." (p. 8)
7. *Tell the whole story*—reflecting "not only our achievements, but our shortcomings; not only our triumphs, but our pain; and not only our failures, but our successes and ideals. This is not to say that all cultures or civiliza-

tions are 'equal', but it is to say that students are capable of understanding the complexity of human nature and the human experience, and an education which does not help them do so sells them short." (p. 8)

8. *Maintain scholarly standards, and include up-to-date scholarship*—recognizing that history is continually reinterpreted.

9. *Be sensitive to language and representation*—without sacrificing accuracy.

10. *Avoid "hypostatization"*—"Treat the issues of race, ethnicity, and culture as one way [not the only way] of understanding American history and American society." (p. 10)

Responding to criticism of the 1991 *One Nation, Many Peoples* report and its perceived implications, Commissioner Sobol's recommendations in "Understanding Diversity" (July 12, 1991) also included the following summary of what was *not* being advocated because, he said, "the issue of 'multicultural education' has been subject to so much misunderstanding and misrepresentation by the public and the press" (p. 12).

> *NOT recommended: trashing the traditions of the West.*
> *NOT recommended: an Afrocentric curriculum.*
> *NOT recommended: ethnic cheerleading and separatism.*
> *NOT recommended: distorting history.*
> *NOT recommended: a curriculum of self-esteem.*
> *NOT recommended: a study of American history based on ethnicity or culture alone.*

It is significant here that Sobol used the language of the 1990 Committee of Scholars and other critics in saying what he was *not* recommending, for example, "ethnic cheerleading" and "trashing." Thus the critics' language was influential in shaping the debate. At the same time, Sobol's effort to gain support had little impact on the critics of New York State's efforts toward more multicultural history and social studies education.

The following excerpts provide a sample of opinion on the second of two widely publicized New York State reports—the June 1991 *One Nation, Many Peoples* and the "Understanding Diversity" policy—and of multicultural education more generally:

> *Multiculturalism.* That jawbreaking word has already caused huge controversy. The furor is sure to continue now that a committee of scholars has recommended revisions in New York State's school curriculum that would place greater emphasis on cultural diversity. But the report should be read with care and an open mind. It squarely faces a tough question: Should public schools stress the common elements that define America or the differing cultures that often divide it? The committee's answer is that a revised curriculum can wisely encompass both. (*New York Times* editorial, June 23, 1991)

> The traditional notion that Columbus "discovered" America—as if before it was known to Europeans it didn't quite exist—is just one of the more apparent examples of what is wrong with the way schools have often

taught social studies. When schools virtually dismiss the Native American culture that was here when Europeans arrived, schoolchildren get a picture of history that isn't just incomplete but misleading as well. . . . And that incompleteness is what the controversial report from a state review panel is all about. The panel's goal is to make the teaching of history and social studies more accurate by including the contributions of, and impacts on, non-white cultures. (*Buffalo News* editorial, June 30, 1991)

[The NYS Report *One Nation, Many Peoples*] denigrates the basic tenets of our American heritage. It is a divisive, far out, liberal sham that should be eviscerated immediately. (William Powers, New York State Republican party chairman, July 14, 1991)

We're in the midst of an important change in our school curriculum. By including the contributions of many different groups that have not previously been recognized, we're trying to make a multicultural curriculum that accurately reflects our society. However, some groups, including the New York Board of Regents, which has just accepted guidelines for a new social studies curriculum, may end up sacrificing accuracy for diversity. They seem to think that, in order to give kids varied points of view, it's perfectly okay to teach ideas and theories that few or no reputable scholars accept. (Albert Shanker, President of the American Federation of Teachers, February 1992)

In the summer and fall of 1991 the renewed America debate was apparent both in the national media and in professional education circles, spurred by the Fourth of July holiday and the following year's Columbus Quincentenary. *Newsweek, Time,* and *U.S. News & World Report* all ran cover stories.[2]

Derisive Discourse: Misunderstanding Diversity?
Social studies curriculum and classroom practice may be formed less by official state policy than by the continuing debates about history, social studies, and multicultural education. How the debates are shaped and played out influences the perceptions and practices of policymakers, teachers, and other school personnel whether they are active participants in, or occasional observers of, these debates.

Life in the United States can be so complex and turbulent that it often takes a "crisis" to gain public attention. Government bureaucracy and social schisms seem so unfixable that mere "problems" are endemic and fail to garner much notice. Crisis rhetoric has become an integral part of everyday political and social life (see Edelman 1977). Proposals for reform are presented as antidotes to what are perceived as serious crises, and opponents of reform predict more crisis as a consequence of the changes they oppose. Thus critics predicted that more inclusive social studies curricula, as recommended by *One Nation, Many Peoples,* could lead to fragmentation of the United States along the lines of Yugoslavia, while proponents suggested similarly severe consequences if the proposed reforms were not realized. As

Gerry O'Sullivan (1992) observed, "cultural contestation is cast as cultural crisis" (p. 18). Both proponents and critics of more multicultural social studies have presented themselves as saviors of America (e.g., MacDonald 1992).[3]

Self-proclaimed defenders of history (e.g., Committee of Scholars in Defense of History 1990; see Chapter 4) focused on the question of legitimate or authentic history, implying that only such an accredited history should be taught in the schools. By their unspecified criteria, much if not most of the range of Afrocentric scholarship did not pass muster. They defined multiculturalism and related scholarship as something other than legitimate history and scholarship. In other words, their discourse delimited historical knowledge to a particular version of history and put alternative interpretations out of bounds. They claimed that only a particular, selective tradition constituted authentic knowledge and therefore was most worthy of inclusion in school curriculum. In contrast to the 1990 Statement of the Committee of Scholars, the executive board of the Organization of American Historians issued a statement in support of an inclusive, multicultural history and curriculum (OAH 1991; see Chapter 4). Although the OAH statement is more representative of the community of academic historians, it was much less adversarial and gained far less public visibility through the media than did Ravitch and Schlesinger's Committee of Scholars' statement.

Examination of the debate surrounding proposed changes in social studies curriculum in New York reveals additional dimensions of the discourse, including tendencies toward polarization with respect to, for example, pluralism or unity, celebration or critique, and political or social history. These aspects of the debate extended the discourse beyond history per se and academic communities of historians to a public discourse about who Americans are and might become, individually and collectively. As suggested earlier, questions of what or whose knowledge is to be included in school curriculum are not solely academic or professional matters. The polarization of opinion spurred by the crisis rhetoric, however, threatened to undermine constructive curriculum discourse.

On another level, particularly striking aspects of the discourse involving events in New York are what might be characterized as a "discourse of derision" and the personal attacks on Commissioner of Education Thomas Sobol. Since the commissioner was the key policymaker supporting New York's multicultural initiatives, attacking him personally could have been an attempt to press him to change course or resign, or to pressure the Board of Regents to replace him. It also was suggested that attacking Sobol would have made Governor Mario Cuomo more vulnerable to criticism if he had become a presidential candidate in 1992.

The "discourse of derision"—a characterization borrowed from Ball's (1990) account of neo-conservative educational politics in Britain—refers to critics' efforts to undermine multiculturalism by caricaturing and then ridiculing it. For example, multiculturalism was linked to an ethnocentric version of Afrocentrism, and then both were scornfully dismissed as "eth-

nic cheerleading" (Ravitch), "self-esteem pablum" (*New York Post*), or leading to "the Tower of Babel" (Schlesinger). Even more strident were claims
that multiculturalism is a facade for efforts to "skew the entire educational
content of public education" in order to serve the perceived needs of, or
cater to the demands of, African Americans (Decter 1991, p. 29). Thus, "by
setting reason against madness" (Ball 1990, p. 44)—that is, history against
multiculturalism—critics of a more multicultural curriculum attempted to
dominate the discursive terrain and thereby shape curriculum policy and
practice.

The professional and public discourse about history, social studies, and
multicultural education redirected attention to the selection of knowledge to
be included in curriculum, particularly to the purposes that different selections might be expected to serve and to the criteria for knowledge selection.
Such attention might well have prompted school districts, schools, and individual teachers to reexamine their social studies programs and modify curricula in multicultural directions. To the extent that the continuing debate
tends toward polarization (for example, separatism versus unity), however,
it serves to sustain the status quo with respect to social studies curricula.
School leaders are mediators who try to avoid controversy and steer a middle course through conflicting demands. In the absence of state mandates or
local pressures, the safest course for local educators is to do little. (See
Chapter 6 concerning experiences in California school districts.)

State Policymaking as Mediation

At the state level, policymakers both respond to and mediate internal
and external demands and interests, including their own. Mediation typically involves transforming demands that are controversial or difficult to
realize into policies that are more widely acceptable and feasible to carry out.
One way to do this is to route the demand(s) through normal bureaucratic
channels. This tactic slows the policy process, during which time strong
feelings may fade. In this way policymakers and the education system attempt to maintain credibility or legitimacy and major change is delayed,
diluted, or avoided (see, e.g., Cornbleth 1990).

In mid-1991 it was not clear how far or how rapidly New York would
move in the direction of the transformative multiculturalism sketched in *One
Nation, Many Peoples*. The subsequent "Understanding Diversity" policy,
while more cautious than *One Nation, Many Peoples*, suggested that movement would continue at a moderate pace—that, in two years, new social
studies programs would be found in New York's elementary and secondary
classrooms. The question was whether and how the largely symbolic policy
of "Understanding Diversity" would be translated into more specific state
education policy regarding social studies curriculum and instruction, the
assessment of students, and the education and certification of teachers.

By the end of 1991, with the incorporation of the state's diversity initiatives into an umbrella state education reform program—the New Compact
for Learning approved by the Board of Regents in March 1991—it remained

unclear whether such incorporation meant that multicultural efforts had been moved from the margins to the mainstream or whether they would be dissipated within normal channels and subordinated to concerns about other social studies outcomes and assessment. It was significant, however, that New York education policymakers had not capitulated to the critics and had not abandoned efforts to make social studies more multicultural in nontrivial and possibly transformative ways. But, three years later, with no social studies program yet being tried in New York's schools, it appeared that the movement toward a more transformative multiculturalism had been muted, at least for the time being.

FRAMING AMERICA

The master's tools will never dismantle the master's house.
    Audre Lorde (1984, p. 112)

In the summer of 1991, despite the derisive discourse, it seemed that the momentum of *One Nation, Many Peoples* and "Understanding Diversity" would carry into the next phase of state-level social studies curriculum revision. At least two sets of circumstances intervened, however, to thwart that movement. One, less heralded in the press than the other, was a major reorganization of SED, for both budgetary and political reasons, and the creation of an organizational mechanism to carry on the curriculum, instruction, and assessment strands of the New Compact for Learning. An overarching or superordinate Curriculum and Assessment Council "of distinguished people with an interest in education" (letter from Commissioner Sobol, January 8, 1992, p. 2) was created in June 1991 with Linda Darling-Hammond, a professor of education at Teachers College, Columbia University, and Nathan Quinones, an education consultant and former New York City Schools Chancellor, as co-chairs. (Later Quinones would withdraw from the co-chair position, and Darling-Hammond would become highly influential.) Over a period of time, seven subject area Curriculum and Assessment Committees were formed, with membership on the council and all the committees being reviewed and approved by the Board of Regents. The reform effort was slowed as relationships were worked out between the council and the committees, and with SED personnel—"inventing it as we go," as one SED staffer put it.

The second set of circumstances dampening momentum stemmed from a July 20, 1991 speech by the controversial Leonard Jeffries, chair of Africana Studies at the City College of New York, at the Empire State Black Arts and Cultural Festival in Albany, a state-subsidized event. Jeffries's wide-ranging anti-Semitic comments (1991), including his characterization of then-Assistant Secretary of Education Diane Ravitch as a "sophisticated Texas Jew" and "Miss Daisy," created a furor in and beyond the media.[4] Media reports implicated Sobol and SED as Jeffries supporters (the Sobol-

SED task force that produced *A Curriculum of Inclusion* in 1989 had hired
Jeffries as a consultant). Such political complications made it more difficult
to move ahead with multicultural curriculum revision without seeming to
endorse Jeffries's views (see, e.g., Chiles 1991; Sobol 1991). Nine months
later Sobol (1992) commented in remarks to the Organization of American
Historians:

> Professor Jeffries' colorful rhetoric and extreme points of view have been
> an inviting target for ridicule and obloquy, and the media have obligingly
> responded by making him a figure larger than life. Unfortunately, his
> views and the publicity they have received have made it difficult for those
> inclined to seek a moderate, balanced position to conduct the debate on a
> thoughtful plane. (p. 17)

Sobol further noted that the damaging effect of erroneous public association of Jeffries with the diversity initiative since 1989 had been:

> to divert attention from what we are actually trying to do, and to make it
> difficult to engage the legitimate, complex issues on which reasonable
> people are not yet agreed. Indeed, I have come to think that at least some
> of the criticism that our project and others like it have received has this as
> its intended effect. . . . How does one account for the intensity of the
> anger, the prevalence of the misconceptions, the insinuations and out-
> right charges of bad faith, the apparently willful distortions and misrepre-
> sentations of what we are doing? I have not read you samples of my
> worse "hate mail." But even many of the critiques which come cloaked
> in the garb of erudition have a stridency, a shrillness, a disproportionate
> ferocity that suggests people who are panicked. I think that many people
> are genuinely frightened by the changes occurring in our society, and
> they resent them. They see individualism losing ground to group identity.
> They see a breakdown of values they hold dear, and they fear a loss of
> control . . . from people like themselves. . . . (p. 18)

Media coverage of the Jeffries speech and its fallout lasted more than two
months, well into the fall of 1991.

After several months of delay, and following appointment of Curriculum
and Assessment (C & A) Committees for Math, Science, and Technology and
for English Language Arts, the Social Studies C & A Committee was appointed in December 1991. The 21 members included nine from the previous Review Committee: Kermit Ackley, Mary Carter, Catherine Cornbleth,
Lloyd Elm, William Fetsko, Nathan Glazer, Jorge Klor de Alva, Susan Sagor,
and Virginia Sanchez Korrol. By the end of the C & A Committee's first year,
Glazer (who had agreed to be a co-chair) was no longer attending meetings,
while Elm and Sagor attended only occasionally. The committee came to be
co-chaired by Jorge Klor de Alva, Professor of Anthropology at Princeton,
and Linda Biemer, Professor and Dean of the School of Education and Human Development at SUNY Binghamton.

The C & A Committee's charge differed from the plan for syllabus revision outlined in the July 1991 "Understanding Diversity" policy. Syllabus revision was not explicitly mentioned since, under the New Compact for Learning umbrella, the familiar course syllabi that specified what should be taught at each grade level might be replaced by less prescriptive curriculum guidelines for social studies K–12. The Social Studies C & A Committee was charged instead with identifying desired learning outcomes for social studies education in New York consistent with the Regents Goals for education (1984, revised 1991) and "Understanding Diversity." The committee also was asked to recommend "elements of a statewide program of educational assessment" to measure progress toward desired learning outcomes (Draft Charge to the State Curriculum and Assessment Committee for Social Studies, November 7, 1991). The charge explicitly stated that the committee was to "advise the Commissioner and the Board of Regents"; all of the C & A committees and the council were advisory bodies.

The correspondence from Commissioner Sobol and SED staff during December 1991 and January 1992 sent differing messages regarding task and direction, suggesting uncertainty regarding how both the diversity initiative and the broader social studies reform would proceed. The mixed messages seemed to reflect the "inventing it as we go" comment mentioned earlier, as did the social studies committee's originally being scheduled to meet in November 1991 but not being appointed until December, and not holding its first meeting until February 1992. In a letter of January 8, 1992 discharging members of the earlier Review Committee, Sobol explained why he was forming a new committee:

> When the [Review Committee] was formed, the Compact was still in the early stages of discussion. We had not yet envisioned the Council and Committee structure. In light of the direction we are now taking with all the disciplines, I believe that it would be confusing and unproductive to have two Committees charged with overseeing the development of curriculum and assessments in the social studies. The presence of nine members from your committee on the new one will help us make sure that its work remains true to your vision.

Rather than recount the Social Studies C & A Committee experience through its 14 meetings over nearly two years, from February 1992 to January 1994, three major themes are explored below, with illustrations drawn from meeting and interview notes and from a range of documents. Then, the emerging Social Studies Curriculum, Instruction, and Assessment Framework is considered. The themes, which both characterize the committee's operation and point to the conclusion that multiculturalism became muted, are (1) business more or less as usual, (2) bridging pluralism and unity, and (3) chains of command.

Business More or Less as Usual

The seemingly heady days of the prior Review Committee had ended with the presentation of *One Nation, Many Peoples* to the New York State

Board of Regents in June 1991 (although, technically, the Review Committee continued to exist until the January 1992 discharge letter from Sobol just cited). The crusading spirit and relative independence of that group was followed by the more matter-of-fact, direction-following C & A Committee. Where the Review Committee had been ballyhooed as "blue ribbon," the C & A Committee was only one of seven. More typical of SED committees of recent memory, it was composed of "21 leaders in the field of social studies" (SED press release, December 20, 1991), what the police prefect in *Casablanca*, Captain Louis Renault, would have called "the usual suspects."

The C & A Committee was not entirely "business as usual," however, primarily because normal channels had been disrupted by the continuing reorganization of SED, and a broad reform program was under way. Also significant was the desire of some of the carryover members from the Review Committee, and a few of the new members, to see the multiculturalism of *One Nation, Many Peoples* and "Understanding Diversity" carried through into learning outcomes, means of assessment, and what became known as curriculum, instruction, and assessment guides, or frameworks. The previously noted tensions between tradition and change, and between ideals and realities, were very much in evidence.

Of the 21 members of the C & A Committee, seven were teachers, five were supervisors or other administrators (one of whom was a former SED social studies staff member), six were university faculty, and three were other educators. By contrast, there were 13 university faculty among the 24 members of the Review Committee. Half the C & A Committee members were female (compared with one-third of the Review Committee), and two-thirds were European Americans (compared with half the Review Committee). Four teacher or supervisor-administrator C & A Committee members also represented organized groups: the state social studies council (NYS Council for the Social Studies), the NYS Social Studies Supervisory Association, and the dominant teacher union (NYS United Teachers); two members represented the NYS Historical Association. Only two members were from out-of-state (compared with five on the Review Committee), and they both were continuing members of the Review Committee and became the C & A Committee's original co-chairs.[5] Compared with the Review Committee, the C & A Committee was more home-grown, more gender balanced, less diverse, less weighted toward university perspectives, and more closely linked to the status quo in social studies education, schooling, and society.

Clearly, the committee was not stacked with people desiring substantial, let alone radical, change in social studies curriculum. For the most part the C & A Committee was composed of people who were used to and comfortable with the way things had been and were not eager to see, or be responsible for, major changes in social studies curriculum, instruction, or assessment. At least four committee members, for example, had been involved in writing the existing social studies grade level syllabi, which they defended regularly. Even some of the committee members who voiced willingness to change their own practice seemed reluctant to impose change on their colleagues. Familiarity and comfort with the status quo was evident in that most committee members sought direction from SED staff, some committee members defended traditionally high-status (Regents) state exams, and a few vocal committee members preferred to keep diversity at the margins of social studies education.

Seeking direction. Much of the committee's first meeting was spent in asking and talking around and about what the group was "supposed" to do, how to interpret the charge, and so forth. Responses from SED staff were vague—in part it seemed because there were no definitive answers to many of the questions. The committee was to "invent" in the spirit of the New Compact for Learning and consistent with "Understanding Diversity." The seeming ambiguity of the committee's tasks continued to rankle several members.

In the past, such committees had specific tasks with considerable guidance from the Social Studies Bureau of SED, which was no longer in existence. Accustomed to a highly centralized education system in New York State, the expectation was for direction from Albany to the committee—and for committee directives to be passed on to social studies teachers across the state. In other words, most committee members expected what came to be called "high guidance" from SED, and more than a few wanted to provide "high guidance," by way of curriculum prescription, to teachers. A year or so later, however, direction and changes in direction from the superordinate C & A Council would generate resentment within the committee (see "Chains of Command" below.)[6]

Evolving tensions. Early tensions between carryover members from the Review Committee and new members of the C & A Committee, and tensions between university and other members of the committee, tended to give way to tensions between advocates of more, or less, multiculturalism (see "Bridging Pluralism and Unity" below), and between advocates of more, or less, curriculum direction to schools and teachers.

The nine carryover members were familiar with the "Understanding Diversity" policy and were accustomed to a degree of respect and independence from SED that was not familiar to new members. At least initially, there appeared to be an insider–outsider split. Some of the outsiders, however, were "old-timers" from previous SED committees, and one had been a SED staff member. As it became clear that this was an ordinary rather than a special committee, as new members brought themselves "up to speed" on "Understanding Diversity," as all members came to understand the New Compact for Learning, and as the C & A Council came to be seen as an adversary of sorts, tensions between old and new members faded.

Of the six university members of the C & A Committee, four were carryovers, two of whom were the committee's initial co-chairs (Jorge Klor de Alva and Nathan Glazer). True to prevailing stereotypes, which had some basis in fact, university faculty were portrayed by some other committee members as idealistic, radical, and too long-winded, while teachers and other committee members were portrayed by some university faculty as too conservative and tied to existing practice and ways of thinking. For example, after only two meetings, one of the university members wrote in a letter, "It is clear our work is proceeding slowly, to the frustration of many of us" (April 2, 1992). About a year later (February 10, 1993) another university member commented that it wasn't surprising that the group was turning out little that was different from what existed, that some members had difficulty thinking in terms other than existing state syllabi and exams:

> That's what you get when you put together . . . people who don't know anything [about what goes on in today's schools] . . . people who wrote the old ones [syllabi] and don't want any change . . . and people who took their assignment carefully and still came up with what is most familiar, comfortable to them and their teaching.

While tensions between school and university representatives did not disappear, they waned as people worked together and came to know each other. Exceptions to the just-mentioned stereotypes helped to moderate these tensions and redefine them in terms of multiculturalism and prescriptiveness, that is, specifying the subject matter to be taught. For example, one of the most eloquent spokespersons for diversity, inclusion, and confronting racism was Mary Carter, a seventh-grade teacher. In contrast, one of the strongest supporters of curriculum prescription, especially of scope and sequence, came to be Jorge Klor de Alva, a professor of anthropology at Princeton and committee co-chair. Klor de Alva also signed on as a consultant to Houghton Mifflin, and became a co-author of its social studies textbook series (after the series was the only one to be adopted in California. See Chapter 3). Some members raised questions privately then and publicly later about his Houghton Mifflin connection at the same time he was serving as the committee co-chair.[7]

Bridging Pluralism and Unity

At the first few committee meetings, statements about multiculturalism were couched in general terms and were largely positive. Tensions emerged as the group worked toward specific learning outcomes conceived as statements of what students should know and be able to do (skills), and what values they should embody, for example, civic responsibility. From there the committee was to draft a social studies framework, including the learning outcomes, narrative elaborations of the outcomes, and performance indicators at elementary, intermediate, and advanced levels. By mid-1992 co-chair Klor de Alva expressed concern about keeping the group together on diversity issues and urged compromise with more conservative members.

Some members of the committee were leery of "too much" multiculturalism. "If Arthur's worried, then I think we should be too," was one school district administrator's way of expressing it. He was referring to Arthur Schlesinger Jr.'s oft-reprinted dire warnings of Balkanization and Babel. Names like Schlesinger, Ravitch, and Shanker—especially Schlesinger— were referred frequently to with deference to support a "moderate" position against "radical" change in the knowledge included in social studies curriculum. Echoing Schlesinger's dissenting commentary in *One Nation, Many Peoples,* one teacher member commented that, "reading between the lines of *One Nation, Many Peoples,* there's too much diversity." It seemed clear that several committee members were influenced by American Federation of Teachers (AFT) publications which featured articles warning of the dangers of multiculturalism by Shanker, Ravitch, and historian Paul Gagnon, as well as by the position of the state-level union (New York State United Teachers, NYSUT) in support of the national union and against local flexibility in matters of curriculum and assessment.

One indicator of the pluralism-unity divide and efforts to bridge if not reconcile it was the iteration of the "pluralism and unity" learning outcome. It had been first in a list of 18, was moved to second (in a reduced list of nine) in the fall of 1993—so as not to arouse opposition among readers right off the bat—and then returned to the lead-off position late in 1993. A sample of various versions of the outcome statement as it evolved follows, with the most contentious words and phrases italicized. The differences and nuances are subtle but significant:

> (May 2, 1992)   Students will employ methods of inquiry from history and the social sciences to understand that the people of the United States are *united* by *shared* values, practices, and traditions *drawn from diverse sources* and *modified by the American* experience.

> (September 1, 1993)   Students will employ methods of inquiry from history and the social sciences to understand how the people of the United States are *diverse yet united* by *shared* values, practices, and traditions *drawn from many sources* and *modified by the North American* experience.

> (September 29, 1993)   Students should understand the ways in which the people of the United States are *diverse and yet are united* by *many shared* values, practices, and traditions.

From May to September the "history and the social sciences" lead-in had been dropped, as had the "diverse sources" of what Americans had come to share and the recognition that values, practices, and traditions found in or brought to America changed over time. Added was "many," although the "many shared values, practices, and traditions" were unspecified by the committee members supporting the language of unity over diversity—not unlike the rhetoric employed by neo-nativists. Then a further change in this learning outcome, making it even more regressive, triggered strong reaction from committee members who had not attended one or both of the committee meetings at which the just-described changes had been made:

> (October 19, 1993)   Students should understand the ways in which the people of the United States, *although diverse, are united* by *many shared* values, practices, and traditions.

How the October version of this learning outcome came to be and then was modified further illustrates the tension within the committee and, more broadly, the state policymaking process, including the mediation of conflicting demands. The tension here was between committee members who favored more multiculturalism and those who preferred less. SED staffers tried, at this point, to mediate conflicting demands by including most of them. Staff were taking a more active role, in part because they were doing more and more of the writing, based on committee deliberations and members' rough drafts of various segments of what was to become the Social Studies Curriculum, Instruction, and Assessment Framework. Also significant is that SED staff seemed to want to placate representatives of significant constituencies. In this context, the following excerpt from a memo from two SED staffers that accompanied the October version of the learning outcomes is significant:

> We have incorporated suggested changes . . . wherever possible. . . . Walter and Lloyd [Walter Tice, NYSUT representative, and Lloyd Bromberg, New York City social studies director] . . . wanted to refocus the concept of unity which we included in Outcome 2. . . . Please fax any remaining changes. . . . We will be preparing another draft. . . . (October 19, 1993, memo from Edward Lalor and George Gregory to members of the Social Studies C & A Committee)[8]

Among the several responses was a memo of October 22, 1993 from Cornbleth to Lalor and Gregory, which read in part:

> Since I believe that the outcomes revision is getting out of hand, I'll only respond to one example . . . and try to address a larger issue. The larger issue: if it only takes two people to change a learning outcome, I suspect that I could find at least one other committee member who agrees with me on what follows—and probably other changes as well. Is this how the game is now being played? As revised in the October 19, 1993 materials, Outcome #2 is very different than it was. Diversity has become an "although," and the dynamic nature of diversity and unity has been lost—the message is now static, which is a misrepresentation.

Surprisingly, the initial SED staff response to Cornbleth's memo was to remove the reference to diversity altogether!

In a subsequent telephone conversation (November 4, 1993), Gregory talked with Cornbleth about trying to reconcile various versions of the learning outcome statements or deciding which version to use for the next draft. Gregory preferred the most recently discussed version, while Cornbleth pointed out that the most recent version was not agreed to by most committee members. If the committee remained divided, Gregory said, the decision could come back to SED and Ed Lalor, now Assistant Commissioner for Curriculum and Assessment. That had happened with previous projects, he said. Also relevant here was that both committee and SED staff recommendations only would be advisory to the commissioner and to the Board of Regents.

Another draft and an early November committee meeting resulted in formal agreement on the following version of the pluralism-unity outcome:

(November 17, 1993)   Students should understand the ways in which the people of the United States are *diverse and yet united* by *many* values, practices, and traditions.

This remained the working version as of January 1994. Diversity and unity were now on a par. The deletion of "shared" and the maintenance of "many" was a compromise, reflecting if not indicating that, while few values, practices, or traditions are *shared* by everyone in the United States, *many* are shared less widely, in criss-crossing patterns that serve to unite people. The loss of diverse sources and change over time and place was mourned by only a few committee members; most seemed to see these ideas as unnecessary or as cluttering the main intent of the learning outcome statement.

Although they also underwent modification, the related "multiple perspectives" and "changing interpretations" learning outcomes were not debated as heatedly by the committee. The January 1994 versions were

(Outcome 2)   Students should understand that people from diverse national, ethnic, religious, racial, socioeconomic, and gender groups often have varied perspectives on the same events and issues as a result of their differing experiences.

(Outcome 3)   Students should be able to analyze and evaluate differing, competing, and changing interpretations of historic, social, cultural, economic, and political events, eras, ideas, and issues, and the roles played in these by individuals and groups.

For most committee members, the pluralism-unity question, as it had been defined by the neo-nativists and their supporters in the America debate, was most salient. Few seemed to understand or take an interest in the larger multicultural issues such as the different assumptions and implications of additive and revisionist compared with transformative versions of multiculturalism.

Very few active committee members seemed to advocate a transformative multicultural position and reach out effectively to others in the course of committee meetings. Transformative ideas and approaches made modest headway, at least temporarily, in the smaller working and writing groups. The absence of more than Mary Carter's strong, progressive, persistent African American perspective and voice against racism was in marked contrast to the prior Review Committee. The C & A Committee had no Ed Gordon or Diane Glover or Ali Mazrui or Elleni Tedla supporting Carter's efforts. The few other supportive voices, like Sanchez Korrol's and Cornbleth's, seemed to carry less weight.

The previously noted tensions between more, or less, multiculturalism and between more, or less, curriculum direction—as concrete manifestations of broader issues of tradition and change and of ideals and realities—

merged into a single conflict late in 1993. Providing for less state direction and more local flexibility as called for by the New Compact for Learning could mean making multiculturalism voluntary. That is, teachers could, conceivably, choose to incorporate very little in the way of diversity, multiple perspectives, or changing interpretations in the history and social studies they taught. Moreover, without directions and examples, teachers who lacked the subject matter knowledge would not be able to make their social studies teaching more multicultural, even if they wanted to do so. So a significant issue became how to provide varied multicultural examples without becoming too prescriptive or incorporating what one committee member had called "too much" multiculturalism. "Too much" multiculturalism was defined implicitly as whatever would require major revision of what teachers taught or whatever would prompt renewed controversy. Anything more than additive multiculturalism was too much for some committee members, while others supported multiple perspectives, and a few sought more transformative curricula. This issue reached beyond the C & A Committee to the committee's relations with the C & A Council, as indicated in the next section.

Chains of Command

The "diversity initiative," as New York State's multicultural curriculum policy activity came to be called in and around Albany, was folded into the New Compact for Learning. Two major problems for both the C & A Committee and the diversity initiative emerged during the committee's second year. One was committee members' resentment of being told to do one thing, and then being told to do something else, by the superordinate C & A Council; the other was the apparent desire of SED and the Council to minimize controversy over the New Compact's proposed changes in state curriculum and assessment (for example, Regents exams). Minimizing controversy meant, among other things, slowing action on a social studies framework and downplaying its already moderate multiculturalism. Whether these were astute political tactics or were means of muting multiculturalism in curriculum policy remained to be seen.

Direction and changes in direction. In his December 1991 letter to C & A Committee members just appointed by the Board of Regents, Commissioner Sobol said the council's role was "to oversee and coordinate" the activities of the seven C & A Committees. When Sobol joined the social studies group at its first meeting in February 1992, he said that "work will flow back and forth" between the council and committees. He also said that the council was not likely to review specifics. At that meeting a key SED staffer referred to an "iterative process" where the work of the council and committees would inform each other. Another SED staffer, responding to a committee member's question, said that in the case of council-committee disagreements SED staff would try to bring people together to resolve differences. At this point most Social Studies C & A Committee members appeared concerned about clarifying their task and position in the hierarchy, their challenges to both task and position did not emerge until a year or so later.

Throughout 1992 the C & A Committee worked to create learning outcomes and an assessment plan for K–12 social studies in New York State. Most of this work was done in two-day meetings (Friday and Saturday or Sunday and Monday) in one of the hotels near the Albany airport. By October 18 learning outcomes had been agreed upon (later, they would be modified and reduced in number); an interim report was prepared (to become part of the council's October 1992 Interim Report); and attention turned to elaborating the learning outcomes and considering alternative curriculum models. During this time there was little direction from the council.

Then circumstances changed. Word circulated in late 1992 that Sobol either wanted to move on social studies and the diversity initiative, or he was being pressured to get something out. There was talk of identifying a small group of "writers" from within and outside the committee to draft a curriculum framework, because the 21 member committee was too large to accomplish this task effectively. Outsiders were to include at least one university historian, apparently to ward off potential criticism from history advocates who continued to be wary of both social studies and multiculturalism as threats to the long-standing dominance of conventional history in the schools. The committee co-chairs and SED staff mulled over numerous names.[9] There was talk that writers would work during December and January to have a draft framework out by spring 1993. Meanwhile the council was working on a description of what it wanted in the way of a framework and was specifying the desired relationship between the council and the committees.[10] The Social Studies C & A Committee, however, did not meet between December 1992 and June 1993 mainly because SED was in disarray.[11]

During the first half of 1993, SED was undergoing a major reorganization, there was talk of budget problems for C & A work, and Linda Darling-Hammond was emerging as a key figure guiding the New Compact reforms. For example, materials shared with the committee at its December 1992 meeting entitled "Tasks for Curriculum Committees and SED Staff (with Council Guidance and Review)" were photocopies of materials that Darling-Hammond at Teachers College had sent by fax to SED staff. It became clear that references to "the council's" wishes or questions were in fact references to Darling-Hammond's.

At the end of March 1993, Cornbleth and historian Robert Harris of Cornell, two of the five SED-selected "writers," met with two SED staffers in Syracuse to plan how to proceed with drafting a social studies curriculum framework. People were "so consumed" with the SED reorganization, one staffer had said when the meeting was being scheduled, that they were "in limbo" and were now just beginning to move again. The other staffer concurred, saying that they couldn't sit on their thumbs much longer. Cornbleth and Harris were urged not to "sit here and wait" for the council to decide what it wanted.[12] Hopefully, the senior SED staffer said, there would be a draft framework by fall 1993: "The Commissioner and I both want to move ahead." Getting something out to schools and the public would allay fears and spur movement. This, however, was not to be.

For reasons that were not at all clear but probably included the reorganization of SED as well as staff and/or council desires to keep the seven C & A Committees on a similar time schedule, the writers did not meet and begin work until July, four months later. By that time the council had decided what it wanted by way of a framework. Meanwhile, a number of C & A Committee members, some apparently disgruntled that they had not been selected as writers and others frustrated by the apparent slowdown, questioned the legitimacy of the process and the turn of events. At an informal meeting with C & A Committee members attending the annual state social studies council (New York State Council for the Social Studies, NYSCSS) meeting in early April, SED staffers made an effort to bring members up to date about what was happening within SED, and with the council and writers. Commissioner Sobol, the Friday luncheon speaker at the NYSCSS meeting, reiterated that the New Compact policymaking process was fluid and developmental. Everyone had access and influence, he said, but no one's influence was unlimited.[13]

By early fall 1993 it seemed clear that both the committee and the writers (and perhaps SED staff as well) were to do as they were told by the council. For example, the committee and writers were to engage in council-directed tasks and make council-directed revisions in draft documents. Council direction came less from formal decisions made at meetings than from reported communications from Darling-Hammond, relayed verbally by SED staff. The committee was directed by the council to prepare a section on social studies for the council's next report to the Board of Regents (eventually submitted for Regents' discussion in November 1993) as well as a framework. Drafts of the chapter and framework were returned to SED staff and the committee with marginal comments and directions for revision from Darling-Hammond. Sobol's earlier statement that the council was unlikely to review specifics turned out not to be the case. Several committee members voiced resentment at being told what they should write, suggesting instead that the council write its own report. For example, Cornbleth said that it was unacceptable to tell an advisory committee what to write, or to make major revisions in its work, and then use members' names to justify what had been written. In what was a minor revolt, the committee considered but did not always adopt the council's recommendations—to the visible distress of a few SED staffers.

By the November 1993 committee meeting, members' irritation had turned away from the writers to focus on Darling-Hammond, the council, and SED staff who seemed to be following her lead unquestioningly. At the December 1993 committee meeting, an administrator member threatened SED staff with "armed rebellion" if the planned agenda and task for the next meeting (January 1994) were changed without consultation as had happened for prior meetings.

The continuing salience of questions about the committee's responsibility and relationship with the council and SED meant that energies often were directed elsewhere than addressing questions of the knowledge to be included in social studies curriculum, how the selected knowledge would be organized, and how diversity would be understood. At times it seemed that the diversity initiative had been overwhelmed—not buried by bureaucracy as might have happened in an earlier era, but mired in the tangled web of an uncertain bureaucracy in transition and the personalized political relations of council, committee, and SED staff. Many committee members, most of them school people, indicated that they were unimpressed with Darling-Hammond's reputation as a noted policy analyst. They saw her as a nonspecialist, not as a prestigious university consultant.

Minimizing controversy. A final thread in this continuing saga of multicultural policy-in-the-making was the apparent desire on the part of the council and SED staff to minimize if not avoid likely opposition to proposed changes in curriculum and assessment that were key to the New Compact reform. Concern with minimizing controversy was voiced initially by continuing members of the Review Committee who hoped to avoid some of the rancorous opposition following *A Curriculum of Inclusion* and *One Nation, Many Peoples* by means of careful language, and by being proactive instead of allowing issues to be defined by critics. At the beginning of the committee's second meeting in early March 1992, someone commented that of all the C & A committees, social studies was "the most visible and dangerous." By late 1993 council and SED concern with minimizing controversy came to mean slowing down movement of the social studies framework to the Board of Regents, schools, and public as well as downplaying multiculturalism in the framework itself. While more conservative members of the committee appeared impatient with the slowdown but supported more modest multiculturalism, the more progressive committee members were impatient on both counts.

Curriculum, instruction, and assessment frameworks instead of content-focused syllabi, and Regents exams involving "performances" as well as multiple-choice and essay questions, were major changes being proposed under the New Compact rubric. These changes, not the diversity initiative, were SED priorities. Council and SED concerns about opposition to these changes from the Regents, education professionals, and the public meant that draft frameworks were not sent to the Regents for authorization to circulate them to the field for review in either the spring or the fall of 1993. Instead, SED staff and Darling-Hammond made presentations to the Regents throughout 1993 about curriculum frameworks and especially performance assessments. A second council "report" was presented to the Board of Regents in November 1993. This report included brief subject area sections that suggested, in general terms, what was to come in the frameworks. The more specific frameworks would appear later.

News stories reporting criticism of the generality of the subject area recommendations in the council report may have prompted a decision to begin sending the draft frameworks to the Board of Regents. John Hildebrand

(1993) of Long Island's *Newsday*, reporting on the November Regents meeting, noted:

> The curriculum proposals, the product of more than two years' work, immediately were attacked by some education policymakers as a porridge of vague abstractions that would be difficult to explain to teachers and students alike. Saul Cohen, a regent and former college president [and geographer], referred to proposed changes in social studies as "pap."

Council members, according to Hildebrand, said that details were omitted deliberately to avoid the appearance that the state was mandating teaching methods. With respect to the social studies portion of the council report, Hildebrand wrote:

> But that generality drew criticism yesterday—in marked contrast to fears expressed in the past that the state's curriculum changes might prove too radical in their condemnation of traditional western values. State Education Commissioner Thomas Sobol, who conceived the curriculum project, had insisted this was not his intent. Curriculum outlines made public yesterday seemed to confirm the point. A chapter in the advisory council's report dealing with social studies, while calling for lessons on historical discrimination against women and minorities, also recommends heavy emphasis on common values that unite Americans, such as their belief in democracy, freedom of religion and social justice.

By early December 1993, decisions had been made to send the Math, Science, and Technology draft framework to the Board of Regents that month (at its December meeting, the board agreed to send the draft to the field for review and comment) and the English Language Arts draft in early 1994. Social studies would not go forward earlier than March or April 1994. Meanwhile the Social Studies C & A Committee was directed to strengthen, in part by making more explicit, the subject matter base of the social studies framework, particularly in history, geography, and civics—areas that received federal monies to support projects to devise national standards. The working strategy seemed to be that the less contentious subject areas would go first, hopefully paving the way for the more problematic social studies framework.

News articles in October and November by David Bauder (1993) of the Associated Press and Debra Viadero (1993) of *Education Week* raised questions about the delay in revising New York's social studies curriculum, noting that the effort was two years behind its original schedule. Both Commissioner Sobol and the Regents (with the notable exception of J. Edward Meyer, who was one of three Regents voting against "Understanding Diversity" in 1991) indicated that the time lag did not mean that they were backing down on diversity.

Instead of responding to public pressure to move more rapidly by pushing the social studies framework, Sobol indicated in a December 1993 conversation with Cornbleth that he would take as much time as needed to get it right—about three or four months, he estimated. After review during spring 1994, piloting might begin during the 1994–1995 school year. Time was needed, he said, to deal with questions of academic rigor and the national standards projects as well as to respond to new members of the Board of Regents and questions from the legislature's Black and Puerto Rican Caucus. He couldn't automatically go to the Regents, Sobol said, with whatever the C & A Committee handed him. He referred to public failure to distinguish between the 1989 *A Curriculum of Inclusion* report and his recommendations based on it, and the angry opposition to both. If the committee did not come up with "what makes sense and is viable," Sobol said, he might need to bring in a person or two to do some writing; he would prefer to have the committee, rather than the "world," angry with him.

In response to a question as to whether or not there was a desire to minimize if not avoid controversy over the New Compact's standards and assessment reforms that could diminish the diversity initiative, Sobol volunteered that Darling-Hammond, while a supporter of multiculturalism, was concerned about controversy. Saying that the diversity message was part of the social studies framework drafts that he had reviewed, but with the "language tempered," he asked Cornbleth whether she agreed. Cornbleth said that she disagreed; she saw the diversity message being diluted.[14]

Asked what he might do if the C & A Committee, council, or Board of Regents sought to weaken the diversity message, Sobol was adamant that he would "fight against it," that he would "rather have the Board of Regents reject something I felt honest about" than water it down. He made it clear that there would be "no retreating"—he wasn't giving up on dealing honestly with the realities of diversity in U.S. history and contemporary society as he saw them. There would be worse problems ahead if we didn't, he warned.

Efforts to downplay diversity in the social studies draft framework came from within and outside the C & A Committee as indicated by the following comments in response to the first draft of a social studies framework assembled by SED staff with contributions from the group of designated writers and the committee:

> Sounds like [a] rationale to justify the teaching of "history" based on the emotional or political needs of those who create new "interpretations" based upon no authentic base. (union representatives and teacher member of committee, September 15, 1993)

> "the multicultural nature of our society" is not an "also" and should not be presented as an add-on or afterthought. (university member of committee, September 14, 1993)

> [With respect to sample assessment tasks] No information about immigration today—to fully explore this issue would hope to have stats on Asians, Hispanics, West Indians as well as Europeans. . . . Westward

Movement for whom . . . "the people they encountered"—these were Americans also. (teacher member of committee, September 13, 1993)

In response to Darling-Hammond's marginal comment, "Don't focus exclusively on race/ethnic differences," writer-consultant Robert L. Harris Jr. wrote:

> I don't think that our examples focus exclusively on racial and ethnic differences as we also include references to religion, gender, socio-economic status, and generational differences. (September 21, 1993)

The previously cited changes in the pluralism-unity outcome also are relevant here.

The council directed the committee to cut the number of references to *One Nation, Many Peoples* and "Understanding Diversity" in the opening sections of the draft framework, which could be seen as a controversy-minimizing tactic or as an attempt to downplay multiculturalism. As of January 1994 the following position had been maintained in the issues and trends section, albeit in a briefer version than previously:

> *Multiculturalism.* . . . The position taken in this curriculum framework goes beyond the tokenism of "heroes and contributions" to the authenticity of transformative multiculturalism. A transformative multiculturalism would mean (a) different themes or emphases, (b) multiple perspectives, and (c) attention to mutual influences among groups. Racism, for example, has affected its perpetrators as well as its targets. (For more information, see *One Nation, Many Peoples,* "Understanding Diversity," and the 1992 revision of the NCSS "Curriculum Guidelines for Multicultural Education" by James A. Banks.) (p. 11)

At the same time, reducing the number of "competencies" and "performance indicators" provided as "illustrative examples" of the learning outcomes meant that the intended multiculturalism was sketched but not fully drawn in the framework drafts. Further specification, a task set for the December 1993 committee meeting, was set aside in order to review emerging statements of national standards from the history, geography, civics, and social studies projects. Broad curriculum models were to be reviewed at the January 1994 meeting, with diversity being only one of 16 considerations in the review—similar to the lack of prominence given to diversity in the 1990 textbook review in California.[15]

A key committee supporter of the diversity initiative, Mary Carter, was unable to attend the December meeting. Referring to the apparent backing away from the specifics of multiculturalism, Carter said in a phone conversation a week or so later that "this has always been the problem in this country." But, she said, committee members couldn't give up the effort to see changes made.

What the draft framework that eventually would go to the Board of Regents and the field would say remained to be seen. Further revision could be expected before statewide use in 1995 or 1996. And what goes out to the schools is not necessarily what will happen *in* the schools. A state curriculum, instruction, and assessment framework is only one of several factors influencing classroom curriculum practice.

MEDIATING MULTIPLE DEMANDS

Education and other policymakers respond to and mediate various demands and interests. One way of mediating "worthy" demands that are controversial or otherwise difficult to realize is to slow the policy process in the hope that strong feelings will fade and "solutions" will emerge. In addition to the typically slow pace of normal bureaucratic channels, policy change can be slowed by task forces, pilot projects, and incorporation of an issue into a larger project. In these ways the education system and its policymakers attempt to maintain legitimacy in the eyes of their various constituents—while major changes are delayed, diluted, or avoided altogether. From another perspective these processes are simply the workings of political compromise, the so-called "art of the possible."

More than two and one-half years after the New York State Board of Regents adopted "Understanding Diversity," recommended by Commissioner Sobol based on the Review Committee's report, *One Nation, Many Peoples,* the largely symbolic policy of "Understanding Diversity" still had not been translated into operational policies for curriculum and instruction, assessment, or teacher education and certification. Efforts to make social studies more multicultural—the diversity initiative to incorporate more inclusive knowledge, in transformative ways, into social studies curriculum and classroom practice—had been moved from the margins to the mainstream New Compact for Learning education reform program. While not dissipated within normal channels, the diversity initiative was subordinated to concerns with standards and alternative forms of performance or authentic assessment. This subjection to other priorities was less a purposeful muting of multiculturalism in curriculum policy, at least by Sobol, and more an effort at political compromise. Perhaps, as a university member of the C & A Committee suggested, it was simply the desire not to allow the social studies "elephant" to bring down the entire tent. If the diversity initiative had not been incorporated into the New Compact, it would have had to compete on its own with other issues (including school funding formulas, asbestos removal, AIDS education, and SED reorganization) for the attention of policymakers and probably would have "gotten lost" altogether.

Obstacles in the Way of the Diversity Initiative

A review of apparent impediments, within and beyond the C & A Committee, to adopting a transformative multicultural curriculum policy in New York State during the early 1990s can both aid understanding of this case of policy-in-the-making and inform future efforts to change curriculum policy. Seven interrelated obstacles are considered briefly.

1. *The neo-nativists and their followers.* Opposition to "too much" multiculturalism remained an ideological concern for some C & A Committee members and a concern about image for others, even though the America debate was relatively low key in 1992 and 1993. Clinton's election in November 1992 removed some key neo-nativists from public office and deprived them of their "bully pulpits." However, the debate could be expected to reignite with the presentation of a New York social studies framework and possibly when the finished products of the history, geography, civics, and social studies national standards projects were issued.

2. *Other priorities.* The larger New Compact for Learning education reform was the SED priority. Its call for major changes in state-level curriculum guidance and assessment was controversial. The Regents, for example, reportedly were not eager to modify "their" Regents Exams, several of which (including U.S. History and Government) had been in place for over a century. So a likely contentious social studies framework would not be presented to the Board of Regents until the idea of curriculum frameworks and alternative assessments had been accepted in principle and until frameworks in less controversial subject areas had been approved for field and public review.[16]

3. *Bureaucracy.* According to Commissioner Sobol, SED lacked the needed funds and appropriate staff to do the work of the New Compact and fulfill the diversity initiative in a more timely manner.

4. *The banner of academic rigor.* The presence of the national standards projects, especially in history and geography, and the claims of members of these academic communities and their supporters to "academic rigor" and the value of their disciplines vis-à-vis "social studies," slowed movement of the social studies framework. Social studies was seen to need to justify its existence, once again, as a school subject in late 1993, both by making the framework's history and geography elements more explicit and by showing how the framework responded to or incorporated key standards from the various national projects. The banner of academic rigor, while a favorite of the opponents of a transformative multiculturalism, was carried as well by some conservative religious organizations.

5. *Opposition to outcomes-based education (OBE).* Organized opposition to state-level OBE proposals (for example, from the California-based Citizens for Excellence in Education and from the Christian Coalition) in several states (including Pennsylvania and Virginia) targeted, among other things, attention to values rather than "basics." To keep such opposition from gaining ground in New York, it was decided late in 1993 to further specify the subject matter in the presumably vulnerable social studies framework and leave less local flexibility than previously envisioned.[17]

6. *Uncertainties of social studies (and multiculturalism).* Just about everyone thinks they know social studies (compared with, say, science), but few know very much, as indicated by Benjamin Barber's adroit commentary (1992,

chap. 6) on what our 47-year-olds know. Consequently, more people are quicker to criticize social studies than other subjects—for being vacuous, soft, or "pap"—while failing to recognize its substance (for example, that "in the context of time and place" means drawing on history and geography). A misunderstanding of social studies, encouraged by some single-subject advocates, makes multicultural social studies appear even more suspect.

As suggested in Chapter 2, while multiculturalism is a robust concept, there are as yet few school curriculum models. Policymakers and educators who want concrete examples will have to create them. Transformative multicultural curricula are "in-the-making." To those who are uneasy with multiculturalism or accustomed to ready-made curriculum packages, transformative multiculturalism is worrisome. To others, it is simply new, untried, and not yet very well understood. The obstacle here is less a purposeful attempt to mute multiculturalism than a hesitancy or unwillingness to risk the largely unknown.

7. *Time.* Time is an obstacle in at least two ways. One is that the passage of time is accompanied by the waning of attention and energy, especially among supporters of change, wearing them down. Members of the C & A committee, for example, found it difficult to maintain momentum for upwards of two years—whether or not delays were intended. A second way in which time is an obstacle is that its passage allows for further impediments to emerge. Major examples in this case are the subject area standards projects, the single-subject advocates (such as geographers), and the conservative religious organizations opposed to OBE. While one obstacle is being addressed, another one appears.

These seven factors, separately and in combination, appear to have impeded movement toward a transformative multicultural curriculum policy in New York either by slowing it down or by moderating the message over the course of events from 1992 to 1994. Whether and how the obstacles are overcome is a chapter yet to be written.

A Continuing Story

This account of multicultural curriculum policymaking in New York is a continuing, not an unfinished, story. As of September 1994 the issues were not resolved, nor were they likely to be, once and for all. As noted in the opening chapters of this volume and illustrated in the case study chapters, curriculum is continually contested. This case is, literally, an instance of policy-in-the-making.

In one sense, official or authoritative curriculum policy will have been made when the New York State Board of Regents agrees to send a draft social studies framework to the field for review; even more authoritative will be the revised framework that eventually is adopted and phased in statewide along with new forms of assessment.[18] In another, perhaps more important, sense, policymaking is ongoing. Policy is continually reinterpreted if not remade at and within various levels of the education system. Social studies teachers are curriculum policymakers, and teachers in the same school have been known to make very different curriculum policies. Despite the presence of state curriculum frameworks and exams (or assessments), teachers continue to be key gatekeepers to the social studies curriculum that is made available to their students. Curriculum policymaking, consequently, is persistent, and practice is locally contingent.

This second chapter of the New York case also illustrates how influence on state curriculum policy is exercised by school and university educators—for example, by staying with the project, by writing and rewriting drafts, and by speaking out. It also illustrates that capable, energetic, and well-placed individuals, like Linda Darling-Hammond, can exercise considerable influence.

Meanwhile, the continuing discourse of history, social studies, multiculturalism, and curriculum reform—and the movement toward national standards—continues to shape as well as to reflect curriculum knowledge and classroom practice across the 50 states. The America debate, for example, has shaped curriculum policymaking in New York and probably has shaped practice as well. Various arguments in the debate supported the diversity initiative and convinced some C & A Committee members and state policymakers to be wary of "too much" multiculturalism. While the America debate was relatively subdued in 1992 and 1993, some who remembered its heat from 1989 to 1991 dreaded its return. So societal dynamics can have an impact even during a period of relative calm.

In addition to the intersections of national issues and education policy questions, the New York case illustrates the interaction of multiple reforms—the diversity initiative and the New Compact for Learning. Neither a single policy issue nor the policymaking process can be understood adequately out of context, that is, apart from its location in an education system, national society, and period of time.

POSTSCRIPT

Co-author Cornbleth writes:

On March 22, 1994 I resigned from the Social Studies Curriculum & Assessment Committee. In my letter to Commissioner Sobol and the New York State Board of Regents, who appointed the committee, I said that resignation was a sad but necessary step on my part given that committee efforts to realize the goals of the 1991 "Understanding Diversity" policy were stymied by lack of committee leadership and SED's apparent unwillingness to risk further controversy about multicultural curriculum. I also had become increasingly uncomfortable with Klor de Alva being both a committee co-chair and a Houghton Mifflin consultant and co-author.

I believed, and told Commissioner Sobol and the Board of Regents, that to continue serving on the committee would be condoning unreasonable delay that served only those interests opposed to the diversity initiative. I did not see how I could have any further positive impact by remaining on the committee, and I hoped that a serious and public resignation would prompt movement toward realizing "Understanding Diversity."

Commissioner Sobol responded in a letter dated March 29, 1994, in which he not only expressed his regrets but also indicated a further delay (at least to fall 1994) before sending the draft social studies framework to the field for review and reaction. He said in part:

> Later this spring or summer, proposed curriculum frameworks [an apparent reference to national standards] in History and Geography, commissioned by OERI [the federal Department of Education's Office of Educational Research and Improvement], will be published. Although we are in no way bound by these proposals, it would be imprudent for New York State to publish its own work before first examining this new national body of work. [The committee already had reviewed and incorporated aspects of the work of all four standards projects relevant to social studies at its December 1993 meeting.]

As of mid-April 1994 the state social studies council, its affiliate association of social studies supervisors, and some Social Studies Curriculum & Assessment Committee members were planning to write to the commissioner and Board of Regents urging that they move immediately to send the draft framework to the field. As of the summer of 1994, both the committee and the draft framework were languishing.

Although there were grounds for hope for action on the draft framework, my optimism has been tempered by the weight of New York State's history of central, top-down direction of curriculum and assessment in social studies and other school subjects. Teachers and other school people—and parents and community members—*expect* Albany to create and send out syllabi and exams. Regents exams, for example, have a history of more than a hundred years, and considerable status. Despite the decentralizing intent of the New Compact for Learning reform effort, New York's history of education regulation is a habit hard to break. But, at this writing, SED seems paralyzed by fear of conservative opposition. Its once-groundbreaking first steps toward transformative multiculturalism seem likely to be redirected—slowly—to more familiar, additive or revisionist paths.

REFERENCES

Ball, Stephen J. 1990. *Politics and policymaking in education.* London: Routledge.
Barber, Benjamin R. 1992. *An aristocracy of everyone: The politics of education and the future of America.* New York: Ballantine.
Bauder, David. 1993. State's educators two years behind on minority project, but they deny they've abandoned a rewriting of history curriculum. [Rochester] *Democrat and Chronicle* (October 10): p. 20A.
Bernstein, Richard. 1993. Jeffries reinstated. *New York Times* (August 8): p. E2.
Chiles, Nick. 1991. Suspicion in Jeffries controversy: Supporters say target is multiculturalism. *New York Newsday* (August 19).

Cornbleth, Catherine. 1990. *Curriculum in context.* London: Falmer.

Decter, Midge. 1991. E pluribus nihil: Multiculturalism and black children. *Commentary* 92 (3): 25–29.

Edelman, Murray. 1977. *Political language: Words that succeed and policies that fail.* New York: Academic Press.

Hildebrand, John. 1993. Education blueprint. Dissension greets plan for revamped curriculum. [Long Island] *Newsday* (November 20).

Jeffries, Leonard. 1991. Text of Jeffries's July speech. *New York Newsday* (August 19): pp. 3, 25–29.

Lorde, Audre. 1984. *Sister outsider.* Freedom, Calif.: Crossing Press.

MacDonald, Heather. 1992. The Sobol report: Multiculturalism triumphant. *New Criterion* 10 (5): 9–18.

New York State Education Department. (1991). *A new compact for learning.* Albany: Author.

O'Sullivan, Gerry. 1992. The PC police in the mirror of history. *Humanist* 52 (2): 17–20, 46.

Sobol, Thomas. 1991. Jeffries is not the point. *New York Newsday* (August 28): letter to the editor.

———. 1992. Paper presented to the annual meeting of the Organization of American Historians, Chicago, April 4.

Social Studies Review and Development Committee. 1991. *One nation, many peoples: A declaration of cultural interdependence.* Albany: New York State Education Department.

Viadero, Debra. 1993. N.Y. wrestles with social-studies framework. *Education Week* (November 17): p. 10.

NOTES

1. In New York, social studies syllabi are booklets of approximately 100 pages for each grade level that specify the content to be taught and suggest learning activities and non-textbook materials that might be used. They are more detailed than a course outline and less specific than daily lesson plans. Revision of K–12 social studies syllabi by the (now defunct) Social Studies Bureau, begun in the early 1980s, was completed in 1987, the year Thomas Sobol became Commissioner of Education and appointed the Task Force on Minorities that produced *A Curriculum of Inclusion.* While progressive in some respects (such as the global studies sequence in grades 9 and 10), the 1987 revision was regressive in others (such as a return from thematic to conventional chronological U.S. history).

2. "Afrocentrism, Was Cleopatra Black? Facts or Fantasies—A Debate Rages Over What to Teach Our Kids about Their Roots" (*Newsweek,* September 23, 1991); "Who Are We? American kids are getting a new—and divisive—view of Thomas Jefferson, Thanksgiving and the Fourth of July" (*Time,* July 8, 1991); "America before Columbus, The Untold Story" (*U.S. News & World Report,* July 8, 1991).

3. Similar arguments about threats to "the American culture" also could be heard 75 years ago. See, for example, O'Sullivan (1992), who traces "the intellectual lineage of the current opposition to 'multiculturalism' " (p. 19).

4. Later Jeffries was removed from his department chair position at City College and then, following his court battle, was reinstated by the Federal District court ruling in August 1993 that his removal simply for making a speech containing "hateful"

statements about Jews violated his First Amendment rights to free speech (Bernstein 1993, p. E2). The film *Driving Miss Daisy* featured an elderly white southern woman and an elderly black southern man who worked as her chauffeur.

5. Elementary social studies teachers and Asian Americans were not represented directly. Linda Biemer, a new member, was appointed as a co-chair after the committee's first meeting. Nathan Glazer, who had noted that the original co-chairs (Jorge Klor de Alva and himself) were not representative of New York or the committee, later withdrew from the co-chair position.

6. The C & A Committee co-chairs seemed to have much less leeway than the co-chairs of the Review Committee. The C & A co-chairs were guided by council decisions and SED staff advice. While often taking an active role vis-à-vis committee members, they did not appear to challenge the council or SED.

7. The shift in Klor de Alva's position and role, from a progressive member of the Review Committee to a moderate-to-conservative co-chair of the C & A Committee, was noticeable to and commented on by carryover members.

8. Identifying SED staffers by name, now but not earlier, is not only for purposes of citation but also to indicate that they were taking more active roles in directing committee activity than previously, both at and between committee meetings. Both Lalor and Gregory were SED veterans. In April 1993 Lalor was appointed Assistant Commissioner for Curriculum and Assessment. Gregory, from the pre-reorganization curriculum unit, became the SED liaison to the Social Studies C & A Committee; he had a background in history education and had worked with Lalor.

9. The five "writers" were committee members Cornbleth and Claire Deloria, a retired social studies teacher and staff development specialist from the Syracuse area, social studies supervisor Kenneth Hilton from the Rochester area, secondary teacher Louise Kuklis from Westchester County, and U.S. historian Robert L. Harris Jr., from Cornell University. Only Kuklis was nominated from outside the committee and SED staff, reportedly recommended by Darling-Hammond. "Writers" also were identified for the Math, Science, and Technology and for the English Language Arts C & A Committees.

10. The emerging conception of "framework," relatively new in the United States, borrowed more from Australian examples of curriculum frameworks via Darling-Hammond than from California's versions. Eventually a framework came to include the following sections: (1) Setting (introductory background information such as Regents Goals and the "Understanding Diversity" policy); (2) Rationale, Issues, and Trends (in the subject area, such as multiculturalism); (3) Outcomes (statements of desired learning outcomes, accompanied by related concepts and illustrative competencies and performance indicators at elementary, intermediate, and secondary school levels); (4) Assessment (with an emphasis on authentic, performance measures); (5) Exemplars of Performance (sample assessment tasks); and (6) Resources.

11. After ten meetings in 1992, the committee met only four times in 1993: in June, September, November, and December.

12. A draft document on curriculum frameworks prepared by Darling-Hammond in December 1992 was not approved by the council until late spring 1993. The actual sections and format of a framework did not take shape until August–September 1993.

13. Sobol's references were primarily to the major teachers union, NYSUT, which had put out a flyer critical of the council's October 1992 Interim Report.

14. Later in the conversation Sobol said that he hoped Cornbleth and others would "keep the committee faithful" to *One Nation, Many Peoples* and "Understanding Diversity."

15. Several committee members were quite vocal in pressing for consideration of curriculum models (program scope and sequence outlines) despite the council's opposition to grade level specification of subject matter. Why SED staff went along with this subgroup, except perhaps to hear them out or to take up time before moving the framework to the Board of Regents, is unclear.

16. Another possible obstacle was that the frameworks for Math, Science, and Technology and for English Language Arts might unduly shape expectations about the form and substance of the social studies and other subject area frameworks. In the national curriculum development projects of the 1950s and 1960s, math and science also led the way, "imposing" conceptions of discipline structure that fit less well in the social sciences and humanities.

17. Early in 1994 the language of "learning outcomes" was changed to content and performance "standards" because of anticipated opposition from groups opposed to Outcomes-Based Education.

18. Assessment was not addressed in the New York case study because little more than the general outlines of a new system of assessment had been devised by January 1994. Actual social studies assessment tasks and scoring criteria will become increasingly important in shaping classroom curriculum practice—insofar as what is tested is what gets taught.

6
California:
Making the Grade

I didn't know he tortured Indians. He was brutal.

Cameron Rodriguez, sixth grade student at Lawton Elementary School, San Francisco, 1992, during a unit on Christopher Columbus

Following the contest at the state level over adoption of K–8 history–social studies textbooks in 1990, a handful of California school districts voted to reject them and seek alternatives. These districts were located in highly heterogenous communities—among them, Oakland and Hayward in the East Bay, across from San Francisco, and East Palo Alto, south of San Francisco. There were partial or total rejections elsewhere, but these three cities, along with San Francisco—which did adopt the books with the proviso that they be used in conjunction with an extensive supplementary reading list—were emblematic of some of the curricular and pedagogic changes districts began making to accommodate their increasingly diverse student bodies.

The textbook dispute sensitized school district administrators and teachers to the existence of strong perspectives and concerns outside their own experience, and in these local districts teachers and community activists came to work together to steer history curriculum and teaching into new waters. Teachers began creating their own curricula in their classrooms; in dispensing with the textbooks that some of the writers of the 1987 *History–Social Science Framework* had actively promoted, they attempted to follow the spirit and letter of that part of the framework, which

> calls on teachers to recognize that the history of community, state, region, nation, and world must reflect the experiences of men and women and of different racial, religious, and ethnic groups. . . . The experiences of all these groups are to be integrated at every grade level. (1988, p. 5)

Following the adoption of the textbook series by the California State Board of Education in October 1990, people who had raised concerns in

157

Sacramento began to raise them in several local districts. There were particularly tumultuous public hearings during the spring and summer of 1991 in Oakland, Berkeley, East Palo Alto, and San Francisco, in the Bay Area, and in Los Angeles. In Hayward, a Bay Area city south of Oakland, school officials, fearing stiff community opposition, did not even bring a proposal to adopt the textbooks to the school board. (Hayward in 1993 did take a formal vote rejecting the textbooks, and it developed a literature-based social studies curriculum that the state board eventually approved.) Of the communities where the debate was most vociferous in 1991, only Oakland and East Palo Alto formally rejected the Houghton Mifflin textbooks. The reasons included both displeasure over perceived omissions of multiple perspectives in the textbooks and anger over the lack of choice—the fact that the state had given them only one option for grades K–7; in past adoptions, there had been more.

SAN FRANCISCO

In San Francisco, Lawton Elementary School teacher Dianne Talarico and several other teachers were appointed to a committee to review the textbooks and make recommendations. Oakland had a similar review process. After assessing the strengths and weaknesses of the books, the San Francisco committee reluctantly recommended approval provided that the district supplement them with biographies, novels, and a variety of other materials offering alternate perspectives from a list of some 200 titles that teachers had identified. In its statement to the board, the teacher review committee said it had found the Houghton Mifflin books to be strong in the areas of learning activities and in teaching strategies to address special needs. But regarding the criteria of cultural diversity, they found the Houghton Mifflin books to

> contain disturbing stereotypes, omissions, and distortions. . . . We cannot endorse this textbook series to be the primary component in the implementation of the district's history/social science program. We can view this textbook series to be, at best, only a part of a more comprehensive history/social science package including many other resources coordinated and delivered by our district. (statement to the school board, June 19, 1991)

Committee members were upset that the state, adopting only one K–8 series (Houghton Mifflin) and one other eighth grade U.S. history book (Holt, Rinehart and Winston), had left them with no alternatives. Talarico commented:

> Because we know that the majority of people rely heavily on the textbook as a guiding kind of force, we felt that it was risky just to give them nothing for the next year. I think that's why we ended up with them, even though

we were extremely disappointed with what we had available to us. I mean, if the state only gives us one [series] to look at, they only give us one to look at—which was Catch 22, because we were damned if we did and damned if we didn't. (interview, November 23, 1992)

School board president JoAnne Miller used the same "Catch 22" language as she and four other board members voted to approve the textbook/supplements package, and as one member voted no. The vote came after a tumultuous five-hour hearing during which Miller called recesses several times because of the din and even threatened to adjourn the meeting. More than 50 people representing dozens of community organizations queued up at the microphone to denounce the textbooks, while about eight, including representatives of Houghton Mifflin (and its newly named editor, an African American man), spoke passionately in their defense. There was no doubt the evening was an extremely emotional event for the adults attending; a few children ran wild on the stage, prompting Miller to call one of her recesses—and at the end, one school district official, overwhelmed with emotion, walked out of the auditorium in tears.

But the pressures had not been felt only by district staff and board members. TACT—The Association of Chinese Teachers—went through agonizing deliberations, changing its position on the textbook approval issue twice in the period leading up to the June 19, 1991 board vote.

An organization of some 200 teachers in the district, TACT had opposed the textbooks the year before in Sacramento, challenging them for barely touching on the role of Chinese immigrants. TACT members felt the books were totally inappropriate for a district in which 45 percent of the students were Asian, including 25 percent of Chinese descent. There was virtually nothing in the textbooks dealing with Chinese Americans—which co-author Gary Nash defended by saying that one textbook could not possibly include and reflect all the myriad ethnic groups living in various regions of the nation. TACT, said then-president Helen Joe-Lew, had wanted to "head them off at the pass" at the state level. Failing to prevent approval of the textbooks (as had every other opponent), TACT turned to supporting a district effort to find supplementary materials to fill in the textbooks' perceived cultural gaps. The group then was prepared to support the textbook/supplement package, when, the weekend before the board vote, the group was lobbied by influential supporters to return to a stance consistent with its earlier opposition, in order to send a "strong message" to publishers to produce more multicultural textbooks. So TACT reversed course and once again officially opposed the district's package proposal.

Roger Tom, the district's curriculum director, found himself in a similar bind. As a member of the state board's Curriculum Development and Supplemental Materials Commission, he had been one of three commissioners who voted against the textbooks in 1990. Since then, in his role as curriculum director in San Francisco, he was acutely aware of the dilemma districts like his were caught in, and he worked to develop a supplementary list that

would give teachers extra materials to flesh out the perceived shortcomings
in the textbooks. The supplementary list eventually selected by teachers and
reviewed by Muslims, Native Americans, and many others featured books
dealing with Chinese immigrant pioneers, black cowboys, Chicanos, gays,
and lesbians.

"It's a tough decision," Tom said before his school board's vote on
whether to reject the textbooks or accept the new package. "No one wants to
be called racist. But it's no longer reasonable for me that the kids and
teachers will not have textbooks" (Waugh 1991b, p. A7).

School superintendent Ramon Cortines (who in 1993 would move on to
become chancellor of the New York City schools) earlier had said the state's
decision to adopt only one series had hamstrung districts like San Francisco.
He had said the decision "politically smells," and that the state could have
allowed local districts to take the instructional materials money and use it as
each district saw fit. "Somebody needs to be a risk-taker. That's what I was
talking about when I said it smells. Nobody wants to take leadership. I think
the [state adoption] decision was political, rather than educational" (Waugh
1991a, p. B1).

But as the vote approached Cortines too decided it would be better to
purchase the new textbooks than have students continue using outdated
ones. In his message to the board, he said the textbooks, "though not perfect,
have been judged to be better than the existing textbooks and are closely
aligned with the state curriculum framework which is the foundation of our
core curriculum" (memo to Board of Education "Re: Adoption of New
History/Social Science Materials," May 30, 1991).

During his presentation to the school board, Tom referred to a survey of
K–8 teachers of whom 83 percent approved of or were neutral about adoption of the new textbooks.

Yet some teachers seemed to be stimulated by the questions raised by the
controversy over the textbooks. John Michaelson was part of the cadre of
social studies teachers, which also included Talarico, that studied the new
history–social science curriculum and then ran workshops demonstrating to
other teachers how to implement it in their classrooms. Interviewed two
years after the 1991 board approval, Michaelson, who had since become an
elementary school principal, was asked if the controversy and attention to
multicultural issues had affected how history was being taught in the classroom. "I know it made me think a lot about how I taught history," he said,
"and to make sure it was an inclusionary study of the past and that everybody had a part in it" (interview, May 21, 1993).

During their workshops for other teachers on the state's framework, and
on the district's curriculum and the textbook/supplement package, he said:

> We tried to promote the idea that the textbooks were a resource, and they
> weren't holy writ, to be followed line by line everyday, but would be
> used to support the curriculum. And the curriculum is composed of a lot
> of other things, including novels, videos, audio tapes.[1]

Did he think teachers were still relying primarily on the textbook, and not utilizing the supplemental materials? Sitting in his principal's chair, and looking back at his own classroom experience, Michaelson said:

> I can't say for sure. I'm not in every classroom. But my hunch is that more rely on that than take the plunge into really using the total curriculum. I think some people plug into it at different places, but I think for the most part those materials are not being utilized to the max.

He added, however, that he did not mean to fault teachers who didn't always use the other materials:

> Very few teachers are given the time to stop and plan something carefully, so it's "get in and use this." And it's also the way most of us have been trained, that you use the book as the core of teaching. It's just now that we're realizing that that's very confining, it's very limiting.

Irene Dea Collier, a kindergarten teacher at Spring Valley Elementary School in San Francisco, is one of those teachers who measures the utility of district and state curriculum policy against what she perceives as the particular needs of her students. Collier, who served on the district's textbook adoption committee in 1991 and was active in TACT, was especially vigilant when it came to reviewing textbooks she would use or recommend to others.

Because of the broad diversity in her classroom, which usually includes many children of Chinese descent as well as Latinos and African Americans, she introduces books that go beyond the "nuclear family" found in most primers. One of the books she uses shows a mother and her two children visiting the children's father in jail. Another shows pictures of different kinds of families, including gay and lesbian. According to Collier:

> You start hearing kids call others "faggot" at the kindergarten level. They may not even know what it means, but they know it's hurtful. So it's something we even have to deal with at the kindergarten level, but we haven't been able to deal with it very well. Sometimes we've had kids whose parents are in jail, and they talk about it: "They did something wrong, yet you still love them." It brings up a lot, allowing them to talk about things they might not be able to talk about. (interview, March 24, 1992)

Another book she uses is about hair, including the style of braiding called cornrows:

> One of the first things kids are curious about is hair. Chinese children are always fascinated by black children's curly hair, and vice versa—black kids are fascinated with the straightness of Asian hair.

Collier said a survey taken of teachers in the district found that most had no strong problems with the Houghton Mifflin textbooks.

So we have a long way to go to convince teachers they even need supplementals. . . . It's so much easier for them to buy a textbook and hope the textbook does everything for them.

The Columbus Quincentennial: Multiple Perspectives

Five centuries after what anthropologist Jack Weatherford (1991) called "the accidental arrival of three Spanish ships lost in the Caribbean" (p. 4), the Quincentennial of Christopher Columbus's journey across the Atlantic provided a unique opportunity for teachers eager or simply willing to try new approaches to an old subject, new ways of looking at a pervasive mythology that had been built up around discovery and conquest. Numerous books and magazine articles attempted both to reexamine the Columbus myth and to issue summary judgments on the debate over the myth. *Time* magazine, for example, wrote: "The next century will not be America's to call its own—or any other single nation's. We are all in one boat together, and Columbus must travel with us now as a fellow passenger, no longer the skipper" (*Time* 1991, p. 61).[2]

Were Columbus and other Europeans "discoverers" who brought a heady breath of civilization, or were they avaricious invaders—or just lucky that they managed to find land? The Quincentennial became ideal subject matter for young students and adults alike, inasmuch as Columbus raised or touched upon most of the central issues in the debate over multiculturalism that had gained widespread currency in the mass media during the previous three years, ever since the issuance in 1989 of a New York task force report, *A Curriculum of Inclusion,* and a seminal newspaper article in the *New York Times* the next year by Richard Bernstein (1990) that propelled the term *political correctness* into the public consciousness.

The challenge of interpreting Columbus was just as intriguing to historians and social commentators outside the classroom. "This is no ordinary time for Columbus studies," wrote Larry Gordon (1991) in the *Los Angeles Times*. The Smithsonian Institution offered a major exhibit, "Seeds of Change." A curriculum based on it, called by the same name, steered a middle course through the political shoals of the debate, emphasizing the very real if not always positive exchanges that took place between Europe and the "new" world—those commodities and misfortunes having the most impact being sugar, infectious diseases, the horse, corn, and the potato.[3] James E. Davis, a co-author of the Smithsonian curriculum, described it in workshops in school districts around the country, including San Francisco in the spring of 1992. San Francisco, like many other districts, was developing teaching units on Columbus for the fall term.

The activist Rethinking Schools project in Milwaukee produced a 96-page booklet called *Rethinking Columbus* (Bigelow, Miner, and Petersen, 1991), which had as its goal "not to present 'two sides,' but to tell the part of the story that has been neglected" (p. 3). It sold more than 200,000 copies nationwide. San Francisco, with its 60,000 public school students coming from more than 40 ethnic or non-English-language backgrounds, purchased 1,000 copies for distribution to teachers. The booklet featured such articles as "Talking Back to Columbus: Teaching for Justice and Hope," by Bill Bigelow (1991), a high school social studies teacher in Portland, Oregon. Bigelow visited the San Francisco school district to conduct workshops on "Rethinking Columbus," focusing on how teachers could "critically explore the contours of the traditional myth of 'discovery.' " The district also brought in representatives from the Italian, Mexican, Spanish, and Native American communities, from foreign consulates, and from cultural organizations to provide their own points of view.

One of Bigelow's techniques, which he recounts in his workshops, is designed to inspire students to think about the notion of "discovery." In San Francisco, at least, it was emulated widely by mentor teachers (those who, like Talarico, also develop units and conduct workshops) and others. Bigelow begins typically by taking a purse from one of his female students that he finds on the floor by her chair. He carries it up to the front of the room, looking puzzled when students wonder why he is carrying a purse. He states that, since it's in his possession, it's his purse: What's the problem? At first the students object: It clearly isn't his purse; he stole it. Some teachers using this role-play might say at this point that it's their purse because they found it. Bigelow says he likes to emphasize the point by dumping the purse on his desk and going through the contents: Of course this lipstick is his. How can you argue? It's in his possession.

Finally he asks: "What if I said I 'discovered' this purse? Then wouldn't it be mine?" In the context of a lesson plan about 1492, the students usually grasp the distinction between a purse being "stolen" and "discovered."

At Lawton Elementary, teacher Dianne Talarico used the same strategy during a unit on Columbus in September and October 1992. Although the voyages of Columbus weren't strictly part of her sixth grade curriculum, which according to the state framework deals with ancient world history, she decided to introduce it because of its timeliness. In addition to teaching her class, Talarico also conducted Columbus workshops for other teachers, passing on her own experience as well as information she'd received from workshops given by Bigelow and others. Her workshop wasn't always well received: For those who grew up on the Columbus myth, all of this revisionist thinking was just so much "Columbus bashing," as one disgruntled teacher told her at the end of one of her sessions.

But the workshops had their effect. According to Jonetta Leek, then the district's social studies K–8 curriculum coordinator, even those who were reluctant to dethrone Columbus often said afterward that they agreed that historical events like those of 1492 could no longer be taught from the single perspective of European "discovery."

In Talarico's classroom one day in October 1992, students were thumbing through a variety of sources to learn about Columbus and the subsequent colonization of the Americas—magazine articles, maps, and books that conveyed not only Columbus's view but that of his crew members, contemporary historians, the Taino Indians and other native peoples of the

Caribbean where Columbus first landed, as well as the Africans who were brought over to the Caribbean islands as slaves in the early 1500s. A textbook would not be the solitary source for her students. She asked them to break up into groups and told each group to pick a particular aspect of the voyages and report back to the class. More important, she asked them to think critically about everything they read, and she posed a series of questions for them to think about: Whose point of view is the story told from? How much space does the book or magazine give to discussing Columbus and the Europeans? How much is given to discussing the Native Americans and Tainos? How is Columbus portrayed? How are the Tainos and Native Americans portrayed? Look at the book or magazine illustrations: What do they communicate about Columbus, about his men, about the king and queen of Spain, and about the Tainos/Native Americans? What new or different information did you learn from reviewing the book or magazine article you read? What do you still wonder about after reading your assignment? In this day and age of space exploration and deep sea expeditions anything is possible. Who will be the one to find new lands? Who will be the one to find other beings? Perhaps it will be you? If it is, how will you treat those beings?

Like Bigelow, who said he thinks the best use of textbooks is treating them as "foils," Talarico said she wanted her students, when reading a textbook or any other account, to try to figure out what was missing as well as what was included. For instance, she said her students found a book in the school library about Columbus that was published in 1969 and which "doesn't say anything about Native Americans at all."

Some of her students thought deeply about her questions. Troy Lionberger, 11, said in a classroom interview:

> I worry about what we'd act like if we found a new place to live. Would we kick out the people who were there? Would we make people slaves like the Europeans did the blacks? The Tainos were having a good time before Columbus came and just took over their lands. . . . The next time we find some culture that's new to us, we have to be careful what we do. We have to consider their feelings.

Columbus Day should still be celebrated, said young Lionberger, "because he found America, but he shouldn't be a hero."

Another 11-year-old student, Cameron Rodriguez, said he "didn't know he [Columbus] tortured Indians. He was brutal." But he said Columbus Day that year should not become a day of protest. "It's a day for thinking," he said.

Changes

Let us put our heads together and see what life we will make for our children.

Tatanka Iotanka (Sitting Bull, Lakota Nation, as quoted in *Rethinking Columbus* [Bigelow et al. 1991, p. 1])

Talarico is typical of those inspired teachers who, faced with the amazing diversity of their classrooms, are continually striving to adapt to new situations. Although varying in enthusiasm, veteran teachers often joined their younger colleagues in recognizing they had to provide a different kind of nurturing and learning context for their students. Their ideas were formed not only by their own backgrounds and education, and education reform movements, but by the reality of California's rapidly changing demographics—and the issues those changes engendered in the communities, the media, and their own personal lives and careers. She related:

> When I went to school all I heard about were the Europeans. And I wasn't in school with a bunch of different ethnic groups or races. But now, I think it's a disservice to all of my students to stand up there and only show the contributions of European people. I can't do it. I go out of my way to provide it because the textbooks do not. Because I think it's important that all students in my classrooms see that people of all cultures contributed to what we have today. But I can only share what I know. There's a lot I don't know.

Talarico, asked whether the state controversy in 1990 had affected her thinking or teaching of history, smiled. She said it was something she had "lived through" because of her role at the district level on the evaluation committee that found serious inadequacies in the Houghton Mifflin books. But even before the controversy she brought to her classroom an appreciation of the need to reach out to her students, who were from Pakistan, Malaysia, India, Laos, Cambodia, Vietnam, China, and Mexico.

The active learning strategy that Talarico, John Michaelson, and others in the district started using is referred to in San Francisco as an "integrated curriculum," in which students are involved in active research, analysis, and interpretation; they do oral histories with their parents and families, they build models of Sumerian cities, and they do role-playing. These teachers break up their classrooms into small groups and then "jigsaw" by dividing the topic of study into chunks. Each group investigates one aspect of the topic and reports what it has learned to the class as a whole.

Michaelson was enthused about bringing history alive through these kinds of activities. He said: "This isn't some dead thing sitting in a book and you talk about an abstract date. You get up and relive it."

One activity Michaelson referred to involved the teacher showing a slide of a boat of immigrants leaving Italy for the United States, and then having the students do interviews of those on the boat. Another has students arguing the pros and cons of joining the Revolutionary Army, asking them to think about the consequences: Would you lose your farm? Would you be hanged as a traitor if your side lost? Do you feel you have any choice over joining? To Michaelson, this kind of interactive curriculum promotes in students higher-order thinking. And it provides a kind of curricular approach that regards textbooks as one more resource, not an end-all.

Cheryl Lee, who was a fifth grade social studies teacher at Cabrillo Elementary School in San Francisco in 1993, used many of the same techniques and delved into a bookcase of supplemental readings and activities to engage her students, of whom in recent years as many as half might be immigrants. An African American who served on the same textbook review committee as Talarico and Michaelson, Lee had few qualms about using the Houghton Mifflin textbooks—mainly because of her confidence in other teaching materials and strategies to supplement the textbooks.

Of the textbooks, she said:

They are so much better than what we had before. . . . There could be a lot of improvement, but textbooks, you can only take them to a certain point and then you have to use other things to get your curriculum across to the kids. I start with the textbook, and then take off using books from the library, and taking off from their own experiences. . . . We do a lot of research. (interview, May 21, 1993)

At the beginning of the year she focuses on the diversity she finds in her classroom:

That's always the jumping off point for the first month of school—who makes up the United States, who makes up San Francisco, who makes up our classroom. And I try to instill in the children that everybody has something to offer and every culture has contributed something to the United States. So we start there and go on, dealing with acceptance, and differences.

She too uses the Bigelow "discovery" activity when discussing Columbus:

I always do this little performance. I take something that belongs to a child, and tell them it's not theirs, to get them to understand that Columbus had his own agenda, and what happened once he came over here. And I talked about that when I was a child, Columbus was this "hero," this great person, who discovered America. We talked about what does it mean to discover something, can you discover a land of people who are already there, and we talked about what happened to the indigenous people after Columbus came. It kind of gives them a different perspective. . . . They understand what it means.

As in Talarico's classroom, the textbooks San Francisco approved and purchased after a grueling public and political fight are used today in classrooms like Lee's largely for general information and for the study questions: Students don't read every word of every chapter. Lee said she would have no problem dispensing with textbooks altogether, and, by following the framework as guide, using literature and other materials. But with the many subjects she has to teach besides history, "There's just not enough time."

SOUTH OF THE CITY

The southern planters and their slaves lived very different lifestyles.
  America Will Be (Armento et al. 1991, p. 414)

Slavery is not a lifestyle.
  Joyce E. King (interview, October 15, 1990)

The heated public controversies over the textbooks largely bypassed most California communities. But in those districts that escaped public hoopla, whenever people or organizations with specific concerns—such as the Jewish Community Relations Council—did raise questions, school officials generally responded. Thus curriculum in some cases was shaped by whether the district was even made aware of questions about the textbooks; it seemed that, often, it was only through public initiative that school officials and teachers got the message that there were issues to be addressed.

"Detecting bias and stereotypes in textbooks can all be a matter of perspective," wrote *Peninsula Times Tribune* reporter Holly A. Heyser (1991, p. A1) of school districts in the area south of San Francisco. For instance, in the Los Altos School District, where about four-fifths of the students were white, administrators were unaware of criticisms until they heard from the Jewish Community Relations Council, based in San Francisco, Heyser wrote. The council had located several passages in the sixth grade Houghton Mifflin book, which introduces students to Judaism and Christianity, that the council said seemed biased toward Christianity by portraying Judaism in ways that, in their analysis, might nurture anti-Semitism in young readers. The district responded by saying it would have teachers skip over the criticized passages (p. A10).

Teachers in Los Altos and other largely middle-class white districts down the peninsula from San Francisco also were unaware of serious concerns that African Americans in San Francisco, East Palo Alto, Oakland, and elsewhere had raised about the sixth grade book's section on human evolution: that it reinforced old stereotypes and downplayed the importance of Africa by describing primitive humans in Africa and then moving on to Europe, where it suggested that culture and civilization began with the Cro-Magnon man, who (as pictured in "A Moment in Time" illustration) looked "just like us." Who, exactly, African Americans asked, was the "us" supposed to be? And why was there such a remarkably time-condensed contrast between bone-marrow-eating people in Africa and Cro-Magnons in Europe eons later? Was it the intent (conscious or unconscious) to reinforce the idea that the ancient people of Africa were savages and that civilization only started in Europe?

Educators said that they didn't dispute the validity of the complaint but that none of them had noticed it on their own. Los Altos Schools' Superintendent Margaret Gratiot expressed the difficulty: "If no one has pointed out the flaws, especially if teachers were brought up with the same stereotypes . . .

whether all of them would pick up on these things, I don't know" (Heyser 1991, p. A10).

No protests had been raised in ethnically diverse Sunnyvale, either. When apprised of some of the specific criticisms, an assistant superintendent responded: "I wouldn't see it. I doubt many other people would see it. But I think that through the use of other supplemental materials, these things can be taken care of" (Heyser 1991, p. A10).

There was no public outcry in Palo Alto, a school district with about 75 percent white students, but there also school officials heard from people unhappy with the portrayal of Judaism, and they responded accordingly. Interestingly, the Palo Alto district had had a history of responding to community complaints about instructional materials. These community protests started during the early 1970s, when Asian American parents raised questions, particularly about the failure of textbooks to include an account of the internment of Japanese Americans during World War II, when 120,000 people of Japanese descent, most of them American citizens residing on the West coast, were pulled from their homes within only a few days and sent to hastily built inland camps.

Repressed memories of the internment experience, revived by the Civil Rights Movement and the ethnic studies campaign on college campuses during the late 1960s, led to one of the first instances of ethnic community protest over textbooks and local district response in California. The Japanese Americans who led that campaign during the early 1970s went on to challenge at the state level the lack of mention in California history books of the devastating internment camp experience of World War II, and eventually won acknowledgment through legislative resolutions calling for inclusion of the wartime internment in California's curriculum. But by the 1990s most of these Japanese American veterans of the early textbook conflicts in Palo Alto and statewide were involved in other activities. The Palo Alto school district had had a stretch of quiet years. In 1991 it was in the process of reviewing the textbooks and developing supplementary materials. According to Jack Gibbany, the district's curriculum director:

> We were looking at the textbooks as being one component of an instructional program . . . identifying what we considered to be some of the weaker points or some of the flaws, and then working at a scheme of providing additional support for teachers in instructional programming. (interview, March 3, 1992)

This review process and "building some teaching units that were outside the textbooks" was "really not unique," said Gibbany, given the district's past experience with community concerns. But in this year, he said,

> the thing that was unique about this was that, partly because of the [state] controversies, people were very aware of what was going on. . . . We were to look at the issues that were being raised statewide and then see if in fact those were things we felt were weaknesses or not.

Seminars and workshops were conducted for teachers by people from the religious communities. Former Curriculum Commissioner Joyce King also made a presentation about problems with the textbooks.

Gibbany said district educators had not noticed the problematic areas until King and others pointed them out. He said he valued the input: "It's good that people look at these things, because some of that kind of stuff, depending on what your perspective is, you might look right over it."

Thus the issues raised in the 1990 dispute over the textbooks reached beyond urban areas, affecting districts that were otherwise untouched by the kind of public outcry that threw school board meetings in Oakland and San Francisco into virtual chaos. Districts like Palo Alto, however, escaped the kind of turmoil that gripped districts like Oakland, a city of 300,000 people, half of them African Americans, and with large numbers of Latinos, Native Americans, Southeast Asians, and whites.

OAKLAND: THERE IS PLENTY OF THERE THERE

On June 5, 1991 the Oakland school board rejected the Houghton Mifflin textbooks after a scabrous meeting during which textbook supporters were greatly outnumbered and, according to a number of press accounts, were loudly outshouted by textbook critics. As Oakland school board member Sheila Jordan sardonically remarked, it was "Democracy in action" (cited in Gross 1991, p. B7). For the next couple of years, a community effort was led by local college education professors Kitty Epstein and Fred Ellis to create an alternative history—social science curriculum, but it eventually collapsed in misjudgments, happenstance, and district politics. When the fall term started in 1991, according to press reports (Gross 1991), teachers at one school were so desperate for curriculum material for the seventh grade in particular that they were lining up at copying machines duplicating pages from review copies of Houghton Mifflin's *Across the Centuries*.

Two years later, on a pleasant autumn day in 1993, some 30 fourth grade teachers gathered for a California history workshop in the Oakland school district's Harper Building, located in an urban pocket of old homes and light industry. The teachers who came were about to be introduced to a newly developed unit called "The First People: Indians of California." These teachers, selected by their principals to attend the workshop, then would return to their schools and pass on what they'd learned to the other fourth grade teachers. Many of the teachers at the workshop seemed glad to receive the new unit; for the previous two years, ever since the Oakland school board rejected the recommendation of teacher review panels to purchase the Houghton Mifflin textbooks, the fourth grade teachers had been using 10-year-old textbooks or none at all. While most had adjusted, "Some are still pretty mad about it," said Oakland's curriculum director, Shelly Weintraub (cited in Li 1993, p. B1).

However, those who came to the workshop seemed to hold no bitterness.

These were teachers who for the most part had been coping fairly well during the previous two years, resorting to old textbooks and using other material they'd gathered on their own. Nonetheless, they appeared eager for the new unit.

Those who developed the new unit were helped immensely by the district's own Office of Indian Education. It had been established during the years following the federal government's designation in the early 1950s of Oakland as one of 11 sites for its relocation program, which was aimed at resettling Native Americans who lived on reservations in South Dakota, Oklahoma, California, New Mexico, Arizona, Alaska, and elsewhere into urban areas. As a result of the program, thousands of Native Americans moved to Oakland, and their presence attracted others. The Intertribal Friendship House, established in Oakland to aid those who had moved off reservations, estimated that by 1990 some 40,000 individuals from at least 200 tribes had moved to and then lived in the Bay Area, which rivaled only Los Angeles as home to the greatest number of urban Native Americans. The school district's Office of Indian Education came into existence after "a group of Indian parents with school age children got together to discuss the lack of acknowledgment for Indian culture and curriculum in the Oakland schools" (Patterson with Lobo 1988, p. 23). Concerned parents and teachers developed strategies to keep Native American students together in "learning strands" and "core groups" as they moved from elementary to middle to high school to alleviate a traditionally high dropout rate (p. 24). The district's Office of Indian Education worked to infuse Indian content into regular classroom activities (p. 24).

The office collaborated with teachers and UC-Berkeley's Clio Project (named after the Greek Muse of history) to develop materials for the unit, including a 200-page binder encompassing six weeks of lesson plans. In addition to the binder, teachers would be given what usually is called an artifact box, but which in Oakland was to be called a box of cultural objects. "Artifacts seemed to reflect a dead culture," explained Weintraub. The Clio Project and its director, education professor Matthew Downey, for several years had been working in a consortium with local school districts to develop new history units aligned with the 1987 framework.

Introducing Downey to the teachers, Weintraub said the unit on California's indigenous peoples was one of three new units that had been developed for the fourth grade, which focuses on California history. The other two units, which would be presented in workshops a few months later, would deal with the period of the Spanish missions and ranchos and with the Gold Rush. Local Native Americans had been significantly involved in formulating the new unit, and one of the first things the unit asked teachers to address during the six weeks of lesson plans were the different kinds of preconceptions or stereotypes of Native Americans that other young students often brought to school. Recognizing the incredible diversity in Oakland's schools—where about 90 percent of students are African Americans, Southeast Asians, Latinos, and

Native Americans—teachers in the district had often told Weintraub, she said, that "our materials need to be multicultural."

To demonstrate an exercise that the teachers could use with their students, the items from the cultural objects box were handed out and passed from table to table so that the teachers could examine each one and then write down what they imagined each once had been used for. Some were easily recognizable: an arrowhead, an animal pelt, and a thin round stick accompanied by another piece of soft wood with a notch (the two to be used, most could figure out, for creating fire by spinning the stick).

Other objects were more puzzling, causing head scratching and wild guesses. What was the purpose of a series of small sticks with marks on them? (They were counting sticks used by early California Indians in counting games, Downey later explained.) What about a small object made of reeds? (It was a doll for Pomo children.) The questions and discussions that buzzed around the room as teachers puzzled over the objects was exactly the purpose of the exercise, said Downey: to get students immersed in early Indian life and ask questions. "What was it like to be an Indian? What was it like to be living in an Indian village? This gets at everyday things," said Downey, adding:

> The principal goal of the curriculum is not to see how much history kids can regurgitate later on a quiz. Rather, it encourages what I call historical thinking, multiple perspectives. During the Spanish period students should understand how the friars viewed their missions, but they should also understand how the Indians felt.
>
> It's a multicultural history. You can't teach California history without being multicultural. (workshop, October 21, 1993)

Several of the teachers in conversations later said they were enthused about the integrated approach outlined at the workshop. "I feel very much in harmony with what they've come up with," said Lorna Baird, a teacher at Lazear Elementary School.

"A lot of teachers already have been doing this kind of thing," said Carin Geathers, a teacher at Grass Valley Elementary School who was one of the teachers who had helped develop the California Indians unit. "The integrated approach, using cultural objects, moving it [history] from the afternoon to morning so it doesn't get shoved aside, and using a multicultural perspective" (interviews, October 21, 1993).

Oakland's rejection of the textbooks had had its positive effects, said Geathers. "I think this"—she waved at a table in the room laden with three dozen books about Native Americans and the unit binder about California Indians—"is the best thing to come out of it. The kids benefit from an integrated approach."

The Oakland board's rejection of the textbooks in 1991 reflected a mixture of racial, political, and cultural attitudes. No one factor explained why officials voted the way they did, either at the state level or at the district level, when confronted with community protests (see Der 1992). The Oakland school district had been roiled with financial problems, a state trustee had been appointed to steer the district back into solvency, reform candidates had been elected to the school board, and a new superintendent had come aboard during the same year that the state began its cyclical review and adoption of new history textbooks.

The voting that ultimately rejected some of the textbooks was not unanimous. The elected board members in Oakland—four of them black, one Asian American, and one white—regardless of race or political affinity, were primarily attentive to community opposition to the textbooks. There was strong, organized opposition by parent and educator activists to the textbooks in a city where the overwhelming majority is nonwhite. That kind of constituency did not exist at the state level, since whites constitute the majority of registered voters. Moreover, state curriculum commissioners are hand-picked by the State Board of Education whose members, in turn, are appointed by the governor.

EAST PALO ALTO AND HAYWARD

The students attending East Palo Alto's K–8 schools are almost entirely young people of color: about 45 percent Latino, another 45 percent African American, and the rest Pacific Islanders (Samoans, Tongans) and European Americans. A few years before the school board voted against purchasing the Houghton Mifflin textbooks in July 1991, the district had decided to adopt a literature-based language arts program and to develop an integrated thematic approach to teaching social studies. With the rejection of the history-social science textbooks, the teachers and curriculum specialists began integrating English and history lessons through use of novels, biographies, and other reading material. Although it rejected the textbooks, the board opted to buy the Houghton Mifflin teacher editions, for use as a resource guide, and also to purchase copies of the state *History–Social Science Framework* for each teacher.

"It works very well and it's a meaningful, powerful way to teach students, but it is also a difficult way to teach and very time-consuming, when it comes to planning," said Paulette Johnson, the district's curriculum director, adding:

> You can't turn to page "x" in the teacher's guide and write your lesson plan based on what the teacher's guide tells you you're going to cover in the history books with the kids, and the kids can't flip to the last page each week and answer the questions. (interview, November 4, 1993)

The framework provides the chronology and identifies the major themes to be taught; the teachers—assisted by Johnson and by attending workshops—develop a year-long plan. Classroom and homework activities make extensive use of literature: For the fifth grade U.S. history class, for instance, teachers draw from a list of books such as *Little House on the Prairie, Indians before Columbus,* and *Sounder,* as well as ethnic folk tales. "What I've seen teachers do with the teacher's guide is to get background information for themselves, and that's one of the things that's time consuming about this way of teaching, because they become researchers," said Johnson. She went on:

> It's particularly difficult for new teachers, and we have a lot of turnover in our district, so it means that people like our mentors and principals really have to be there to help them, and I have to do on-going staff development in how to plan thematically, because people are not being taught how to do it in colleges and universities. The whole idea in what we're doing is trying to really broadly expose students to history by giving them a chance to reflect on it. The framework says we need to connect the past to the present. Well, we can't do that with any single volume. We've got to use the newspapers, we've got to have them read broadly, we've got to get them involved in research, we've got to get them questioning.

Yet Johnson agrees that many teachers, given a textbook, "would be ready to go back to it. I think they would never teach the same way again, but I think they would go back. It's kind of saddening, but I think we have to be realistic" (interview, November 4, 1993).

Across San Francisco Bay from East Palo Alto, the Hayward school district in June 1993 won approval from the State Board of Education of its application for a waiver to use state textbook money to buy instructional materials other than the state-approved textbook series. Hayward became the first and only district in California to jettison history—social science textbooks altogether and design a literature-based curriculum. Led by Etta Hollins, a consultant and education professor at California State University at Hayward, a committee of teachers, administrators, parents and concerned community activists, and teachers union and elected school board representatives developed the curriculum entitled "From Many Perspectives: A Shared Vision." It draws on a list of more than 400 trade books, ranging from traditional favorites like *Little House on the Prairie* to less frequently used works like *Black People Who Made the Old West* and *Tales of a Korean Grandmother.*

With 64 percent of Hayward's students from minority groups and speaking more than 50 languages (including Spanish, Farsi, Vietnamese, and Hindi), it became imperative to provide multiple perspectives beyond that which a single textbook could offer, said Hollins (interview, April 6, 1993). The curriculum had its origins two years earlier when parents active in Hayward's African American Parents Alliance protested the state-approved textbooks. One member, Harriet Moore, said at the time that "a group of parents got together and approached the board, with a formal letter asking them to hire consultants to write a core curriculum." In their view, she said, the textbooks really did not meet the needs of our diverse community. It's a very diverse community, with so many different ethnic groups, and the direction the book was written, many of us were excluded, and when we were included they were either inaccurate or biased. (interview, June 12, 1991)

Moore said she and others in her alliance had read "every single one" of the K–8 textbooks. "We agree they are much better than textbooks written in the past, but we do not find them acceptable. They are not improved enough."

By lobbying the board and later working with Hollins, community activists like Moore helped mold local education policy. But it took two waiver applications, thoroughly scrutinized by California State Department of Education reviewers, before the state board approved the program; and in a district plagued by demanding financial and political concerns, as were many other urban districts, Hayward's progress toward a literature-based social studies program was excruciatingly slow.

LOS ANGELES AND HOUGHTON MIFFLIN

In Los Angeles pressure from teachers to buy new textbooks to replace outmoded ones overrode protests from a coalition of religious organizations (Muslim, Jewish, and Christian) whose leaders wanted to be sure that teaching about the world's religions—now called for by the framework to begin in the sixth grade—would be approached with caution and sensitivity so as not to elevate one religion over another. The complaints from racial and ethnic groups, and from gays and lesbians, that were raised elsewhere also were heard in Los Angeles, a vast, sprawling district where more than 80 percent of the students are from ethnic and racial groups once considered minorities. In the past the district had simply accepted the textbooks approved at the state level and had allowed individual schools to place their own textbook orders. But because of the community concern and the negative reaction the textbooks had drawn in some areas, the board took the unusual step of holding up the schools' textbook orders until the board had had a chance to review the books and assess public opinion.

In March 1991 the board voted 7–0 to approve the K–8 books for use in Los Angeles schools—but only after Houghton Mifflin agreed to produce a series of "ethnic specific monographs (African American, American Indian, Asian Pacific American, and Latino/Hispanic American), a women's monograph, and possibly a monograph on people with disabilities" (Board resolution submitted by the superintendent February 4, 1991). The publisher also agreed to develop, with the involvement of interested organizations, a monograph on the teaching of religion and to provide bibliographies listing primary and secondary sources to be used with the textbooks.

Houghton Mifflin downplayed the board's requirements. The day after the board's vote, in a press release put out by Hill and Knowlton, the public relations firm hired by the Boston publishing company, John Ridley, Houghton Mifflin's vice president and editorial director of elementary education, was quoted as saying: "These books represent the beginning of a new era in the teaching of history in the United States. The real winners are the children and teachers of Los Angeles who need these textbooks in order to meet the state's new guidelines for the teaching of social studies."

In adopting the Houghton Mifflin series in 1990, state officials did require certain changes in response to opposition to negative statements and images raised by the Jewish Community Relations Council and Muslim groups, including the Southern California–based Council on Islamic Education. For example, at the Curriculum Commission's direction the publishers removed an illustration depicting the Prophet Muhammad, such depiction being offensive to most Muslims. But the commission did not require the publisher to replace one of its "A Moment in Time" illustrations that became a recurring sore point between the Islamic council and the publisher over the next few years. It was called "A Caravan Camel." Shabbir Mansuri, the council's founder, and two consultants met with Houghton Mifflin executives in Boston in June 1993 to renew their concerns. "It is quite remarkable that all of the other 'Moments' involve people, but Islamic civilization rates only a camel" they wrote in an extensive review of the 7th grade textbook, *Across the Centuries,* in which the camel appeared. Unlike many other textbook critics, the council offered an alternative that they developed, "A Moment in Time: An Abbasid Scholar." But as of October 1994, 16 months after their meeting, Mansuri had not received any response from the publisher.

Houghton Mifflin, following the textbook challenges in 1990 and 1991 at the state and local level, made some text revisions. For the 1994 copyrighted edition, two more names were added to the four other authors of the series: J. Jorge Klor de Alva, a professor of anthropology at Princeton University and co-chair of the New York Social Studies Curriculum and Assessment Committee, and Louis E. Wilson, an associate professor of Afro-American Studies at Smith College. (Wilson had been flown to California by Houghton Mifflin in 1990 to testify in favor of the textbooks at the state board's hearing in Sacramento.)

In the 1994 edition of the fifth grade U.S. history textbook, the "A Moment in Time" illustration of the "Escaping Slave" that Joyce King and others had felt demeaning was removed and in its place appeared an illustration of "A Black Abolitionist"—which provided a more positive reflection of African American struggles than had the earlier illustration.

There were other changes, too—some striking, some subtle. A discussion of racism was moved up from page 491 in the 1990 California version to page 146 in the copyrighted 1994 edition. The discussion was included in a sidebar box, "Understanding Colonialism." Although a similar box appeared on the same page in the 1990 version, the 1994 edition included a much stronger statement (Armento et al. 1994):

European people were of a different race, or skin color, than the Indians. The feeling of being better than the people of another race is called *racism*. The racism of many Europeans made them think it was their right to take away the land of the Indians. Europeans also forced the Indians to work, sometimes as slaves. Believing themselves to also be superior to the Africans, the Europeans brought them as slaves to the Americas. (p. 146)

None of this was in the earlier version. CURE (Communities United against Racism in Education), a group of parents and educators formed by Berkeley parent and activist Beverly Slapin and others following the October 1990 state adoption, had studied the textbooks and disseminated a lengthy list of examples similar to one put out by the Rochester, New York, school district. Among other things, CURE's critique (1991) pointed out that in the 1990 version of *America Will Be* (which actually was copyrighted 1991), the textbook had introduced racism late, and only to

> describe the discriminatory laws and policies against immigrants to the United States in the late 1800s and early 1900s. This first introduction of racism does not include the oldest and enduring expression of racism in the U.S.—racism against indigenous peoples and African-Americans. (p. 47)

Typical of other corrections in the 1994 edition was one made to a caption that in the 1990 version read, "Here a group of *Mexicans* ride in a parade in Santa Fe, New Mexico"; the not-so-unimportant change that appeared in 1994 was: "Here a group of Mexican *Americans* ride in a parade in Santa Fe, New Mexico" (Armento et al. 1994, p. 21, both books, emphasis added). Another correction reflected the benefit of paying closer attention to extant research. In his lengthy, point-by-point rebuttal to criticisms of various passages, co-author Nash (1990) had quarreled with an objection concerning a picture caption that said, "John Wesley Powell talks with an Indian in the Grand Canyon in this 1873 photograph." In her objection, Ellen Swartz (1990), the Rochester school district's multicultural coordinator, had said, "If this man's name is not known, then his Nation could at least be stated." In his rebuttal, Nash said: "The tribal identity was given wherever possible. This is a guiding principle throughout the K–8 series, as is evident in hundreds of examples. In this case, the tribal affiliation could not be found. *(text verified as accurate)*" (attachment A, p. 1) But in the 1994 edition the "Indian's" identity had been discovered and was included in the caption: "In this 1873 photograph, John Wesley Powell talks with Tau-Gu, Chief of the Paiutes, near the Grand Canyon" (Armento et al. 1994, p. 33).

Another transformation occurred in the introductory paragraph to Unit Three, "Life in the English Colonies." In the earlier version it had read, in part, "English settlers who came to America in the 1600s often faced disease, hunger, and battles with Indians. But as the English colonies grew, life for many settlers improved" (Armento et al. 1991, p. 152). In many ways those two sentences typify the problem of perspective that concerned people in cities that rejected the textbooks—and even in some cities that ultimately approved them. The comment from CURE (1991): "Again, here is the perspective of the invaders as defenders, with indigenous peoples as aggressors. And life for the settlers improved at the expense of life for the Native peoples" (p. 65).

Houghton Mifflin changed the passage in its 1994 edition:

> English colonizers who came to America in the 1600s often faced disease, hunger, and battles with Indians defending their land. But as English colonies grew, and the Indians were forced to move or were killed by diseases, life for many of the new residents became more settled. (p. 152)

While some of the changes in the 1994 edition might have been made regardless of outside influence, other changes were remarkable. One doubts whether they would have occurred in the absence of criticism from parents and educators desiring a history less preoccupied with the great movement west by European immigrants. As Frances FitzGerald (1979) has noted:

> The school establishment is not the only group that shapes American history in the textbooks. It is often private-interest groups or citizens' organizations that bring about the most important political changes in the texts. . . . Today, texts are written backward or inside out, as it were, beginning with public demand and ending with the historian. (pp. 35, 69)

In California, clearly, public demand had a decided impact on textbook publishers.

"I am taking a positive approach," said Rochester's Ellen Swartz in 1990, when it still was not clear what effect her objections would have. "I think publishers will make changes, if they are helped. It makes sense. It's a big market. They can sell books" (interview, July 31, 1990). Later, however, Swartz (1992) offered a more critical analysis:

> Though slightly increased numbers of men and women of color now sit as silenced sentinels on scattered textbook pages to meet the ethnic and gender counts of publishers, they are effectively robbed of their indigenous analyses and oppositional voices and perspectives. Their biographical presence, usually presented as textual vignettes or side-bars, becomes side-barred in classroom practice because of the lack of contextualized information that would centralize their voices in the broader historical discourse. (p. 343)

TEACHERS, TEXTBOOKS, AND CURRICULUM POLICY

The conjunction of media attention to multicultural issues surrounding Columbus, political correctness, non-Western inroads into the literary canon, the debates over these K–8 textbooks—the America debate—

reverberated through the schools. These debates may not always have directly changed policy, but they influenced teachers, who of course are the ultimate arbiters of curriculum policy and practice. Even though some districts and teachers, as shown above, have moved beyond reliance on textbooks, in many places curriculum practice is still textbook driven, and consequently textbooks remain an ongoing object of scrutiny.

Textbook "use" by teachers like Cheryl Lee doesn't mean the same thing as it does to other teachers. Some rely on the textbook as a virtual source book, while others treat it as a guide, much as a motorist who is basically familiar with the terrain will check a road map to follow the intended route. Teachers—and staff—don't always have the requisite knowledge or critical sensitivity to detect cultural or historical flaws in instructional materials.

Teachers—and elected school board officials—can be influenced by outside pressures; if parents and community activists feel strongly enough and organize effectively around a particular issue, they also can affect curriculum policy—whether they are against multiculturalism as with the "Rainbow Curriculum" in New York City, or opposed to the textbooks as in Oakland and Hayward. In the case of the California *History–Social Science Framework*, anecdotal evidence seems to suggest that many California teachers accept the framework's direction, at least in concept. But there are some who are not always happy with the textbooks provided them. That these teachers do not constitute a large number is understandable considering that, statewide, the teaching force is about 80 percent white, and educated in college programs that rarely included multicultural imperatives. A 1976 National Science Foundation study led James P. Shaver, O. L. Davis Jr., and Suzanne W. Helburn (1979) to conclude that "teachers tend not only to rely on, but to believe in, the textbook as the source of knowledge. Textbooks are not seen as support materials, but as the central instrument of instruction by most social studies teachers" (p. 151). It's likely that that reliance and loyalty have not changed much in the intervening years.

Those teachers who aren't dependent on textbooks respond to unsatisfactory materials by fashioning their own curriculum, using a variety of instructional materials in addition to the textbooks, although—as East Palo Alto's Paulette Johnson pointed out—that approach takes time that many teachers, especially elementary teachers, simply do not have.

Since adoption of the history-social studies textbooks in October 1990, the California State Department of Education has put out a small number of curriculum guides for teachers, but much more remains to be done, said Glen Thomas, director of the Department of Education's curriculum and instructional materials division. "I don't intend to criticize Houghton Mifflin, but a big need, even greater than the framework, is the need for instructional resources," said Thomas, referring to a coherent package of textbooks, primary sources, and literature. "There are a lot of fragmented pieces out there. . . . The social studies area is replete with a whole bunch of pieces of stuff. That's still a major challenge for teachers to search through and make it a coherent learning experience for students" (interview, October 26, 1993).

In the absence of surveys or other data, Thomas guessed that across the state there was "quite extensive" acceptance of the 1987 framework by teachers, and a "general verbal agreement" by districts to implement it, although he suspected that actual implementation of the framework had fallen "far short of that . . . for a variety of reasons [including], probably, lack of resources." With the state providing $27.94 per student for instructional materials in grades K–8 and $18.85 per student in grades 9–12 in 1993, California ranked close to thirtieth nationwide. And, said Thomas, "We're slowly working our way downward."

Teachers have directly influenced official state curriculum policy by their participation in instructional review panels and in framework review committees. Another such opportunity was scheduled for mid-1994, when under the state's current curriculum cycle the 1987 *History–Social Science Framework* would be up for review. By 1993 the state had sent a copy to every district superintendent, and, as described above, some districts used instructional-materials funds to purchase copies for teachers to use as guides. In addition, said Thomas, "I'm sure we've sold many hundreds of thousands around the country." The mandatory review might lead in any of several directions, Thomas said (in October 1993), adding that it was then too early to predict how extensively the framework might be revised, if at all. It was unlikely, however, that it would not undergo some modification, he said, citing the precedents of earlier reviews of the visual arts and language arts frameworks. In both cases the Curriculum Commission affirmed the direction taken in the two frameworks but asked that several parts be modified or that additional teacher assistance, in the form of monographs, be developed to address problematic areas.

By October 1994, the commission had held several hearings and according to Commissioner Eugene Flores, the dominant theme was "we like it, leave it alone, don't change it." Final approval of any changes would not come, he said, until as late as December 1995. "We fought the curricular wars about history back in 1987, and they were wars. . . . We could open up that battlefield again—(but) there's a hesitation. . . . I like to tell people it's more like the inverse of Pandora's Box: nobody ever wants anything out, everybody wants more in. And we already know our teachers are saying 'How do I teach what we have already?' " (interview, October 2, 1994).

One of the most thorough reviews of the 1987 framework's treatment of U.S. and world history came in July 1994, from Mansuri's Council on Islamic Education. While lauding the framework's lofty goals, the framework fell down, it said, in its course descriptions, primarily because they lacked "consistency, clarity and balance" (p. ii). As for non-Western religions and civilizations, they are presented relatively briefly in grades 6 and 7 and "Thereafter, all of these magnificent cultures are dropped from history, only to reappear as corpses in the twentieth century, passive victims of colonialism or objects in the study of 'unresolved world problems' " (p. iv).

In preparation for the 1994 framework review, the California Council for the Social Studies (1993) called on its membership to submit their ideas and suggestions for improvements. Several responses printed in the council's publication, *Sunburst,* in December 1993 gave some indication of what teachers were thinking about:

Two teachers, Lyn Reese from Berkeley and Tess Henry from Claremont, wrote that "the Framework is not an equitable presentation of the history of half of humankind. What is missing are the women!" They said the framework, in listing what students should learn, must include a statement requiring an examination of the beliefs about gender and a study of women's roles, and that scholars of women's history should be asked to amplify the framework with regard to women's roles in "every historical period" (p. 9).

James H. Bell, a teacher from Poway who served on the 1987 History–Social Science Framework Committee, said the seven-year cycle for reviewing frameworks was too short a period for proper implementation and

> that in this era of lean budgets for curriculum development and textbook and materials purchasing we would be ill-advised to do more than an updating of the 1987 Framework, leaving the *basic structure* as is. (p. 10)

Finally, in a statement that most likely reflected the mainstream thinking among California's teachers, Marilyn E. Lubarsky, of Upland High School in Upland, listed several areas of concern but concluded: "The framework is a fine piece of work which needs honing, and the honing should be done by the experts, classroom teachers" (p. 9).

Yet, as McCarthy (1990) points out, teachers as a group do not necessarily have that kind of autonomy:

> In a society where the government has clearly reneged on the promise of racial equality raised during the Kennedy and Johnson administrations in the 1960s, educators are being bombarded with new and contradictory demands. They are being asked to generate an ethos of harmony and equality at the same time that the government pressures them to foster competitive individualism. This emphasis on competition reflects itself in the dominant role of standardized testing and in the narrow range of classroom knowledge that actually gets taught in the urban setting. Teachers feel compelled to be conservative about what they teach. Multiculturalism, in this context, is regarded as something of a supplement to a school curriculum that is oriented toward "the basics." (p. 125)

Despite the fact that teachers in the 1990s, particularly in urban areas, were becoming more aware of the inadequacy of curriculum and materials carried over from a halcyon time when white students were a majority, it is clear that teachers alone cannot effect the kinds of changes that are needed in the classroom. Active, engaged parents, culturally sensitive and informed administrators and curriculum specialists, and elected school board officials more committed to student learning—all must take part in the work ahead. It can't be left to the "experts," whoever they are.

REFERENCES

Armento, Beverly J., Gary B. Nash, Christopher L. Salter, and Karen K. Wixson. 1991. *America will be*. Boston: Houghton Mifflin.

———, J. Jorge Klor de Alva, Gary B. Nash, Christopher L. Salter, Louis E. Wilson, and Karen K. Wixson. 1994. *America will be*. Boston: Houghton Mifflin.

Bernstein, Richard. 1990. The rising hegemony of the politically correct. *New York Times* (October 28): sect. 4, p. 1.

Bigelow, Bill. 1991. Talking back to Columbus: Teaching for justice and hope. *Rethinking Columbus*, Milwaukee, Wis.: Special edition of Rethinking Schools, pp. 38–43.

———, Barbara Miner, and Bob Petersen, eds. 1991. *Rethinking Columbus*. Milwaukee: Rethinking Schools.

California Council for the Social Studies. 1993. *Sunburst* 17 (23): pp. 8–10.

Communities United against Racism in Education (CURE). 1991. Untitled analysis of Houghton Mifflin textbooks. Berkeley: Oyate.

Council on Islamic Education. July 1994. *Assessment of the California History–Social Science Framework*. Fountain Valley, CA: Council.

Der, Henry. 1992. Cultural context of Oakland protests against Houghton Mifflin history textbooks. Unpublished paper.

FitzGerald, Frances. 1979. *America revised: History schoolbooks in the twentieth century*. Boston: Little, Brown.

Gordon, Larry. 1991. Charting new courses in teaching about Columbus. *Los Angeles Times* (December 26): pp. A1, 36, 37.

Gross, Jane. 1991. A city's determination to rewrite history puts its classrooms in chaos. *New York Times* (September 18): p. B7.

Heyser, Holly A. 1991. New text survives bias debate. *Peninsula Times Tribune* (July 18): pp. A1, 10.

History–Social Science Framework. 1988. Sacramento: California State Department of Education.

King, Joyce Elaine. 1992. Diaspora literacy and consciousness in the struggle against miseducation in the black community. *Journal of Negro Education* 61 (3): 317–340.

Li, David K. 1993. Teachers write own curriculum. *Oakland Tribune* (October 22): pp. B1, 2.

McCarthy, Cameron. 1990. Multicultural education, minority identities, textbooks, and the challenge of curriculum reform. *Journal of Education* 172 (2): 118–129.

Nash, Gary. 1990. Attachment A, p. 1, enclosed with a letter from John T. Ridley, Houghton Mifflin Vice President and Editor-in-Chief, Elementary School Division, to Joseph D. Carrabino, chair of the California Board of Education, September 6.

Patterson, Victoria, with Susan Lobo. 1988. Oakland's Indian education programs: A success story. *News from Native California* 2 (4): pp. 23–24.

Shaver, James P., O. L. Davis Jr., and Suzanne W. Helburn. 1979. The status of social studies education: Impressions from three NSF studies. *Social Education* 43 (2): 150–153.

Swartz, Ellen. 1990. America will be: A text critique. Rochester, N.Y.: City School District, Multicultural Project.

———. 1992. Emancipatory narratives: Rewriting the master script in the school curriculum. *Journal of Negro Education* 61 (3): 341–355.

Time magazine. 1991. The trouble with Columbus (October 7): pp. 52–61.

Waugh, Dexter. 1991a. Schools mixed on buying new history text. *San Francisco Examiner* (January 27): p. B1.

————. 1991b. New texts on San Francisco school agenda. *San Francisco Examiner.* (June 19): p. A7.

Weatherford, Jack. 1991. *Native roots: How the Indians enriched America.* New York: Crown.

NOTES

1. Michaelson's school also invested in a packaged interactive curriculum developed by Stanford University graduates who had formed a company to produce them. It comes in a thick binder filled with photographs, slides, and suggested activities. The Oakland school district, following its rejection of the textbooks, ordered the same U.S. history binders.

2. See also "America before Columbus," *U.S. News & World Report,* July 8, 1991, pp. 23–37; "Discovering Columbus," by John Noble Wilford, *New York Times* magazine, August 11, 1991, pp. 25–55; and Wilford's book *The Mysterious History of Columbus* (New York: Knopf, 1991).

3. See also Jack Weatherford, *Native Roots: How the Indians Enriched America* (New York: Crown, 1991).

PART III

Possibilities

7
America Not Yet

This world is white no longer, and it will never be white again.
    James Baldwin (1955, p. 175)

Black History does not seek to highlight the outstanding contributions of special black people to the life and times of America. Rather our emphasis is on exposure, disclosure, on reinterpretation of the entire American past.
    Vincent Harding (1970, p. 279)

T he failure to adopt as state policy a history–social science curriculum representing a transformative multiculturalism in California, as well as the slowness and uncertainty of movement toward that end in New York, does not negate the possibility that it will be achieved in the future, although the obstacles have remained intractable thus far. Joyce E. King's (1995, in press) analysis goes to the heart of the issue of race and power:

> Disagreements about education and curriculum transformation among liberals, progressives, and conservatives—that appear to be about what should be included in the literary canon or taught in the school curriculum—are as much about the society's failure to resolve the problems of racial hierarchy and cultural hegemony in a purported democracy. (p. 2)

Henry Giroux's (1992) critical view of the discourse of multicultural education is more descriptive of white, particularly neo-nativist, discourse than that of the "others" to whom he refers. He says that the discourse

> generally fails to conceptualize issues of race and ethnicity as part of the wider discourse of power and powerlessness. . . . Multiculturalism is generally about Otherness, but is written in ways in which the dominating aspects of white culture are not called into question and the oppositional potential of difference as a site of struggle is muted. (p. 117)

It is the case, however, that non-mainstream work, by people of all colors, has been marginalized by dominant intellectual communities within and outside the academy.

What made the California textbook controversy a particularly interesting debate, in Beverly M. Gordon's view (1993), was its illustration of black resistance to Eurocentric discourse and "the level of ferocious attack and challenge made by dominant establishment scholars" (p. 453) in defense of their position. A similar observation could be made of the New York social studies curriculum controversy, particularly the vitriol that greeted the 1989 report of the Task Force on Minorities, *A Curriculum of Inclusion.*

Our intent in this concluding chapter is not only to recap and compare key aspects of the California and New York case studies and to consider the implications of impending national standards (and assessments) but also to attend to historically marginalized or suppressed voices and to consider the curriculum policy and practice implications of casting light into what has been the shadowed world of alternatives for most curriculum policymakers and practitioners.

LESSONS

It is my conviction that there are always two nations in every nation: the dominant on-going nation, enchanted with its self-proclaimed virtues, values, and glorious traditions, and another nation that exists on sufferance, half-buried, seldom surfacing, struggling to survive. . . . Oddly enough the enduring historical values of the nation—the values it celebrates but does not always observe—are kept alive by this half-suppressed, half-buried sector. Again and again, despised, outcast groups in this country, by struggling for "equal enforcement of the law," "due process," and "equal opportunity," have kept such values alive.
     Carey McWilliams (1973, p. xxi)

The critical objections raised by African and Asian Americans and many others in California to new textbooks in 1990, and in some cases to the 1987 *History–Social Science Framework* that provided a blueprint for the textbooks, heightened sensitivities in many school districts. Teachers and administrators were impelled to consider and rethink previously unconfronted questions, such as, what sort of history is to be taught today? and how is it to be taught, now that the majority of students in California classrooms are racial and ethnic "minorities"?

Similarly, in New York, the 1989 *A Curriculum of Inclusion* task force report challenged in forthright language the Eurocentric ground on which existing social studies curricula had been constructed, while the 1991 *One Nation, Many Peoples* report, employing more moderate language, sustained and extended the challenge.

In both states opposition came swiftly. In New York the opposition initially focused on what was perceived as unduly harsh, angry language in *A Curriculum of Inclusion,* and the fact that no historians had been involved in its preparation. The establishment counter attack, diligently attended to by the New York and national media, resulted in a retreat by state education officials. Education policymaking, always a political process, followed a zig-zag course of give-and-take. The issues in New York influenced the debate over American identity then captivating the media and academic discourse, and the America debate in turn influenced curriculum policymaking in New York. As recounted in Chapter 5, the process of reshaping social studies curriculum in New York to reflect multiple perspectives was slowed if not redirected by these outside influences.

In California the critical voices raised from traditionally marginalized sectors were, in terms of the battle over the textbooks, essentially quashed for the time being. But, as shown in Chapter 6, their message spread far beyond the public hearings held in Sacramento in 1990, influencing decisions and teaching in numerous school districts. The victory of the framework and textbook advocates was hailed by media commentators and partisans such as then-NEH chair Lynne V. Cheney, who held up the California framework as a model for the nation while simultaneously denouncing New York's task force report, as noted in Chapter 5. As Debra Viadero (1992) reported, quoting Cheney:

> "It's no longer a question of whether we're going to have a multicultural education. The question is whether we're going to do it well or do it badly." Taking a swipe at New York's plan for making social-studies teaching more multicultural, Ms. Cheney said, "New York has often been the leader in doing things badly." . . . In contrast, Ms. Cheney said, California's framework is "a model" because it "emphasizes what we share as well as what makes us different." (p. 25)

The incessant drum beating by Cheney and other advocates of California's approach inevitably began to grow tiresome, as evidenced by remarks made in October 1994 by California Curriculum Commission member Eugene Flores (who was not a member when the textbooks were adopted in 1990) at a world history conference in Southern California sponsored by the Council on Islamic Education. Although some states had emulated California's new curriculum frameworks and were watching its attempts to develop new means of student assessment, education officials in the Golden State were beginning "to perceive this attitude of ABC—'Anything But California,' " said Flores. In a follow-up interview, Flores said, "eventually, you know, the criticism comes back—'Is the capital of the U. S. in Sacramento now, or is it Washington, D.C.?' " (interview, October 2, 1994)

The California conference, a gathering of Muslim scholars and teachers also attended by representatives of various textbook publishers (Houghton Mifflin's scheduled representatives could not make it—one had recently resigned from the company and the other pleaded workload) showed that resistance to the neo-nativists' agenda was still strong. The keynote speaker was Ali Mazrui, the Albert Schweitzer Professor in the Humanities at the State University of New York at Binghamton, who had served on the New

York Review Committee that produced the *One Nation, Many Peoples* report. Referring to the committee, Mazrui said that "the majority of us did feel our children were receiving an excessively Eurocentric approach to the study of the United States and to the study of the world, although there were one or two dissenters in our midst. Considering how controversial that subject was, I think there was substantial consensus."

Nationally, Mazrui noted two complementary reform movements. One, he said

> is indeed the multicultural movement, which seeks to sensitize syllabuses, teachers, textbooks, publishers, to the cultural diversity of this country. The other movement is . . . in global studies which seeks to restore balance in the study of world history and world affairs. . . .
>
> The multicultural movement seems to believe that while the United States has been the greatest asylum for diverse peoples, it hasn't been the greatest refuge for diverse cultures. The multicultural movement seeks to end this anomaly, seeks to end Eurocentrism in the study of American history and culture. It seeks to establish the fact that the United States as a pyramid was not built just by the pharoahs, called the founding fathers, but by women as well as men, blacks as well as whites, non-Christians as well as Christians. . . . The global studies movement also insists that world civilization is a product of many cultures and not merely of the triumph of modern Europe.

The New York and California cases demonstrate that education policymaking, especially in areas such as history and social studies, is highly political and abutted by diverse pressures; among the main ones are parents, ideologues, business interests, school board politics, internal district politics, classroom practice, and teacher calls for autonomy. A primary lesson from our studies, however, points to a paradox if not a hypocrisy: At the same time that many education policymakers and liberal scholars gave lip service to the need to expand and multiculturalize the curriculum, their actions served to minimize such expansion and, in effect, to contain the degree of change. Underlying this braking effect appears to be a basic suspicion, probably a fear, of the ramifications of going beyond simple acknowledgment and modest accommodation of demographic changes. The suspicion that racialethnic separatism awaits just around the corner has been expressed most prominently by Arthur M. Schlesinger Jr. (1991): "The bonds of cohesion in our society are sufficiently fragile, or so it seems to me, that it makes no sense to strain them by encouraging and exalting cultural and linguistic apartheid" (p. 138).[1]

Voices such as Schlesinger's have influenced the debates in California and New York, as noted in earlier chapters, giving a neo-nativist twist to the movement toward fashioning national standards in several subject areas—a movement that has many of its origins in the debate over what and who is the America and American of the future.

STANDARDIZING AMERICA

The eighteenth century marks not only the dawn of the age of national-
ism but the dusk of religious modes of thought. The century of the En-
lightenment, of rationalist secularism, brought with it its own modern
darkness. . . . What then was required was a secular transformation of
fatality into continuity, contingency into meaning . . . few things were
[are] better suited to this end than an idea of nation.
    Benedict Anderson (1991, p. 11)

The 1990s movement to develop "world class" national curriculum standards in at least five subject areas—English, mathematics, science, history, and geography—had its official birth at the 1989 education summit of the nation's governors, culminating later in the 1994 enactment of the Educate America: Goals 2000 legislation.

The movement's recent antecedents can be found in the 1983 report *A Nation at Risk* (National Commission on Excellence in Education 1983), which called the nation's education system mediocre and urged higher expectations for students in the "new basic" subjects (the "old" basics of English, mathematics, science, and social studies plus computer science); curriculum-based exams (a nationwide system but not national exams); improved teacher preparation; and longer school years.[2] The 1989 summit followed several widely publicized studies that found U.S. students to be lagging compared with students in other industrialized nations.

National curriculum standards tied to assessments drew widespread support during the early 1990s, support often linked to the beliefs that the nation's economic standing in the world community depended on drastic curricular reform, that drastic reform required tougher standards, and that tougher standards could be realized only nationally, through federal policy. As PACE (Policy Analysis for California Education) put it: "Since the United States is involved in worldwide economic competition, solely local control of tests and curriculum is a luxury the U.S. can no longer afford" (Guthrie et al. 1992, p. 2).

Others disagreed. Herbert M. Kliebard, an education professor at the University of Wisconsin at Madison, asked how a national curriculum would resolve economic problems:

> When there is a real or perceived crisis, there's a tendency in the United States to focus on education. But I don't think that a national curriculum, national standards or anything like that will have any effect on our economic position in the world. (quoted in Celis 1993, p. 16)

Theodore R. Sizer, Brown University education professor and chair of the Coalition of Essential Schools, said: "I see this as the tip of the iceberg. The iceberg is the arrogation of authority over children by the central government, in the name of high standards and international competition" (quoted in Rothman 1992, p. 8).

Once again California was held up as the model by supporters of national standards. As American Federation of Teachers president Albert Shanker (1992) wrote: "They say our country is too diverse to get agreement on curriculum. But California has done it, and its population is as diverse as that of the U.S." (p. E7).

While noting opposition to the movement toward national curriculum standards, including disagreements over the federal role and the need to insure equity for all students, Guthrie et al. (1992) echoed then-Secretary of Education Lamar Alexander in claiming that "the political momentum behind these national reform efforts is impressive and growing" (p. 6).

Yet some proponents of national standards recognized early on that there was serious opposition to national standards, assessments, and curriculum. Such concerns included that local control over schools might be lost, that a national curriculum would hinder classroom innovation and could well become as rigid as those found in some European countries, and that national policy would undermine state curriculum reform efforts. Seeming to anticipate opposition, Henry Kiernan and John Pyne (1993), both participants in the National History Standards Project, said in support of standards:

> The mere mention of "standards" sends shivers up the spines of many educators. . . . Yet it is important to remember that the push for national standards is not a "neo-conservative" plot orchestrated by a coterie of Reagan-Bush zealots out to "homogenize" our schools and indoctrinate our students with "politically correct values." The movement for national standards is a broad-based movement supported by a variety of people representing all sections, classes, races, and political viewpoints. (pp. 3–4)

"A national curriculum—*not*" became a repeated refrain: "It cannot be said often enough: national standards do not mean a national curriculum" (Gagnon 1993, p. 11); "They are not mandates, and they are not a national curriculum" (Bahmueller and Branson 1993, p. 13); "Standards do not entail a national curriculum" (Downs 1993, p. 23).

Clearly, the movement toward national standards, and perhaps national assessments and a national curriculum, raised the stakes and the pitch of the rhetoric insofar as there was more to be gained or lost (or misunderstood) by having one or another vision of America enshrined in those standards.

Other issues, particularly in the early stages of developing standards for history and the social studies, arose over questions of content or curriculum knowledge. Several national education and history organizations that reviewed draft history standards in 1992 said that they were too content-heavy and would overload teachers (Viadero 1993, p. 5). Other reviewers concluded that the draft history standards unduly emphasized Western civilization or were dominated by a Euro-American perspective—the same issues that textbook and framework critics had raised in California. This is not surprising, considering that the director and co-director of the National History Standards project, located at the National Center for History in the Schools at UCLA, were Charlotte Crabtree and Gary Nash, respectively—the same people who helped propel that perspective into California classrooms.

In 1992 Crabtree and Nash circulated the National Center's 300-page monograph, *Lessons from History,* to the standards project's focus groups for review and comment. In his covering letter to the focus groups, Nash (who also was one of the authors of *Lessons from History*) said the monograph originally was produced as a guide for teachers but now was being seen as providing some basis for the development of U.S. and world history standards (Nash 1992).

The American Historical Association's focus group (1992a) responded with a lengthy analysis of *Lessons from History,* saying that despite "very good comments about broader understanding and critical thinking," the chapter on U.S. history was "flawed" (p. 1). The focus group's report faulted *Lessons* for its emphasis on "broad coverage of facts, rather than treating history as a process of deeply interconnected actions," saying that it presented "too simplistic a view of the historical past."

The report, echoing earlier concerns over the Houghton Mifflin textbooks raised by critics in 1990, said the focus group was "troubled" over the document's interpretation of what should be conveyed in the standards concerning historical reality and the American past. It quoted *Lessons from History* as follows:

> To tell us who we are, what we have done, and what we are becoming; the Western, or European past, to understand our moral and political heritage and the causes of its advances and its failures; and the history of non-European civilizations, to know the nations and peoples with whom we have to live out a common destiny. (p. 13)

Said the focus group:

> Underlying the authors' interpretation . . . is a clear presumption that students are of European descent. We note, for instance, that "our" refers solely to West Europeans, and that "non-Europeans" are cast as essentially alien peoples with whom we have to get along. (p. 7)

The American Historical Association's world history focus group (1992b) also criticized *Lessons from History* for using a "Western-oriented view of the world" (p. 2). In the early stages at least, the historians and educators leading the history standards project seemed not to have learned any lessons from the controversy over the 1990 textbook adoption in California.

In addition to questions of how much subject matter content the emerging standards should include and which perspective(s) should be represented, there also was the question of how much content specificity was desirable. Somewhere along the way from *A Nation at Risk*'s call for higher expectations for student learning in 1983, to the world class standards called for by the national goals in 1989, to the finished products of the various standards projects due out in late 1994, the emphasis seemed to shift from broader *performance* standards indicating what students should be able to do (examine and evaluate historical evidence) to more specific *content* standards indicating what information students should analyze. Specific content standards do not preclude more multicultural history–social studies curriculum knowledge, but they do tend to support an additive or modestly revisionist multiculturalism more than a thoroughly revisionist or transformative position—in part because content standards are, by their nature, more likely to be static than dynamic and open ended.[3]

In addition to the National History Standards Project, there were three other national curriculum standards projects relevant to history–social studies education: the Geography Education Standards Project, administered by the National Council for Geographic Education, in Washington, D.C.; the National Standards for Civics and Government, developed by the Center for Civic Education, in Calabasas, California; and the Curriculum Standards for Social Studies, developed by the National Council for the Social Studies, in Washington, D.C. The geography and civics standards projects, like the history group, were supported with federal grants awarded during the Bush administration. The social studies standards project did not receive federal funding. Neither social studies nor civics was on the list of what became seven subjects recognized in the national goals supported by the Clinton administration in 1993 (arts and foreign languages were added to the original five).[4]

By late 1994, it seemed likely that the unveiling of the history and social studies standards produced by the various projects would prompt another round in the America debate. Specific standards in contrast to vague slogans such as common culture and inclusion could splinter existing alliances. Indeed, there were signs that the neo-nativist network of the late 1980s and early 1990s might be coming unglued, that their common culture rallying cry might not have much holding power when it came to specifics. For example, Lynne Cheney, who had provided NEH funds for developing history standards to Crabtree's center at UCLA, denounced them before their release to the general public. Referring to the UCLA center's *Lessons from History,* which she had applauded, Cheney said during a MacNeil/Lehrer Newshour segment on October 26, 1994:

> Mr. Nash and his colleague, Charlotte Crabtree, really promised to deliver X, a version of history that was based on a document that they had already produced which is fine, one that I would be so happy to have my grandchildren learn from, and, instead, they produced Y, this document. . . . I do think that the state of history in higher education has been so radicalized that it's not possible for us to develop standards.

Cheney contended that the American history standards promulgated a politically correct social history that ignored prominent historical figures such as Robert E. Lee and included previously obscure individuals such as Mercy Otis Warren. The split between Cheney and Crabtree-Nash represented not so much a family spat as it did the fact that the neo-nativist network, as suggested earlier (see Chapter 1), was by no means a monolithic cadre. Rather, it was a loose gathering of academics, public figures, and political commentators from various positions and vantage points who shared the warmth of the campfire of ancient, celebratory nation-founding tales. The history standards that emerged from the UCLA project did not satisfy Cheney and perhaps others in part because they challenged the notion that there is a single history to be taught—illustrating once again that curriculum knowledge is continually contested.

The various history-social studies standards projects promised finished products by the end of 1994, and it seemed highly unlikely that any of the projects would, or could, support a transformative multiculturalism. All the standards projects relevant to history and social studies appeared more likely to sustain the status quo vis-a-vis race-ethnicity and power relations than to challenge it.

POSSIBILITIES FOR TRANSFORMATIVE MULTICULTURALISM

In contrast to additive and revisionist forms of multiculturalism that selectively expand the history to be conveyed within existing or slightly modified frameworks or story lines, transformative multiculturalism, as introduced in Chapter 2, challenges and alters the historical narrative framework, thereby restructuring and redefining America. The experiences and perspectives of groups that traditionally have been unseen, unheard, or simply marginalized are not merely acknowledged or mentioned; they are an integral part of the transformed history–social studies curriculum. Transformative multiculturalism serves to enhance understanding of one's own and others' experiences, of how present circumstances have come to be, and to inform social action toward equity and social justice goals. Its action-oriented dimension is similar to what has been called social reconstructionism (Sleeter and Grant 1987; Sleeter 1989), social action (Banks 1988), and "progressive activism" supported by an education that "seeks not just to inform but to transform" (Marable 1991, p. 95).

Next we elaborate and provide illustrations of two forms of transformative multiculturalism—a black studies perspective and a cross-disciplinary approach to reciprocal history—that should be taken seriously in future policymaking and practice.

Black Studies Perspective

Drawing on Carter G. Woodson's 1933 *The Mis-Education of the Negro* and the work of Michel Foucault and others, Sylvia Wynter (1992) argues that the major questions of what knowledge is to be included in history–social studies curriculum and how it is to be organized and used are, at root, epistemological and ethical. In other words, they are questions of underlying if not acknowledged assumptions about the origins, nature, and limits of knowledge (epistemology) and about who benefits or is harmed as a result of the choice of epistemological position and of knowledge for curriculum (ethics).

Woodson (1933) had argued that the public schools taught blacks to despise themselves, and that

> to handicap a student by teaching him that his black face is a curse and that his struggle to change his condition is hopeless is the worst sort of lynching. It kills one's aspirations and dooms him to vagabondage and crime. It is strange, then, that the friends of truth and the promoters of freedom have not risen up against the present propaganda in the schools and crushed it. This crusade is much more important than the anti-lynching movement, because there would be no lynching if it did not start in the schoolroom. (p. 3)

Woodson saw through the myth of the common school to show that the education system supported white hegemony, less by physical coercion than by conveying the dominant ideology of racial hierarchy and black inferiority. He observed:

> No systematic effort toward change has been possible, for, taught the same economics, history, philosophy, literature and religion which have established the present code of morals, the Negro's mind has been brought under the control of his oppressor. The problem of holding the Negro down, therefore, is easily solved. When you control a man's thinking you do not have to worry about his actions. . . . The same educational process which inspires and stimulates the oppressor with the thought that he is everything and has accomplished everything worth while, depresses and crushes at the same time the spark of genius in the Negro by making him feel that his race does not amount to much and never will measure up to the standards of other peoples. (p. xiii)

Sixty years later Wynter (1992) interpreted the continuing, school-supported cultural domination as a consequence of conceptualizing and knowing "our social reality through the prescriptive categories of a 'local' world view." Problems in history curricula and textbooks ensue when it is assumed that one's knowledge of "social reality is a supra-cultural rather than a culture-specific order of knowledge" (pp. 8–9), for example, that the experience of European immigrants to what is now the United States is generalizable to all. Present multicultural alternatives—within the structure of this prescriptive epistemological order—will not resolve education's social or intellectual crises or the broader environmental crises facing the entire human species. In Wynter's view even a transformative multiculturalism will not resolve these crises, unless it is one that challenges the present "regime of truth."

Iterating Woodson's challenge to the extant organization of knowledge in the U.S. education system, particularly the misrepresentation of the past in history curricula, Wynter (1992) argues that the problem is *"precisely our present episteme,* its disciplinary organization of knowledge and 'regime of truth' [from Foucault] that is the root and causal source of these problems" (p. 4).

Wynter says the question "What is wrong with our education?" can be re-posed as "What is wrong with our present local culture?" The challenge to the textbooks, she says, "can be seen as itself being the harbinger of a demand logically generated from our role as Black Liminal Other to the present Judaeo-Christian conception of the True Self. This demand is now no other than that of securing our human autonomy" (p. 61). The Houghton Mifflin textbooks, she says, and the epistemological order in which they were written, relegate non-immigrant students "conceptually to a secondary status" (p. 63). The challenge, she says, makes it possible "for us . . . to recognize that we need no longer, as humans, remain prisoners of our culture's prescriptive categories" (pp. 63–64).

Wynter (1990) has called her alternative a "black studies perspective," which she describes as a cultural model or epistemology with the potential for transmuting knowledge by challenging the "prescriptive rules" of the American "public culture," which over the centuries have rigidly maintained racial hierarchy (see Chapter 3). Despite the racially specific label, Wynter's black studies perspective is not that of a single racial or ethnic group. It is generated from "the group category forcibly constrained to play the role of the *alter ego* to the conception of the ideal [Anglo/Euro-American] Self" (enclosure 2, p. 1). The vantage point of "alterity," Wynter proposes, can provide an alternative way of knowing.

Joining Wynter in developing this approach, King (1995, in press, p. 40) suggests that alterity provides a "perspective advantage." Whereas Euro-American cultural knowledge "serves to *legitimate* the dominant white middle-class normative cultural model," a black studies perspective does not claim to be either a "normative cultural model of being and way of knowing the world" or supra-cultural (pp. 18–19). A black studies perspective is not a mirror image, black version of white Eurocentricity. The deciphering, culture-centered knowledge (see Chapter 2) in the work of Wynter and Toni Morrison, in King's view,

> is not a world dominated by Blackness or a world that multiculturalizes the Other and leaves conceptual Blackness intact. Rather, the social imaginary is the "newly defined world" that will "hold all the people" and constitute an altogether different "order of knowledge" and "changed quality of consciousness." (pp. 41–42).

Wynter is calling, says King, "for liberating knowledge in behalf, not only of African-descent people, but also for the most inclusive interest of human freedom" (p. 47).

Although she does not raise it in such terms, English professor and essayist bel hooks (1990) captures the sense and possibility of marginalization within a normative context. She argues that it can be a place for liberatory thought. "Understanding marginality as position and place of resistance is crucial for oppressed, exploited, colonized people" (p. 150). She observes a "definitive distinction between the marginality which is imposed by oppressive structure and that marginality one chooses as site of resistance, as location of radical openness and possibility" (p. 153). Hooks identifies marginality as "much more than a site of deprivation . . . it is also the site of radical possibility, a space of resistance" (p. 149).

The black studies perspective that King and Wynter offer complements King's conception of deciphering knowledge and its potential to dissolve social myths and centrism. It is compatible with our conception of critical pragmatism (see Chapter 2), particularly the critical edge that questions surface appearances and taken-for-granted practices. Wynter, King, and hooks, for example, raise questions from such different vantage points, each casting light into the shadows of prevailing race- and class-based orthodoxies. Reversing Audre Lorde's epigram, perhaps only the master's tools *will* dismantle the master's house.

The transformative potential of a black studies perspective for history—social studies curriculum lies in its insistence on analyzing and questioning the prescriptive rules of the prevailing social and political power structures and the cultural landscape. Knowledge selected for curriculum would be organized and used to encourage students to raise and pursue "deciphering" questions, in other words, to think critically from their own and others' standpoints.

The purposeful introduction of a black studies perspective prods the raising of questions that might not be imagined otherwise. For example, Wynter (1990) asks how is it that the "dispossession of the indigenous peoples, their subordination and the mass enslavement of the people of Black African descent" came to be seen as "just and virtuous" actions by those responsible. Further, how has the continuation of "this initial dispossession" in, for instance, "the jobless drug and crime ridden inner city ghettos and barrios" come to be seen as "*just,* or at the very least, to be in the nature of things?" (enclosure Two, p. 59). Additional questions in this spirit have included: What beliefs, practices, and circumstances serve to maintain racial (socioeconomic, and other) hierarchy? What privileges do whites, particularly white males, in the United States enjoy that people of color and women do not? (See, e.g., McIntosh 1992.) How have these privileges come to be? What systems of thought justify them? What actions might be taken to minimize if not halt exploitation of one another and the environment? Also, recall from Chapter 6 the kinds of questions that San Francisco teacher Dianne Talarico encouraged her sixth grade students to consider, not only about Columbus but also about the sources they were reading: for example, Whose point of view is the story told from? What do you still wonder about?

Clearly, a black studies perspective and other transformative approaches that question the basis and organization of knowledge in history—social studies curricula by their nature preclude prescriptive curriculum policies or practices that predetermine presumably correct (that is, orthodox) answers or outcomes. After all, who did discover "America"? What does it mean to "discover" something? And, what was/is "America" to those who were here long before the Europeans?

What might America become?

Reciprocal History

A second, complementary if not interrelated approach to knowledge in history–social studies curriculum that represents a transformative multiculturalism is reciprocal history. As introduced in Chapter 2, reciprocal history takes as its focus the interactions and interconnections among diverse individuals and groups over time and in their social-environmental context. It emphasizes how various individuals and groups have learned from and otherwise influenced each other. These interactions and interconnections are examined from multiple perspectives or vantage points. Among the assumptions that underlie this conception of reciprocal history are the following:

1. U.S. history, from its beginnings, has been hybrid and multicultural—"our" histories have been irreversibly intertwined, making America more than the sum of its parts. The "cultures of all Americans have evolved through reciprocal relationships" (Tyack 1993, p. 27).
2. Historically, interactions among individuals and groups in the United States have been shaped by racial/cultural and class-based distinctions and hierarchies (Wynter 1992).
3. U.S. cultures and history have been dynamic as well as multifaceted. Thus, both racial and ethnic cultures have changed over time while continuing to be integral to an ever-changing America (see, e.g., Conzen et al. 1990). Simply put, intermingling occurred from the start and continued over the centuries, modifying nearly everyone's identity.
4. Reciprocity involves gender and sexual orientation as well as race and ethnicity. The various cultural groups that make up America are composed of both women and men, neither of whose thought and action is either unitary or independent of the other.
5. Hierarchical relations have tended to support one-way studies, for example, examining the influence of Euro-Americans on Native Americans, much more than, for example, examining the effects on white Americans of the "Africanist presence and personae" (Morrison 1992, p. 90). By emphasizing mutual interaction and interconnection such as the impact of racism on its perpetrators as well as its victims, and drawing on deciphering knowledge (King 1995, in press), reciprocal history can contribute to flattening hierarchical relations of power and privilege.
6. Reciprocity is open-ended and ongoing, as interaction continues in changing circumstances. In the words of the Organization of American Historians (1991):

> Historical studies should proceed first from the clear acknowledgment that no major group or society has a wholly singular and static cultural heritage. On the contrary, the cultures of all people have become intermingled over time, often in subtle and complex ways that historians are still exploring. . . . a history that asserts or implies the inherent superiority of one race, gender, class, or region of the world over another is by definition "bad history" and should have no place in American Schools. (p. 6)

Such a conception of reciprocal history carries significant implications for transformative history—social studies curriculum policy and practice. Not only would it mean a more encompassing selection of knowledge for curriculum, but that knowledge would be organized so as to highlight interactions and interconnections, and it would be treated as provisional, open to question. Further, it would be used to teach students to "decipher" their past and present, to consider alternative futures. Reciprocity would be examined from more than one vantage point.

For instance, students might investigate what John Edward Philips (1991, p. 228) calls "white Africanisms." It is Philips's thesis that "as much African culture survives now among whites as among blacks in the United States" (p. 227), and he provides a range of examples from music to religious practices to African influences on feminist theory. He suggests that:

> The possibility that whites could benefit culturally from interaction with blacks has not been seriously presented. Pride in their African heritage is something that white children should be taught along with blacks. (p. 236)

Further, examples from literature can be coordinated with history—social studies curriculum, such as considering the effects of slavery on the Shelbys in Harriet Beecher Stowe's *Uncle Tom's Cabin* or Ursa MacKenzie's experience of "biculturality" in Paule Marshall's *Daughters*.

DIALOGUE AMONG DIFFERENCES

In professional education forums and policy arenas as well as school and university classrooms, the America debate would benefit, we believe, from seriously pursuing dialogue among differences. The dialogue we have in mind is informed by the critical pragmatism introduced in Chapter 2. It aims to be non-hierarchical, non-competitive or dominating, and welcoming of diversity. It encompasses what Mikhail Bakhtin characterized as "heteroglossia," that is, "the existence of many voices, some contesting, some cohering, all demanding and deserving attention" (cited in Greene 1993, p. 212). Participants in a dialogue among differences listen to and try to understand one another "without denying or suppressing the otherness of the other" (Bernstein 1991, p. 336). In so doing, participants assume that they can learn from one another. Disagreement is inevitable, and consensus on every topic may not be possible or desirable. A key is moving away from an adversarial stance, which is better aimed at winning arguments than at addressing the larger crises confronting us.

A major goal of such dialogue among differences is to decrease non- and mis-understanding, if not to yield agreement, and thus to better inform action. The intent is not to create unity around a single center, but to foster greater understanding of ourselves and others and of our interconnections.

If extremists, fundamentalists of any stripe, will not engage in critical dialogue among or across differences, their refusal ought not to be allowed to prevent the rest of us from making the effort. It may be, as James Davison Hunter (1991) suggests, that the most ominous "culture wars" in the United States, and perhaps more widely, are *not* those among races or religions or cultures but those between cross-cutting orthodoxies and progressivisms. Yet race does remain the nation's central, unresolved dilemma, and it is to this racial divide—and its ethnic and cultural corollaries—that we address this concluding section.

We assume that dialogue among differences is possible, although admittedly scarce at present. We can, however, imagine such conversations in classrooms, professional forums, and policy arenas. But dialogue is risky and demands engagement. In a March 1994 public lecture in Buffalo, New York, Cornel West called for such a public conversation. "Public conversation," he said, "is a form of struggle. . . . I'm not talking about chit chat."

Dialogue among differences in the interests of understanding and community, and further, to the undermining of domination, is essential to transformative multiculturalism in both policy and practice. Conditions conducive to such dialogue with a focus on the nature of knowledge in school history–social studies curricula include what Nicholas C. Burbules and Suzanne Rice (1991, p. 411) call "communicative virtues" as well as serious engagement with the significant scholarship over the past hundred or more years by African Americans and other scholars of color, both female and male.

Burbules and Rice speak of communicative "virtues or dispositions rather than rules . . . because they need to be interpreted and applied thoughtfully to different situations" (p. 412). What is virtuous, in other words, is context dependent rather than absolute. "Tolerance and patience may be virtues," Burbules and Rice suggest, "when practiced by a teacher striving to understand and appreciate a student's perspective, but not so when invoked to protect racist or sexist speech that intimidates, harms, or silences others" (pp. 411–412). In addition to tolerance and patience, their list of conditions for dialogue among differences includes

> respect for differences, a willingness to listen, the inclination to admit that one may be mistaken, the ability to reinterpret or translate one's own concerns in a way that makes them comprehensible to others, the self-imposition of restraint in order that others may "have a turn" to speak, and the disposition to express one's self honestly and sincerely. (p. 411)

Lists such as these are starting points for consideration, not checklists for scoring and evaluation. For example, we would add the avoidance of what Patricia Hill Collins (1991, p. 42) calls "dichotomous oppositional difference," that is, either-or dualistic thought epitomized here by pluralism-unity. Three characteristics of dichotomous oppositional difference are particularly detrimental to dialogue among differences. One is using difference as the basis for categorization in such a way that the terms in each dichotomous pair "gain their meaning only in *relation* to their difference" (p. 42) from each other. Examples include black-white, fact-opinion, male-female, reason-emotion, and subject-object. A second characteristic is that the pair of terms typically is seen as "inherently opposed"; the difference between them is not complementary. Thirdly, "these oppositional relationships are intrinsically unstable" because they are constructed as unequal. Relative stability has been achieved, Hill Collins suggests, by subordinating one member of each pair to the other—blacks to whites, for example. "Dichotomous oppositional differences invariably imply relationships of superiority and inferiority, hierarchical relationships that mesh with political economies of domination and subordination" (p. 42).

To the extent that differences are construed as dichotomous and oppositional, dialogue among differences will not get very far. This kind of hierarchical, either-or thinking can be seen as a way of deflecting or impeding dialogue and of attempting to impose one's own preferences. If the choices are cast as good or evil, pluralism or unity, for example, what is there to discuss?

The dialogue among differences that we envision encompasses different ideas, interpretations, and perspectives as well as diverse participants. Prerequisite to a transformative multiculturalism is acknowledgment of and interaction with a range of scholarship. Beverly M. Gordon (1993) suggests that "dialogue that does not marginalize Black intellectual discourse allows for scholarly discourse" (p. 468). The case might be stated even more strongly: that discourse or dialogue which *a priori* marginalizes any scholarship on grounds of its origins cannot itself be scholarly.

Assuming commitment and conditions that are more, rather than less, conducive to dialogue among differences, about what would participants talk? We could explore possible visions of America and of social justice, creating meanings that are neither "centric" nor "other" because "we" have constructed meanings together (see, e.g., Banks 1993). We could probe the U.S. tradition of individualism that has obscured group differences and identities and hierarchical social relations (see, e.g., Olneck 1989, 1990). We could reexamine aspects of our joint if not common history and contemporary circumstances—not necessarily as cause for celebration or protest but, following the San Francisco sixth grader's comment about Columbus Day cited in Chapter 6, as a time "for thinking" and learning from each other. We could reconsider what kind of knowledge to include in history–social studies curricula for elementary and secondary students. And we could act on the knowledge gained from such dialogue.

Continuing the conversation—the dialogue among differences—is essential because there is no "once and for all," no "happily ever after." Old issues reappear in different guise, and new ones surface. As Maxine Greene (1993) has put it:

> The heteroglossic conversation moves on, never reaching a final conclusion, always incomplete, but richer and more densely woven, even as it moves through time. (p. 213)

The quest for America is without end:

History, despite its wrenching pain,
Cannot be unlived, but if faced
With courage, need not be lived again.
Maya Angelou, "On the Pulse of the Morning" (1993)

REFERENCES

American Historical Association. 1992a. Report of the U.S. history focus group of the American Historical Association, National History Standards Project.
———. 1992b. Report of the world history focus group of the American Historical Association, National History Standards Project.
Anderson, Benedict. 1991. *Imagined communities.* New York: Verso.
Angelou, Maya. From "On the Pulse of the Morning" by Maya Angelou. Copyright © 1993 by Maya Angelou. Reprinted by permission of Random House, Inc.
Bahmueller, Charles F., and Margaret Stimmann Branson. 1993. National standards for civics and government. *Docket* (Spring): 12–17. (Journal of the New Jersey Council for the Social Studies)
Baldwin, James. 1955. *Notes of a native son.* Boston: Beacon Press.
Banks, James A. 1988. Approaches to multicultural curriculum reform. *Multicultural Leader* 1 (2): 1–3.
———. 1993. Multicultural education: Development, dimensions, and challenges. *Phi Delta Kappan* 75 (1): 22–28.
Bernstein, Richard J. 1991. *The new constellation: The ethical-political horizons of modernity/postmodernity.* Cambridge: Massachusetts Institute of Technology Press.
Burbules, Nicholas C., and Suzanne Rice. 1991. Dialogue across differences: Continuing the conversation. *Harvard Educational Review* 61 (4): 393–416.
Celis, William 3d. 1993. The fight over national standards. *New York Times,* Education Life (August 1): pp. 14–16.
Conzen, Kathleen Neils, David A. Gerber, Ewa Morawska, George E. Pozzetta, and Rudolph J. Vecoli. 1990. The invention of ethnicity: A perspective from the USA. *Altreitalie* (April): 37–62.
Downs, Roger M. 1993. The geography standards project: "Geography for life." *Docket* (Spring): 22–25. (Journal of the New Jersey Council for the Social Studies)
Gagnon, Paul. 1993. Systemic reforms of schools: From national standards to the classroom down the hall. *Docket* (Spring): 8–11. (Journal of the New Jersey Council for the Social Studies)
Giroux, Henry. 1992. *Border crossings.* New York: Routledge.
Gordon, Beverly M. 1993. African-American cultural knowledge and liberatory education. *Urban Education* 27 (4): 440–470.
Greene, Maxine. 1993. Diversity and inclusion: Toward a curriculum for human beings. *Teachers College Record* 95 (2): 211–221.
Guthrie, James W., Michael W. Kirst, Allan R. Odden, Julia E. Koppich, Gerald C. Hayward, Greg Geeting, Mikala L. Rahn, Kevin A. Skelly, and Stephen Wai-Kwok Yan. 1992. *Conditions of education in California 1991.* Berkeley: University of California-Berkeley, School of Education, Policy Analysis for California Education (PACE).
Harding, Vincent. 1970. Beyond chaos: Black history and the search for the new land. In J. A. Williams and C. F. Harris, eds. *Amistad* (1): pp. 267–292. New York: Vintage Books.

Hill Collins, Patricia. 1991. Learning from the outsider within. Pages 35–59 in M. M. Fonow and J. A. Cook, eds., *Beyond methodology: Feminist scholarship as lived research*. Bloomington: Indiana University Press.

hooks, bel. 1989. *Talking back: Thinking feminist, thinking black*. Boston: South End Press.

———. 1990. *Yearning: Race, gender, and cultural politics*. Boston: South End Press.

Hunter, James Davison. 1991. *Culture wars: The struggle to define America*. New York: Basic Books.

Kiernan, Henry, and John Pyne. 1993. National standards and education reform: Prospects and sources. *Docket* (Spring): 1–7. (Journal of the New Jersey Council for the Social Studies)

King, Joyce E. 1992. Diaspora literacy and consciousness in the struggle against miseducation in the black community. *The Journal of Negro Education* 61 (3): 317–340.

———. In press 1995. Culture-centered knowledge: Black studies, curriculum transformation and social action. In James A. Banks and Cherry A. McGee Banks, eds., *Handbook of research on multicultural education*. New York: Macmillan.

Marable, Manning. 1991. Multicultural democracy: Toward a new strategy for progressive activism. *Z magazine* (November): pp. 89–95.

McIntosh, Peggy. 1992. White privilege and male privilege. Pages 70–81 in Margaret L. Andersen and Patricia Hill Collins, eds., *Race, class, and gender*. Belmont, Calif.: Wadsworth.

McWilliams, Carey. [1973], 1981. Introduction to Carlos Bulosan, *America is in the heart*. Seattle: University of Washington Press.

Morrison, Toni. 1992. *Playing in the dark*. Cambridge and London: Harvard University Press.

Nash, Gary. 1992. Letter to focus-group members for National History Standards Project (February 12).

National Commission on Excellence in Education. 1983. *A nation at risk*. Washington, D.C.: U.S. Government Printing Office.

Olneck, Michael R. 1989. Americanization and the education of immigrants, 1900–1925: An analysis of symbolic action. *American Journal of Education* 97: 398–423.

———. 1990. The recurring dream: Symbolism and ideology in intercultural and multicultural education. *American Journal of Education:* 147–174.

Organization of American Historians, Executive Board. 1991. History education in the public schools. *Organization of American Historians Newsletter* (February): p. 6.

Philips, John E. 1991. The African heritage of white America. Pages 225–239 in Joseph E. Holloway, ed., *Africanisms in American culture*. Bloomington: Indiana University Press.

Rothman, Robert. 1992. Standards and testing report is hailed, criticized. *Education Week* (February 5): 8.

Schlesinger, Arthur M. 1964. *Paths to the present*. Boston: Houghton Mifflin.

Schlesinger, Arthur M. Jr. 1991. *The disuniting of America*. Knoxville, TN: Whittle Direct Books.

Shanker, Albert. 1992. Where we stand. *New York Times* (March 1): p. E7.

Sleeter, Christine E. 1988. Multicultural education as a form of resistance to oppression. *Journal of Education* 171 (3): 51–71.

——— and Carl A. Grant. 1987. An analysis of multicultural education in the United States. *Harvard Educational Review* 57: 421–444.

Tyack, David D. 1993. Constructing difference: Historical reflections on schooling and social diversity. *Teachers College Record* 95 (1): 8–34.

Viadero, Debra. 1992. Two federal agencies launch project to develop national history standards. *Education Week* (January 8): 25.

———. 1993. Draft standards to urge three years of U.S. history. *Education Week* (June 23): 5.

Wynter, Sylvia. 1990. A cultural model critique of the textbook, *America will be.* Letter to California State Board of Education Members, enclosure 2.

———. 1992. The challenge to our episteme: The case of the California textbook controversy. Paper presented at the annual meeting of the American Educational Research Association, San Francisco (April).

Woodson, Carter G. 1933. *The mis-education of the Negro.* New Jersey: Africa World Press.

NOTES

1. Like father, like son. In *Paths to the Present* (1964) Arthur M. Schlesinger Sr. wrote:

   > The national purpose has been to create a democracy of diverse cultures which should embody the values and ideals, the arts, knowledge and techniques, of *men* of every *European* background. . . . Efforts to crush out minority heritages violate the national purpose and set a dangerous example for the rest of the world. (p. 85, emphasis added)

   This, of course, was written before the new pattern of massive immigration from Asian countries that began after 1965 and the decline in migration of European countries. One wonders if the non-European face of today's immigrant population would have led Schlesinger Senior into the same den of worry now occupied by his son—or not?

2. In *A Nation at Risk* the language of standards was used sparingly and usually to mean "standards and expectations" (p. 27), that is, consensus on goals and high expectations for students, not as it came to be used ten years later. Also, regarding assessment, *A Nation at Risk* stated clearly that standardized achievement tests "should be administered as part of a nationwide (but not Federal) system of State and local standardized tests." Further, "This system should include other diagnostic procedures that assist teachers and students to evaluate student progress" (p. 28).

3. Tensions between emphases on content versus performance or process standards seemed to be a key factor in the 1994 federal de-funding of the English standards project located at the University of Illinois and involving the National Council of Teachers of English and the International Reading Association. The Department of Education apparently wanted more content specification.

4. Why the Department of Education under Lamar Alexander and Diane Ravitch supported the development of civics standards when civics was not specified in the national goals remains unclear; the Center for Civic Education was awarded $4.3 million by OERI at the end of the Bush administration. By 1994 civics had been added to the subjects listed in the national goals, and economics also was being added.

Index

Ackley, Kermit, 134
Adler, Mortimer, 42
African American, 64, 82, 85
Africanist presence, 39, 46, 197
Alexander, Francie, 78
Alexander, Francie, and Charlotte Crabtree, 60
Alexander, Lamar, 14, 113, 190, 203
Alter, Jonathan, and Lydia Denworth, 113
America debate, vi, 4, 14, 15, 17, 23, 27, 31, 43–49, 74, 100, 131, 152, 187
American Historical Association, 191
American Textbook Council. *See* Sewall, Gilbert
Angelou, Maya, 200
Anderson, Benedict, 35, 45, 189
Ankeny, Kirk, 90
Anzaldua, Gloria, 56
Apple, Michael W., 88
Appleby, Joyce, 5, 45
Appleby, Joyce, Lynn Hunt, and Margaret Jacob, 42
Armento, Beverly et al., 62, 63, 167, 175, 176

Bahmueller, Charles F., and Margaret Stimmann Branson, 190
Baird, Lorna, 171
Bakhtin, Mikhail, 198
Baldwin, James, 5, 39, 185
Ball, Stephen J., 131, 132
Banks, James A., 35, 43, 47, 48, 56, 76, 148, 193, 200
Banks, Sandy, and William Trombley, 20
Barber, Benjamin, 150
Barringer, Felicity, 10, 11
Bauder, David, 146
Beard, Charles, and William Bagley, 50
Becker, Jules, 8
Bell, James H., 180

Bennett, William, 12, 42, 74, 96
Berger, Joseph, 101
Berger, Peter, and Hansfried Kellner, 27–28
Bernal, Martin, 76
Bernstein, Richard, 155, 162
Bernstein, Richard J., 30–31, 32, 198
Bianchi, John-Paul, 105, 117
Biemer, Linda, 134, 155
Bigelow, Bill, 163, 164, 166
Bigelow, Bill, Barbara Miner, and Bob Petersen, eds., 162, 164
Black studies perspective, 38, 55, 195, 196
Blauner, Bob, 4
Bloom, Alan, 125
Bradley Commission on History in the Schools, 16, 18, 95
Bradley, Lynde, and Harry Foundation, 16, 18
Brinkley, Alan, 42
Bromberg, Lloyd, 140
Buffalo Soldier, v
Burbules, Nicholas C., and Suzanne Rice, 199
Bush, George, 14, 15, 51, 113, 203

California Council for the Social Studies, 179
Canon, 41, 42, 96
   historical master narrative, 34, 41
Carr, David, 42
Carrabino, Joseph, 87
Carter, Mary, 105, 107, 111, 119, 125, 134, 138, 141, 148
Cather, Willa, 15
Celis, William 3rd, 189
Chernow, Daniel, 67
Cherryholmes, Cleo H., 55
Cheney, Lynne, 12, 15–16, 17, 18, 42, 60, 69, 71, 85, 86, 96, 113, 187, 192, 193

Chiles, Nick, 134
Chinese Americans, 64, 72, 83, 85, 159
Christian Coalition, 150
Chun, Gloria, 72
Cisneros, Henry, 11
Citizens for Excellence in Education, 150.
    See Simonds, Richard
Clarke, Breena, and Susan Tifft, 113
Clark, Todd, 73
Clinton, Bill, 10, 51, 150
Cohen, Saul, 146
Collier, Irene Dea, 161
Columbus, Christopher, vii, 63, 129, 130,
    157, 162, 163, 164, 166, 177
Committee of Scholars in Defense of History,
    99, 100, 129, 130, 131
Conzen, Kathleen Neils et al., 197
Cornbleth, Catherine, viii, ix, x, 5, 6, 26, 51,
    101, 102, 104, 106, 107, 114, 124,
    125, 132, 134, 140, 141, 143, 144,
    147, 152, 155, 156
Cornbleth, Catherine, and Dexter Waugh, 6
Cortines, Ramon, 160
Council on Islamic Education, 175, 179,
    187
Crabtree, Charlotte, 16, 17, 18, 21, 26, 64,
    68, 69, 71, 73, 75, 76, 78, 82, 87, 90,
    95, 121, 191, 192
Cremin, Lawrence, 11, 14
Crichlow, Warren, Susan Goodwin, Gaya
    Shakes, and Ellen Swartz, 87
Critical pragmatism, 27–34, 41, 105, 196,
    198
    and pluralism, 32–33
Cullen, Countee, 80
Culture
    American, v, 4
    common, vii, 12, 68, 85, 104–105, 119–
    122
    native model, 65
Cuomo, Mario, 131
CURE [Communities United against Racism
    in Education], 176, 177
Curriculum of Inclusion, A, viii, 19, 52, 74,
    94, 95, 96, 97, 98, 99, 100, 102, 110,
    111, 112, 114, 125, 134, 145, 147,
    154, 162, 186

Daniels, Roger, and Harry H. L. Kitano, 7
Darling-Hammond, Linda, 133, 143, 144,
    145, 147, 148, 152, 155
Davis, Angela, 97
Davis, James E., 162
Decter, Midge, 132
Deloria, Claire, 155

Der, Henry, 22, 87, 172
Diamond, Celia, 104, 116
Discourse, viii, vii–viii, 43, 44, 49, 74, 105,
    111, 152
    discursive practices, 44, 45
    discourse of derision, 130–132
Donner Foundation, 17, 18
Douglass, Frederick, 48
Downey, Matthew, 69, 72–73, 170, 171
Downs, Roger M., 190
Du Bois, W. E. B., 28, 29
Dukes, Hazel N., 95

Eagleton, Terry, 55
Edelman, Murray, 130
Educational Excellence Network, 16, 18,
    112
Ellis, Fred, 169
Ellsworth, Elizabeth, 30
Elm, Lloyd, 106, 107, 112, 116, 117, 125,
    134
Emerson, Ralph Waldo, 28
Epstein, Kitty, 169
Erickson, Peter, 15, 35
Euro-immigrant perspective, 60, 62, 63, 66,
    84–85

Fetsko, William, 107, 114, 117, 134
Feynman, Richard, 26
Finn, Chester, 16, 18, 76, 86, 95, 96
Fiske, Edward B., 96
FitzGerald, Frances, 177
Flores, Eugene, 179, 187
Franklin, Benjamin, 127
Fraser, Nancy, 48
Fuchs, Lawrence H., 7, 35
Foucault, Michel, 40, 44, 193, 194
Fuentes, Carlos, 27

Gagnon, Paul, 16, 17, 18, 68, 76, 85, 103,
    116, 125, 139, 190
Gates, Henry Louis Jr., 15, 43, 125
Gays and lesbians, 23, 63, 64, 86
Geathers, Carin, 171
Gergen, Kenneth J., 56
Gibbany, Jack, 168
Giroux, Henry, 5, 13, 185
Glazer, Nathan, 102, 105, 106, 107, 108,
    109, 110, 113, 114, 117, 125, 134,
    137, 155
Glover, Diane, 105, 107, 116, 117, 118, 141
Goodson, Ivor F., and Stephen Ball, 51
Gordon, Beverly M., 186, 200
Gordon, Edmund, 102, 104, 107, 108, 112,
    113, 114, 116, 117, 121, 122, 125, 141

Gordon, Larry, 162
Grant, S. G., 71
Gratiot, Margaret, 167
Greene, Maxine, i, 22, 39, 198, 200
Greenfeld, Liah, 35
Greenman, Jessea, 86
Gregory, George, 140, 155
Gross, Jane, 169
Gunn, Giles, 28, 29, 33
Guthrie, James, Michael Kirst, and Allan
    Odden, 12, 189, 190

Haley, Alex, 67
Hamilton, Harry L., 95
Harding, Vincent, 4, 185
Harris, Robert L. Jr., 143, 148, 155
Harvey, David, 29
Henry, Tess, 180
Heritage Foundation, 15
Heyser, Holly A., 167, 168
Higham, John, 6, 7
Hildebrand, John, 109, 145–146
Hill, Anita, 48
Hill Collins, Patricia, 47, 56, 199, 200
Hilliard, Asa, 116, 125
Hilton, Kenneth, 155
Hirsch, E. D., 72, 95
History-Social Science Framework, vii, 12, 21,
    60, 65, 68–74, 84, 90, 95, 121, 157,
    172, 178, 179, 186
History textbook adoption process, 19, 20,
    21, 22, 23, 74–88
Hoar, Jack, 73–74
Hogeboom, William L., 125
Hollins, Etta, 173, 174
Holt, Rinehart and Winston, 61, 82, 158
Honig, Bill, vii, 17, 19, 59, 68, 71, 73, 77,
    86, 87, 96
hooks, bell, 65, 195, 196
Houghton Mifflin, 21, 26, 37, 61, 62, 63,
    64, 72, 74–79, 82–88, 113, 138,
    152, 158, 159, 161, 165, 166, 167,
    169, 172, 174, 175, 177, 178, 187,
    191, 195
Howard, John R., 111
Huggins, Nathan, 61, 68, 85
Hughes, Robert, 125
Hunter, James Davison, 198

Immigrants, 6
    Chinese, 7–9, 11, 159
Immigration
    discrimination, vii, 7–9
    legal restrictions, 9
    illegal, 10, 11

IMEP (Instructional Materials Evaluation
    Panel), 21, 77–79, 81, 85, 90
Iotanka, Tatanka, 164

Jackson, Charles, 84
Jackson, Kenneth, 16, 17, 18, 102, 106,
    107, 112, 113, 114, 115, 117, 124
Jaenen, Cornelius, 35
James, William, 28, 47
Jeffries, Leonard, 96, 111, 124, 123, 133,
    134, 154
Jennings, Peter, 77
Joe-Lew, Helen, 159
Johnson, Paulette, 172, 173, 178
Jordan, Sheila, 169

Kalantzis, Mary, and William Cope, 29
Kang, K. Connie, x, 20, 21
Kang, K. Connie, and Dexter Waugh, 72
Karp, Stan, 22
Kaye, Harvey J., ii, 5
Kerner Commission, 97, 98
Kessler-Harris, Alice, 48
Kiernan, Henry, and John Pyne, 190
King, Joyce E., x, 13, 21, 40, 41, 65, 66, 67,
    69, 74, 76, 77, 79–85, 86, 88, 167,
    169, 175, 185, 195, 196, 197
King, Martin Luther, Jr., 13, 36, 48, 113
King, Rodney, 10, 14
Kirp, David, 17
Kliebard, Herbert M., 5, 14, 51, 189
Klor de Alva, Jorge, 106, 107, 108, 109,
    110, 114, 125, 134, 137, 138, 152,
    155, 175
Knowledge, 43, 44
    curriculum, viii, 49–52, 152
    deciphering, 40–41, 195, 197
    expanding, 40–41
    invisibilizing, 40–41
    marginalizing, 40–41
    nature of, 43
Kuklis, Louise, 155
Kulchin, Peter, 42

Ladson–Billings, Gloria, i, 75–76, 79, 90
Lalor, Edward, 140, 155
Leach, Frank, 8
Lee, Cheryl, 166, 178
Lee, Robert E., 193
Leek, Jonetta, 163
Legesse, Asmarom, 65
Leo, John, 60, 111, 113
Li, David K., 169
Limerick, Patricia Nelson, Clyde A. Milner,
    and Charles E. Rankin, 42

Lionberger, Troy, 164
Lippmann, Walter, 44
Lubarsky, Marilyn E., 180

Machiavelli, Niccolo, 59
MacDonald, Heather, 131
Malcolm X, 13, 36
Mandella, Nelson, 113
Mansuri, Shabbir, 17, 18, 175, 179
Marable, Manning, i, 193
Marley, Bob, v, x
Marshall, Paule, 198
Maxey, Phyllis F., 70, 71
Mazrui, Ali, 103, 105, 107, 113, 114, 117,
    118, 141, 187, 188
McCarthy, Cameron, 180
McCormick, Erin, and Don Martinez, 10
McIntosh, Peggy, 56, 196
McKay, Claude, 80
McWilliams, Carey, 186
Meyer, Edward J., 146
Michaelson, John, 160, 161, 165, 166, 182
Miller, JoAnne, 159
Minnich, Elizabeth K., 56
Montero-Sieburth, Martha, 56
Moore, Harriet, 173, 174
Morrison, Toni, 38, 39, 46, 56, 197
Multiculturalism, 49, 64–65, 73, 101, 120,
    129
    additive, 35, 36, 38, 141, 142, 193
    revisionist, 35, 36, 37, 67, 141, 193
    multiple perspectives, 37, 38
    transformative, 35, 38, 133, 141, 142,
        148, 151, 193, 194, 199, 200 (see also
        black studies perspective; reciprocal
        history; Organization of American
        Historians)

NAACP (National Association for the Ad-
    vancement of Colored People), 95
Nash, Gary, 17, 18, 21, 26, 68, 75, 76, 83,
    84, 90, 159, 176, 191, 192
National Center for History in the Schools,
    16, 191
National Commission on Social Studies in
    the Schools, 108
Nation at Risk, A, 189, 192, 203
National Council on Education Standards
    and Testing, 113
National Council for History Education. See
    Bradley Commission
National history standards, 16, 18, 189–193
National identity, 43, 64–65, 68, 73, 120
    American exceptionalism, 45, 46
    civic nationalism, 35
    ethnic nationalism, 35

Native Americans, 62, 66, 71, 87
Nativism, 5, 7
Neo-conservatism, 5, 6
Neo-nativism, 6
Neo-nativist, 13, 31, 35, 38, 41, 46, 48, 100,
    103, 121, 150, 192
    neo-nativist network, ix, 15, 16, 18, 68–
    69, 85
New Compact for Learning, A, 94, 132, 133,
    135, 137, 142, 143, 144, 145, 147,
    149, 150, 152, 153

Olin, John M. Foundation, 15, 17, 18
Oliner, Pearl M., 70
Olneck, Michael R., 36, 56, 200
One Nation, Many Peoples, viii, 38, 52, 93,
    94, 101, 106, 114, 115, 119, 120,
    121, 122, 127, 128, 129, 130, 132,
    133, 135, 136, 139, 145, 148, 149,
    156, 186, 188
Organization of American Historians, 118–
    119, 131, 134, 197
Ostrofsky, Susan Wong, 117
O'Sullivan, Gerry, 43, 131, 154
Outcomes-Based Education (OBE), 150,
    151, 156

PACE (Policy Analysis for California Educa-
    tion), 12, 60, 61, 63, 189
Parcells, Bill, 3
Patterson, Victoria, 170
Paz, Octavio, 3, 4
Philips, John Edward, 198
Pluralism and unity (e pluribus unum), 34,
    46, 47, 48, 60, 70, 115, 138–142,
    199
Policymaking, vi, 51, 88, 132–133, 150–
    152
Political correctness, 6, 15, 22, 162
Popkewitz, Tom, x, 51
Powers, William, 130

Quinones, Nathan, 133

Race and racism, vi, 6, 64, 66, 67–68, 119–
    122, 185
Rainbow Curriculum (Children of the Rain-
    bow), 22, 178
Ramirez, Raul, 72
Raskin, Jamin B., 6
Ravitch, Diane, 13, 16, 17, 18, 19, 46, 68,
    69, 71, 73, 86, 95, 96, 99, 100, 111,
    112, 121, 125, 131, 132, 133, 138,
    139, 203
Reagan, Ronald, 12, 15
Reciprocal history, 38, 39, 40, 41, 196–198

Reese, Lyn, 180
Reid, William A., 51
Reinhold, Robert, 68
Religion, 63, 64, 70
  religious right, 22, 23
Remini, Robert V., 7
Roberts, Francis, 104, 108, 112, 116, 117,
  122, 124
Rodriguez, Cameron, 157, 164
Rogler, Lloyd, 103
Rorty, Richard, 31, 32
Rothman, Robert, 190

Sagor, Susan, 104, 107, 114, 117, 134
Salter, Christopher, 75
Sanchez Korrol, Virginia, 105, 107, 110,
  111, 114, 134, 141
San Francisco Examiner, 20–22, 72, 81, 90
Schlesinger, Arthur M., Jr., 15, 16, 19, 74,
  96, 99, 100, 103, 104, 105, 106, 107,
  111, 113, 114, 115, 116, 117, 120,
  124, 131, 132, 138, 139, 188
Schlesinger, Arthur M., Sr., 203
Seller, Maxine, 36
Sewall, Gilbert, 17, 18, 26, 76, 85, 96
Shakespeare, William, 43
Shanker, Albert, 16, 103, 111, 124, 130,
  138, 139, 190
Shaver, James P., O. L. Davis Jr., and Su-
  zanne W. Helburn, 178
Shogren, Elizabeth, and Douglas Frantz, 23
Siegel, Harvey, 34
Simonds, Richard, 22, 23
Singer, Alan, 13
Sizer, Theodore R., 189
Slapin, Beverly, 176
Sleeter, Christine, ii, 66, 193
Sleeter, Christine, and Carl A. Grant, 56, 193
Slotkin, Richard, 42
Sobol, Thomas, 16, 93, 95, 97, 98, 102, 103,
  104, 105, 106, 110, 111, 112, 113,
  122, 124, 125, 127, 129, 131, 133,
  134, 135, 136, 142, 143, 144, 146,
  147, 149, 150, 152, 153, 154, 155, 156
Solomon, Jolie, 113
Spencer, Herbert, 50
Stage, Elizabeth, 61, 82
Stage, Elizabeth, and Charlotte Crabtree, 60,
  61, 63, 64, 83, 86
Steinberg, Stephen, 7, 11
Stimpson, Catherine, 32
Stowe, Harriet Beecher, 198
Sullivan, Andrew, 113
Swartz, Ellen, 71, 83, 85, 176, 177
Swartz, Ellen, and Susan Goodwin, 37

TACT (The Association of Chinese Teachers),
  159, 161
TACTIC (Taxpayers Association Concerned
  about Truth in Curriculum), 81
Taino, vii, 163, 164
Takaki, Ronald, 37, 59
Talarico, Dianne, 157, 160, 163, 165, 166,
  196
Task Force on Minorities, 95, 102
Taylor, Charles, 56
Tedla, Elleni, 117, 119, 141
Templeton, John, 90
Thomas, Clarence, 48
Thomas, Glen, 178, 179
Thomas, G. Scott, 124
Thoreau, Henry David, 50
Think tanks, 12, 15
Tice, Walter, 140
Tifft, Susan, 113
Tom, Roger, 84, 159, 160
Tyack, David B., 9, 197
Tyack, David B., and Thomas James, 48
Tubman, Harriet, 48

Understanding Diversity, viii, 52, 94, 95, 101,
  122, 127, 128, 129, 132, 133, 135,
  136, 137, 146, 148, 149, 152, 153,
  155, 156

Van Cour, Gary, 105, 119
Viadero, Debra, 113, 146, 187, 190

Warren, Mercy Otis, 193
Waugh, Dexter, ix, x, 21, 67, 75, 81, 160
Waugh, Dexter, and Larry D. Hatfield, 13, 15
Weatherford, Jack, 162, 182
Weintraub, Shelly, 169, 171
Weis, Lois, x
West, Cornel, 28, 29, 39, 48, 65, 199
Westlake group. *See* Bradley Commission
White, Hayden, 42
Whittle Communications, 116
Wilford, John Nobel, 182
Williams, Raymond, 50
Wilson, Louis E., 175
Wilson, Pete, 10
Woodson, Carter G., 193, 194
Wynter, Sylvia, x, 13, 38, 40, 55, 59, 61, 62,
  64, 65, 66, 83, 88, 90, 193, 194, 195,
  196, 197

Yourcenar, Marguerite, 3

Zinn, Howard, 37